WAR IS WAR

WAR IS WAR

by

Ex-Private X
(A. M. Burrage)

Pen & Sword
MILITARY

First published in the United Kingdom
in 1930 by Victor Gollancz Ltd.

Reprinted in this format in 2010 by
Pen & Sword Military
An imprint of
Pen & Sword Books Ltd
47 Church Street
Barnsley
South Yorkshire
S70 2AS

ISBN 978 184884 154 3

A CIP catalogue record for this book is
available from the British Library

Printed and bound in England
By the MPG Books Group

Pen & Sword Books Ltd incorporates the Imprints of Pen & Sword Aviation,
Pen & Sword Family History, Pen & Sword Maritime, Pen & Sword Military,
Wharncliffe Local History, Pen & Sword Select, Pen & Sword Military Classics,
Leo Cooper, Remember When, Seaforth Publishing and Frontline Publishing

For a complete list of Pen & Sword titles please contact
PEN & SWORD BOOKS LIMITED
47 Church Street, Barnsley, South Yorkshire, S70 2AS, England
E-mail: enquiries@pen-and-sword.co.uk
Website: www.pen-and-sword.co.uk

AUTHOR'S FOREWORD

This book is a sincere attempt to put on record, albeit from memory, the experiences of one man as a private soldier in France during the war, his own reactions to those abnormal conditions, and his observations concerning the very little that came within his orbit. Its object is to give those who may be curious to know what the war was really like, all the intimate details of the lives we led in and behind the lines.

Many books about the war have been written, and will be written, by ex-officers ; but, as all those who served must realise, an officer, of no matter what rank, saw the war from an angle far remote from the view-point of Thomas Atkins. I will go further and state that a platoon commander, who practically lived with his men, was incapable of appreciating their sufferings and hardships unless he too had been in the ranks. They can record conversations in the officers' messes, describe battles, and tell anecdotes about us. But they were only *with* us, not *of* us, and they cannot get inside our skins.

Unfortunately Private Thomas Atkins is inarticulate. Few professional writers went on active service in the ranks. So, as a humble exception, and quite conscious that my own experiences of war were limited and tame, I have ventured to set down what I remember.

For reasons which will be obvious to the reader this book must appear under a pseudonym. Were it otherwise I could not tell the truth about myself and others. I have altered the names of the characters, each of whom exists or did exist, and every incident is, to the best of my knowledge and recollection, true.

In the cause of Truth I have given my literary style—such as it is—a half-holiday, and written these random recollections and impressions much as I would convey them to a friend by word of mouth. Directly a writer attempts in his best professional manner to describe something that happened to himself he is bound to become impressionistic ; and Impressionism and Truth are only half-sisters and scarcely on speaking terms.

There may be those who will complain of the sudden changes of key throughout this book. The reason is that I was looking back while I wrote and trying to recapture the mood of the moment. Out there Comedy and Tragedy tumbled over each other's heels as in one of the old-fashioned melodramas. If there is a note of irony here and there concerning people and institutions I didn't like, the graver passages of the book were written with the utmost sincerity.

The war had many facets : Bruce Bairnsfather saw Old Bill, and laughed and drew him, and laughed again. Seigfried Sassoon saw only poor ignorant boys sobbing out their last breath for a cause which they knew nothing about. Most of us saw these extremes of Comedy and Tragedy, and the means between them.

I have tried not to concentrate on any particular phase, and have helped myself to a fairly wide canvas to portray the comparative little that I saw. I have not grubbed in the dirt for obscenity and horror in the hope of selling a few extra copies, but I have shirked nothing, and I think I have contrived to be frank without the use of those dirty words which a certain German writer found so essential to his Art. Anyhow, I don't want women readers. If any young man should ask an old soldier, " Was it really like this ? " and the old soldier answers, " Yes, it's all true," this book will have served its purpose.

And I shall not mind if the young man exclaims, " What a very unpleasant fellow the author must be ! "

Perhaps I am.

Ex-Private X.

CHAPTER I

Nearly all of us on the draft were men who had tried to obtain commissions in England, and failed. There was a black mark against one, the personal appearance of another was against him, and a third was hopelessly inefficient. There were therefore three fairly sound reasons why I was still a full private. Never mind. There was a chance of getting gazetted through G.H.Q. over on the other side, and sucking in the War Office.

I was senior to most of the other men on the draft, having had a good long spell in England, and not having shown that impetuous desire to get myself killed which the civilian population was agreed that one ought to feel. I suppose I could have pulled wires and stayed behind longer, but I had done exactly nothing except what I was told—and not always that. I had behaved with the passiveness of a cabbage, and like an exported cabbage I was now going out. Well, thank heaven I'd got away from those desolatingly patriotic old men who had " given " their sons.

Things might have been worse. We were not going up the line at once. Our service battalion was on lines of communication and doing headquarter guards, and looked like continuing so indefinitely. For that reason we were perhaps the cheeriest draft on the boat until sea-sickness reduced us all to one common level of humanity.

We were supposed to be a " kid-glove " regiment recruited from public school, university and professional men. But the war was getting on in years and the regiment could not afford to be so particular. Still, our fellows were intellectually and socially superior to most, and remained so until we were cut to pieces and had to swallow large drafts belonging to other units.

The boat, on which after some vicissitudes we embarked at Southampton, had been designed for the reception of cattle, and I should not have grumbled if it had been kept for its original purpose. A storm was blowing up and we met it as soon as we were outside Southampton Water. The passengers were a pretty mixed bag, containing men of every kind of unit of the British Army, except perhaps the Inland Water Transport. I never have seen any of the I.W.T. and I don't believe they ever really existed.

I stayed on deck—to see the last of England, although I wouldn't confess it—and just as the shores were fading I saw and heard sentiment rebuked. A youngster in the H.A.C. remarked : " Well, there goes England ; I wonder if we shall see her again." To which a gunner, who was clumsily feeding himself with a jack-knife out of a tin of bully beef, made cynical answer : " Well, I'm havin' my tea."

For a while I remained on deck, enjoying the wind, the occasional gusts of rain and the motions of the boat, and marvelled at the British Navy. We had an escort of three destroyers spread out in front of us so as to form a triangle. But they were a long way ahead and I wondered how they could prevent an enemy submarine from sneaking up behind and biting us in the leg, so to speak. But nobody else seemed to think of that possibility, and the destroyers trudged on through the waves with such an air of confidence that I felt sure they must have some means of knowing that there was nothing about.

The storm got worse after a bit and those of us who were still on deck were ordered below. This was rather horrible, because we were all packed on the floor like sardines, and nearly everybody then proceeded to be sick. I didn't, because for some occult reason I happen to be sea-sick proof. However, my two uncomfortably close neighbours made up for my niggardliness in paying tribute to Neptune by bringing up more undigested food than I had imagined the human stomach to be capable of containing. Further, they were both sick over my trousers.

The retchings and paroxysms going on all around were horrible to hear and see. Had there been any empty floor-space the floor would have been swimming. But amid all this unpleasantness the grim humour, which I had already learned to associate with the British Army, was not absent. One of the men next to me, a gunner, entertained us with a prolonged, disgusting, gargling, snarling and really fierce attempt to vomit. When he had quite done for the time being his friend, who had been admiring his effort from the opposite wall, called out : " Still got your teeth, Jack ? "

The light was much too dim for reading, besides the boat was pitching so that one needed both hands to save one's head from being cracked. There was nothing to do, therefore, but to recline half lying on the floor, allow perfect strangers to be sick over one, and to meditate. So it was that I began to review my position. How was this squalid adventure going to end?

Here was I, a young writer (aged twenty-seven), unmarried but with three people to support, going off to the war and leaving them to the mercy of God with a separation allowance of twelve and sixpence a week. While in

England I could earn money by my pen, but how was it going to be on the other side ? While I was training I had spent most of my spare time in earning money for the support of my dependants. Would that still be possible in France ? For myself I had nothing but sixpence a day—that was the rate then for private soldiers with separation allowances—and ten shillings a week pocket money allowed me by a well-to-do friend who was unfit for service.

I began to think that I was rather a mug for being there. I needn't have been. I had joined rather late, but still as a volunteer. Even after conscription had been brought in I might have kept out on compassionate grounds. I was not fit, from the rather high standard of the Army when I joined it, and I had only got past the doctor through influence. I had no inclination at all for soldiering, and privately knew myself to be a coward. Then what the devil was I doing in that rotten cattle-boat, probably on my way out to a bloody death ?

Professor Freud might answer the question. I hated being thought a funk. I had the strongest disapproval of young and fit civilians without dependants, but could not very well express it while I was a civilian myself. I found it very uncomfortable to crawl about in a lounge suit while most men of my age were in khaki. Most of my friends who were worth while had vanished. The three girls with whom I had simultaneous " understandings " —although not actual engagements—were being dazzled even by chronic home-service-ites. Obviously the thing to do was to get into some musty brown material.

Don't think that I wasn't a patriot. I was willing to die for my country if needs were. But dying for one's country may be a very expensive luxury for which others have to pay. I had not a bean to leave to my mother and two other near relatives. For their sakes I could not afford to die—nor could I for my own, for I was then going through a phase of spiritual trouble.

I had been brought up as a R.C., but had given up practising my religion because I couldn't quite believe in it. On the other hand, I couldn't quite disbelieve, and if it were all true I realised that things might be very awkward for me if I happened to die in that state of mind. A very weak character ? Yes, of course I was. It was about the damnedest fool in the world who lay thinking in the bowels of that pitching, sick-smothered tub.

Of one thing I was determined—that I would get a commission if I could through G.H.Q. I meant to see some fighting while I was about it. I thought, in my innocence, that the experience might help me in my career as an author. Still, was I fit to have control of men when my instinct on hearing a gun go off was to bolt like a rabbit ? I consoled myself with the thought that other fellows, no better than I, had managed all right. To anticipate a little, I may add that I was so inept at parade-ground work, and so steeped in petty " crime " from the moment I set foot on French soil, that there was never any question of my being gazetted.

So far my career in the Army had been very unfortun-ate. I could not take it seriously, and officers and N.C.O.'s do not like to feel that they are causing amuse-ment. I had lost my chance of a commission within a few days of gazettement mostly through allowing a hobby for taking illicit week-end leave to become a habit. I had had no discipline of any sort since I left school, and took very unkindly to the bit and bridle. I became in all essentials a schoolboy again. At school I had been considered rather a good joke. In the Army they did not give commissions to Good Jokes—if they happened to notice it in time.

Now that you have some vague idea of the author's personality—although not, I trust, of his identity—we can get on with the rigmarole.

The boat bumped itself over the bar of Le Havre harbour only about three hours after schedule time. I had become thoroughly used to unpunctuality. Punctuality was strongly impressed on the rank and file, but we were the only ones to practise it—because we had to. The practical examples we received were not encouraging. If a general were coming to inspect us at eleven, we knew that he would keep us sweating or freezing on parade until at least twelve before he arrived.

I do not think that this was always through inefficiency on the part of the Brass Hats ; I think it was studied discourtesy to their inferiors. "I'm General A. and I do as I like, and you're dung, damn you!"—that was the attitude. It will be my privilege to write in these pages a few kind words about military mandarins.

Of course it was raining hard when we disembarked. The difference between the French climate and ours is simply this, that in England it is nearly always raining and in France it only rains when you particularly don't want it to. We spent about an hour messing about and carrying things ashore before at last we formed up on the quay.

Captain Jinks, who took out the draft, had been in command of the draft company in England. He was a good-natured old imbecile, a little too old for active service, and he loved to see his men full of good spirits. He had always insisted on the singing of boisterous and full-blooded songs on route marches, and to hear teetotal eunuchs who wanted to suck up to him roaring out songs about wine and women had been one of the pleasures which made Army life not altogether unbearable to me. Although I expect he had been disgustingly sick he was quite cheery to-night, because he knew that he was going almost straight back home again.

Later on, I have heard, he went out and spent six days in a very quiet part of the line for instructional purposes, and came home a changed man. It is on record that he wept for three days and three nights in the ante-room of the officers' mess when, during the shortage of man-power in March '18, there was danger of his being sent out " for keeps."

The base camp was close to Harfleur, and we started on the march through the rain, not quite in the footsteps of Henry the Fifth, for of course Captain Jinks got himself lost. " Follow the tram-lines and they'll lead you home " is not true of the environments of Le Havre, for the tram-lines lead everywhere. For some reason we were not expected to sing—perhaps because Captain Jinks realised that we were now in France and had a theory that the Germans might hear us. It was as well, because nobody wanted to. Wet through, tired, hungry and utterly fed up we reached the camp at about half-past three in the morning.

Anybody knowing the Army will guess at once what happened there. We were not expected. There was no accommodation for us. My suggestion that we should return home was coldly received by the magnificent base-wallah sergeant who had been dug out of his bunk to come and look at us. We were herded into a Black Hole of Calcutta which they had the nerve to call a "reception hut " and remained there until half-past five, when we were harried into some wet bell-tents on a greasy slope—sixteen or so to each tent.

It's funny how experience changes one's point of view. Cold, sodden, hungry, sleepless and already home-sick, we thought we could never be more miserable. Yet this was heaven to what most of us went through later. It was no use trying to go to sleep, for réveillé was at six, and although nobody took the least notice of us for the next three hours we had to stand by our tents until somebody did.

At about nine o'clock we were called on parade for breakfast and conducted to a so-called mess hut. We had cheered up a little, but as soon as we were inside our faces fell. I forget what was offered us to eat, but I know it was quite uneatable. The tea was cold and about as foul as the cooks could brew it. And our bread ration— our half a loaf of white bread a day, ha ! ha !—consisted of a small handful of crumbs, bread and biscuit, tossed into the top parts of our mess-tins by a filthy little swine of an orderly with dirty fingers.

Looking back across the years, and a great deal mellowed by time, I still say that those who were responsible for the administration of the base camps in France should be hanged as high as Haman. Rations were always shortest where there was no excuse for a shortage, and cooking was always at its worst where there was every appliance to hand. Moreover the " permanent base " people of all ranks were indeed permanently base. The unofficial motto of the Army, " —— you, Jack, I'm all right ! " was screamed at one on every hand.

I gave up trying to count the decayed, dug-out old colonels who ought to have died in their beds years since. There they were, purple, alcoholic, pompous, over-fed, strutting and preening, getting in everybody's way and doing nothing except eat a good man's food and draw a good man's money. The N.C.O.'s were futile, brazen-voiced asses, clinging to their jobs as drowning men are supposed to cling to straws. An N.C.O. of that particular type could often get a job at the base and bully the poor fools of better men who were going up the line to die for him. The rank and file consisted largely of professional footballers, pugilists and other athletes who were natur-ally too delicate to endure life in the trenches. But I will say as little as possible about the base because the memory of it still makes me angry.

I must mention, however, that during the few days we were in this paradise we had two " short arm " inspec-tions. Why two, I don't know, but it is perhaps a tribute to the zeal of the medical officers. When the rain stopped the snow started, and it was during the snowy period that these inspections took place. We were made to strip in a marquee with an icy wind whistling through and wait a considerable time for our turn to submit to the rather humiliating inspection. I suppose the idea was that if you hadn't a venereal disease you ought to have pneumonia instead.

Le Havre was out of bounds except to the " perma-nently base," but I got sent to the docks once with another man on a fatigue to bring up coal. We managed to slip away for a couple of minutes to a brasserie and get some bread and cheese and beer, but we couldn't get far. My companion had an intellectual prurience over some brothels in the Rue des Gallennes. In one of them, it was said, one of the sirens wore the uniform of a British captain and was much in demand among the disrespect-ful Tommies. If this were true it was a brain-wave on the part of the lady, and I expect she made enough to retire on, and is now a respected wife and mother.

Naturally there wasn't any coal for us at the docks—something was wrong with the indent or something—so I was ordered to drive the empty coal-cart and pair of horses back to the coal-dump at Harfleur. I had never driven a horse in my life, much less a pair, but an order is an order. The streets were crowded with traffic, there was a double line of trams, and the horses seemed rather jubilant about having nothing to pull. My insular preference for driving on the left of the road did not help matters much, but we got to Harfleur somehow ; indeed, we arrived like a battery of Horse Artillery going into action in the good old days.

We left a few days later and I wasn't sorry. I never saw the camp again, but I saw the site of it a year or two ago. It looked like the Abomination of Desolation—and so it should look.

CHAPTER II

We had what I must call an "officers' farewell" when we left Le Havre. We were paraded before a hut to be inspected by some pompous old ass or other. After keeping us waiting about the average length of time he tottered out rather unsteadily on his pins and breathed whisky all over us—for which I was rather grateful, for I had begun to forget what whisky smelt like. Having done which, he blinked at us owlishly and with some difficulty remarked : " Y're dishghrace to y're reg'ment." Then he tottered back into the hut—to be a credit to *his*.

While I am on the unpleasant subject of base-camps and their permanent inhabitants, I must mention Étaples, whither many weary months later I was to be brought as a casualty. Yes, we went on to Étaples, which on the whole I don't think was quite so foul as Havre ; but perhaps we thought this because the weather had mended or because we were becoming acclimatised to base camps.

We travelled on a train which, when it was going all out, sometimes achieved the incredible speed of five miles an hour, but this was rather marred by long stoppages. I forget now how long it actually took. At one station where we stopped—name now forgotten—there was a refreshment buffet on the platform. We were rather tired of tea made out of water from the engine, and there was a wild rush for the "wet" side of the buffet.

I was well to the fore, but before I could get served a small herd of thirsty officers, who wanted the place to themselves, came and hounded us out.

I was wandering away, dry and disconsolate, when one of them called me from the door. He was a youngster whom I knew very well but hadn't seen since the early days of the war, and he roared with laughter at seeing me rigged out as a Tommy. Then he asked me in to have a drink, and I explained matters to him.

" Oh," he said in a loud and hearty tone, " I suppose I can buy you a drink without these silly bastards messing themselves."

Now as my friend wore only one pip, and as most of the others, although not of his regiment, were of considerably higher rank, I felt slightly embarrassed. But none of the " silly bastards " said anything, so I had two or three.

While on the subject of drink I noticed one peculiar thing about myself. I had never been what one might call a rabid teetotaler. On the eve of the departure of the draft I had returned rather late to barracks and put a sergeant's boots on the fire because I thought—and said—that he was a stupid fellow. On a previous occasion I had been ordered to attend the funeral of another sergeant, whom I had liked, and I was so sorry about his death that I was quite unable to go to the funeral at all, and woke up on a piece of sacking in the cook-house four hours after it was all over. I mention these incidents to absolve myself of any possible stigma of teetotalism.

Yet when I landed in France I found that I didn't want to drink. It wasn't so much that I didn't fancy my beer out of a greasy mess-tin, I'd just gone off it except when I found myself in a position to have it in comfort.

I became a customer of the Y.M.C.A. and other huts and drank as much cocoa as any Nonconformist grocer. It's funny to think that I once enjoyed cocoa. It was hot and wet, and I was cold and wet outside, perhaps that was why.

It was the refreshment huts alone that made the base camps tolerable. What should we have done without the Y.M.C.A.? But they have had so much and such deserved praise that they require none from me. Some of the old men who served in little tents near the line were heroes. I remember one poor old chap in such a tent just behind Ypres, where there was an air-raid punctually every three minutes. Out had to go his one candle when the alarm sounded, and then the brutal and licentious soldiery would come and raid his shelves.

But at the bases every creed had its own canteen, which the non-elect were quite free to use. We used to discuss among ourselves whether the tinned salmon sandwiches at the Anabaptists' Hut were preferable to the sardine sandwiches sold at the same price by the Wesleyans, just as to-day one might discuss the relative merits of the Ritz and Carlton. Nor have I had a word of religion spoken to me in one of these places—except once, and that was not a refreshment hut at all but a place where they gave free stationery to the troops. It serves to bring me back by a circuitous route to Étaples.

Yes, there was a hut where they gave you notepaper and envelopes if you went up and asked for them. I went up and found behind the counter a stout old lady with a funny face. She looked just like a male comedian dressed as a " dame " in order to be the principal boy's mother in a pantomime. So much so that when she smiled at me I thought she was going to say something quite low. However, she only asked me if I wanted some stationery, and when I had gratefully told her that this was so she brought some—but kept her hand on it. Then she asked me if I had a Testament.

I thanked her again, said " No," and that I should like one, but I added that I should prefer the Douai Version. At which she stared at me as if I were a nasty smell and exclaimed : " You're not a Catholic ! " I wasn't a very good one, but you can always get even a bad Catholic up in arms about his Church. I didn't want to argue with the old fool, but she kept her hand on the writing paper so I had to stay. She read me a long sermon on the sins of the Church, the wickedness of the Popes, and seemed in some vague way to hold me personally responsible for the Spanish Inquisition.

She then read me her own Act of Faith. It was all " I believe this " and " I believe that." Meanwhile a crowd of assorted troops was queueing up behind, some amused and others impatient, so I settled the argument for her.

" Yes," I said, " I know what you believe. You believe that Christ came to earth, founded a Church, let it go to pot for fifteen hundred years, and then set two men like Henry the Eighth and Martin Luther to put it right for Him."

Then I got my stationery.

I have no ill-feeling for this poor old creature, but why should she have been allowed to do it ? As a monument of futility she was harmless, but on the other hand she did no good. But suppose she had had personality and logic, what then ? It was not the time to try to convert men from one brand of Christianity to another. If a man whose life was hanging on a thread had any

Christian faith at all, oughtn't she and all of us to thank God for it, instead of trying to plant seeds of doubt when the poor wretch had no time to discard old creeds for new ?

There was also at least one male idiot let loose at Étaples. He was not in Holy Orders, nor was he in the Army, but he wore a kind of khaki uniform which made him look like a cross between one of Lyons's commission-aires and an A.A. scout. As far as I could see he just walked about among the men and tried to do good. He was oh ! so broad-minded. He even did not object to a little mild swearing, and once in my hearing, in a burst of confidence, he admitted that he sometimes said " Damn " himself. When asked what he thought of that popular adjective relating to the deed of kind he blushed and walked hurriedly away.

Now there was a well-meaning idiot who, if he were unfit for soldiering, would have been better at home making munitions or taking over the job of a fit man. You cannot save a man's soul by muttering a pious aphorism in his ear any more than you can damn it by telling him a dirty story.

While in Étaples I was a customer at the hut run by Lady Angela Forbes. I don't know if I saw Lady Angela herself, but her assistants were all very pleasant, and it was rather thrilling to think that the young woman who had just spilt a quart of tea over your best tunic might be a duchess. The refreshments were good and cheap at that hut, but Lady Angela had also another hut beside the railway where, when we were about to entrain, I was charged fourpence for a mess-tin full of tea. However, when I went home on leave more than a year later, all my party received two buns each from Lady Angela

Forbes free gratis and for nothing—so hats off to Lady Angela.

We went on to Hesdin, an echelon of G.H.Q. where part of the battalion was stationed. This was another interminable railway journey, or so it seemed ; but it did end—and for me with a rather unpleasant adventure. From Havre to Étaples we had enjoyed the luxury of French third-class railway compartments, but when we came to entrain at Étaples we were faced by cattle trucks bearing the ominous words, "Hommes 40, Chevaux 8." There *is* room for forty men, forty equipments and forty rifles in a cattle truck. Yes, just room, if you don't mind somebody half sitting on you, and somebody else doesn't mind your putting your feet on his face.

Another snag is that it takes a long time to detrain. It takes a considerable while for men to sort themselves out, put on their packs and equipments and leave the truck by only one door. This was a matter which the French railway authorities seemed not to have taken into consideration, for the train sauntered on, leaving five or six of us in each truck.

Just as it was starting two Fusiliers officers jumped in from the other side, and, when we asked their advice, said that the train would probably be shunted back on to a siding. But when it had covered three or four kilometres we realised that this was not to happen. As it was only doing about five miles an hour we decided to jump for it.

A man named Brown went first, and burdened as he was in full marching order, came a terrible purler on the stones in dropping from the upper footboard. I went next, and one of the officers suggested that he should take my rifle, and I could then run after the train and take it from his hand. (This will seem quite incredible to people who did not travel in troop trains in France during the war, but so it was.)

I fell not too heavily on my hands and feet, ran a little way and took the rifle held out to me. I then became aware of cries of horror and white faces staring and mouthing at me as the trucks rattled slowly past. Evidently something was wrong, and I looked and saw what it was. I was on the six-foot way, and a passenger train was tearing towards me on the other line. There was no time to jump across in front of the oncoming engine, and in another couple of seconds I was going to be caught between the two trains. With a pack and tin hat on my back I hadn't a chance. I seemed certain to be crushed to death or flung into a gap between the coaches.

However, inspiration came to me in the nick of time, and I dived full-length parallel with the rails. I heard afterwards that the engine-driver of the oncoming train had signalled to me to do this, but I did not see him. This saved my life, but my troubles were not quite over. The lower footboard of the train I had left played tunes on my tin hat strapped on to the pack on my back, and I lay waiting, with the wheels grinding in my ears, for a footboard lower than the others to squash me or scoop me under the train. This of course did not happen, and I am grateful to the French railways for keeping their lower footboards so uniform in height.

When the trains had gone I got up and rejoined Brown, who was laughing like blazes at my discomfiture. We went and got some coffee at a hut by a level crossing, and then made our way back along the track to Hesdin, where we reported and were severely rebuked for not getting off the train in time. The other men who funked jumping, having seen what had nearly happened to me, went on to St. Pol, did not return until next day, and had nothing said to them. Justice, where are thy scales?

In Hesdin we were quartered in the romantic old Napoleonic barracks. There the draft was split up into companies and some went straight off to other detachments, so that I lost several old comrades for a month or two. I stayed on at Hesdin where there was very little parade-ground work. We did mostly guards and fatigues, and taking it all round the duties were light, and I found plenty of time for writing.

Hesdin was a typical old French town with cobbled streets and shuttered windows and the inevitable atmosphere of decay. At the back of the barracks there was a soldiers' brothel. It had not been put out of bounds, and even had it been I should have felt compelled to have a look at it. I went with another man.

The interior was rather like that of a Nonconformist meeting house, and never before nor since have I seen commercialised vice made to look so unattractive. The " characters " might all have taken part in one of Shakespeare's tavern scenes or stepped straight out of *The Beggar's Opera*. The *patron*, a hulking bully, and his obscene old consort would have made a perfect Mr. and Mrs. Peacham. There was an appalling serving-wench who could not bring one a drink without making some Rabelaisian remark or an indecent gesture. But to me the most amusing of the whole circus was the spectacled young woman in a severely cut black dress who sat at the receipt of custom and took the wages of sin. You felt that you couldn't say anything out of place to *her*. She made me think of that terrible story of de Maupassant, in which the *maison de tolerance* is shut for the day because of a spiritual event in the life of the little daughter of the establishment.

As for the resident ladies, the least said of them, poor things, the better. They were old and worn and hideous, with death's heads instead of faces.

We sat for half an hour drinking and resisting invitations to " come upstairs." I noticed that the very bad *vin blanc* was five times the price charged at the more virtuous establishments, and since *they* profiteered unconscionably Monsieur and Madame must have done very well out of the drinks alone.

I saw only one man plank down his five francs and march brazenly upstairs. He was a sergeant in the R.A.M.C. I heard afterwards that he went there every night. I had often wondered what was the use of an R.A.M.C. sergeant, and it wasn't until I heard this that I found a theory.

Why were not the " red lamp " houses put out of bounds ? A man was given every encouragement to contract a contagious disease, and once he had caught it he was treated like a criminal. I must say a few more words on this unpleasant subject. At every Casualty Clearing Station and hospital one saw latrines labelled "Venereal Only." These patients were segregated for a very obvious reason, but so far as I know, without being an authority on the subject, there are two kinds of these diseases. Therefore if a man went down with one the medical authorities put him in the way of getting the other. Hardly a useful present, one would think, although doubtless having the two at once would have made the patient more interesting to the medical faculty.

I have as yet said nothing about my friends and as yet given none the fictitious names with which I shall be compelled to provide them. There were many fellows on the draft whom I liked and who, I think, liked me, but there was none with whom I could quite form that intimacy of mind which is called friendship. In other words I had no particular crony. I don't want to try to pose as having been an intellectual, but there seemed nobody to whom I could show other than my superficial —and thoroughly idiotic—side.

There was Tim, a good drinking companion, who joined under one name as a schoolmaster, and whom I met in Fleet Street after the war as a full-blown journalist with a new patronymic. A queer metamorphosis, that ! But Tim had his own pal, another Irishman, who later on in the war smelt a Protestant conspiracy every time a shell fell within a hundred yards of him.

Then there was young Silver, the boy with Chinese eyes who used to put me to bed in our billet in England on those regrettable occasions when the bed wouldn't stay still. He was the son of a Nonconformist missionary and of course a teetotaler, but he was no bigot. We liked each other very much, but he was too young for me. Intellectually and in the ordinary habits of living there was between us a great gulf fixed.

At the base I found a youngster that I could have got on with, but he happened not to belong to my unit. He was in the H.A.C. One evening when I was standing in the queue at the Y.M.C.A., waiting to get a mug of cocoa, a voice behind me began to chant :

> " *From too much love of living,*
> *From hope and fear set free*——"

So naturally I continued :

> " *We thank with brief thanksgiving*
> *Whatever gods may be——*"

And we concluded in unison :

> " *That no life lives for ever*
> *That dead men rise up never,*
> *That even the weariest river*
> *Winds somewhere safe to sea.*"

I was young enough then to worship Swinburne, and to hear him quoted among that obscene, whistling, whooping crew drew me to the boy at once. He turned out to be a son of another Nonconformist parson. How I used to find 'em ! But he had read, and not unintelligently, and we met and talked most evenings before the day when he and some others set off singing down a road lined with poplars. He got through the shambles all right, for I heard from him in 1919 when he was at New College, Oxford.

Strangely enough, the man who became my friend was the man I began by liking least. He belonged to a type which I had never cared for. He had held a rather unimportant clerkship in a London office, and from the ends of his toenails to the roots of his sparse fair hair he was the complete London lowbrow. He was a big fellow, a few years older than myself, with a broad red face, a genial smile and a fair moustache. I don't think he had read anything more literary than *Photo Bits* nor thought of anything less mundane than a woman or a pint of beer.

I began by hating him, his speech, his manner, his outlook on life, everything about him ; and in Hesdin I suddenly found myself liking the old devil. I don't know why. We had nothing in common, and I can't think what he saw in me. But friendship, like love, is often based on no tangible foundation.

Dear old Dave, hearty drinker, good comrade and consummate scrounger, to whom all women were alike so that they were between the age of consent and seventy-five ! Where are you now, I wonder ? But there was a divine spark in you somewhere, as I was to find later, although you never found it for yourself. You are the only man I ever cried over, you big stiff—but that part of the tale shall be told presently.

David Barney and I wandered forth of evenings, explored the local cafés, and penetrated into the sur-rounding countryside where, triumphant among their immemorial filth, dwelt the local peasantry. I found that whatever might be his conversational limitations you could never be dull in old Dave's company. He had such a delightful Marie Lloydish sense of humour.

CHAPTER III

Hurrah ! I am being sent off to advance G.H.Q. on a small detachment, and Dave is coming too. If you get on to a very small detachment you are supposed to have a very good time. There will be only two officers, not much discipline, and everybody will be much more matey.

Spring is coming on, and there has been a persistent rumour that we are going into the line. Most people have been quite shameless in their aversion to this unpleasant prospect. But it can't be true, otherwise we shouldn't be going off on this job.

We are going up Arras way where there is obviously going to be some fighting, and we are going to do guards for Sir Douglas Haig. Haig wouldn't have moved across to Arras if there weren't going to be a show there. But we shall be with the headquarter staff and therefore safe enough. I have put in for a commission and been told that I haven't been out long enough, which is probably another way of saying that they wouldn't recommend me for one at any price. I've done my best, anyhow, and if they won't let me go into the trenches I must stay behind them and be thankful.

So one morning we are paraded, and we clamber into lorries and off we go.

England is not the only country in which spring is fickle. To-day is a perfect beast, and it is raining cats and dogs, and when after a long and bumpy ride we come to our new home, which is called Bavincourt, we don't see it at its best.

Bavincourt is a small and squalid village set in beautiful surroundings about seven miles behind Arras. Dominating the village is a large, four-square white château, with beautiful woods behind it—where later we learn to hide the tins we have been told to take down to the incinerator. This château is to be Haig's headquarters and home—for he had not yet arrived. But an army of Engineers is on the spot to fix up huts for the staff and generally prepare the place, and we are to help them until the time comes to mount guard, for everybody knows that the engineers like giving instructions and letting the P.B.I. do the work for them.

Bavincourt has not been touched by the war, although a trench has been dug just beyond the cemetery. But we are now within sound of the guns and one or two big shells are said to have fallen harmlessly in the surrounding fields.

Our billet is an evil-smelling, rat-ridden barn in a farmyard behind the church, and our beds are roughly constructed bunks of wire netting stretched between beams. We regard our new surroundings with horror. Poor innocents, we do not yet realise that this accommodation is the height of luxury to troops coming out of the line for so-called rest. While we are grumbling and cursing we are actually being pampered. We still look at things from a civilian angle, and seriously imagine that apart from the danger we are just as badly off as the men in the trenches.

There is an hour to spare before the roll is called on our first evening, so David and I, shuddering and depressed in our wet clothes, paddle down the main street of the village to see what it is really like. There are one or two mouldy little shops, but they have nothing to sell that interests us. There seems not to be a drop of beer or a bottle of wine in the whole place. However, I must say this for the enterprising inhabitants of Bavincourt— that as soon as they realised that troops with money to spend were billeted in the village there was hardly a cottage where you couldn't buy packets of chocolate, biscuits and cups of coffee, and the estaminets began to run with wine and beer as if some secret spring had been tapped.

" Bloody awful hole," is my first comment on Bavin-court, but Dave is not so sure. He has already spotted four women—of assorted ages and types but to me equally foul—with whom he covets a closer acquaintance. He cannot speak a word of French, but has addressed them in a universal and perfectly unmistakable language.

" Ah ! " he says to me, smacking his lips, " it's lovely stuff ! "

The corporal in charge of our billet is known derisively, but for no fathomable reason, as " Duckboard Bill." He is a nice ineffectual fellow, and the only one of us who has been in the trenches. He freely owns that he couldn't endure it. Later on we are to have ocular evidence of this, and he was to become a joke in the battalion. Poor Duckboard Bill ! God was very good to him, and eventually he got back to England—I think with shell-shock. Unlike most men whose nerves could not stand the strain of war he never tried to bully. I at least never laughed at him. I, in my glass house, have no stones to throw.

We do not sleep very well that night. For one thing we are not used to having rats running about over us.

Cw

We do not yet realise that we have been introduced to a new sport, that of strafing them with our entrenching-tool helves. Also they assist us in baiting Duckboard Bill.

Duckboard Bill is a sybarite with an air-cushion which he uses for a pillow. This he plants on the beam at the head of his bunk. Rats run along all the beams, but they will not cross Duckboard Bill's face unless they are frightened. The way to make them is to focus one on that particular beam with the light of an electric torch. The rat runs along the beam to try to dodge the light and eventually skips lightly over the corporal's countenance. He wakes up spitting. Great fun for everybody except Duckboard Bill, who cannot understand what makes the rats so fond of him.

Our small detachment constitutes a pretty mixed bag. Among us there is a fellow who has been on the London stage, and gives imitations of " Mrs. May." He is always doing this and we doubt if he will ever rid himself of the habit. All day long he is squawking in the voice of a Cockney virago, " You *woman*, you ! You *woman*, you ! "

Then there is Trewarren, a Cornishman, about the most unpopular of us all. He was a lance-corporal in England, and used to try to bluster like a sergeant-major. He worships spit and polish and used to suck up to Captain Jinks in England by inventing new stunts for cleaning up. He dropped his stripe when coming out to France, and now most of us won't speak to him. He is to die bloodily—for which I, even now, can feel no honest regret. Since most of us had to die, it was just as well that he should be one.

Then there are Walters and Makepeace. Walters has

been a scoutmaster and Makepeace a boy scout, and they still play at being boy scouts. They rig up a tent in the orchard and decorate the interior with scout-like inscriptions. They too are both doomed, poor chaps.

Maynard has had all the bad luck, and is to become a very tragic figure. He has been cashiered from a crack regiment in the very early days of the war, and has joined us as a private in the hope of getting back his commission. He is to be gazetted again—but only on the day of his death.

Jones too is among the doomed. He is an Old Salopian, a little Welsh boy hardly of military age, very foul-mouthed but quite amusing, and dead nuts on the rats.

These are a few of the names and personalities that linger in my mind, but were they all living to-day and I met them, I don't suppose I should remember their faces. There is also a teetotal, non-smoking, non-swearing section whose smug piety, even if sincere, is rather irritating. There is nothing funny or clever about swearing, but if a man doesn't swear when he's in the Service there must be something the matter with him.

Three cheers ! We wake up to a fine day, and Bavincourt takes on a different aspect. With the warmer weather approaching we begin to feel that it is going to be " rather bon." Moreover, we find that there is a mess hut for us at the end of the orchard, so we can actually take our meals sitting at a table. At eight o'clock we parade in rough dress for working parties, and Dave and I find that we have been sold into slavery for the time being to the R.E.'s. I keep well in the rear of the party, because I know to which end the soft jobs will be given.

Dave, however, prefers to work rather than to sit down and smoke and think beautiful thoughts, so we are separated. By the time I step forward all the tasks are safely allotted, and the sergeant plainly does not know what to do with me.

" Oh," he says, " go and report to Corporal Williams and see if he can find you a job. He's putting up a hut in that field over there."

In my new environment I do not yet know the ropes sufficiently to risk wandering away and losing myself. Plainly I am not wanted, and if I knew what I was to learn during the next few days I should be " missing, believed asleep." As it is I make in the direction indicated and come to a very small field surrounded by—of all rare things in France—a hornbeam hedge. Some men are busy with the skeleton of an officers' hut, but to make sure that I have come to the right place I call through the hedge : " Is Corporal Williams there ? "

On my side of the hedge I am invisible, and a small dapper figure springs smartly to attention, salutes and says, " Yes, sir."

" Stand easy ! " I shout back. " I'm only a private. The sergeant sent me to you to see if you can find me a job."

The men roar with laughter but Corporal Williams is evidently slightly deaf, for he remains at attention and says very respectfully : " Beg pardon, sir, I can't quite hear."

I repeat what I have said in a louder tone while the men laugh louder than ever, and then a dreadful change overtakes Corporal Williams. Evidently he is angry and at the same time he has lost all respect for me.

" *Come* 'ere ! " he roars. " *Come* 'ere, you something barstard, and I'll find you a job."

I make my way round to the gate while the rest of the party are still enjoying the joke. I rather wish they wouldn't enjoy it so much, because things are likely to go hard with me. There is nothing that a N.C.O. hates so much as making that kind of mistake, especially in the presence of others. I wonder what he is going to say when I reach him.

I was always one of those unfortunates who seemed fated to extract strong invective from earnest young non-coms. A musketry instructor, fresh from Hythe, always hated me to refer to the muzzle of the rifle as the spout. One of our own corporals once called me a " bloody yellow dog-faced Antichrist "—which, for a bit of impromptu, I thought rather good. On another occasion when a full equipment had been served out to me for the first time I did not know how to put on the pack, so rather than be late for parade I ran on with my pack in one hand and my rifle in the other. Smoke seemed to come out of the company sergeant-major's ears. " What do you think you are ? " he demanded. " A something commercial traveller ? "

I fully expect Corporal Williams to excel these mere amateurs in the matter of language, but his vocabulary is limited and alliterative, and evidently he had not read the poetry of John Masefield. In fact, he is only taciturn, and evidently he already has all the men he requires. I know nothing of the mysteries of putting up huts in sections, so after a while he addresses me bitterly as " Harry Tate." So I accidentally drop a beam weighing about a hundredweight on to his toe, and then he says he doesn't want me any more and tells me to report back to the sergeant.

The sergeant cannot be found—at least I can't find

him, and I am not going to spend half my life looking for
R.E. sergeants. So I skip into the woods like a faun,
sit down and begin a short story. And that's the last
the R.E.'s see of me for the day.

The two officers in charge of our detachment are
both decent chaps. Most of our officers are. They have
all been in the ranks of our regiment, and we all are
supposed to be more or less socially equal. That,
however, has tended rather to tighten up discipline.
Social values are at a discount in the Army, otherwise
we should have the Colonel's batman addressing him
as " Bertie."

Medville, a full "loot," is the senior. He is a quiet, sad,
kindly, decent chap. Later I am to go over the top with
him, and then I find him to be a fine soldier. Lucey, the
other, who has only one pip, is not a bad sort either, but
he is only twenty, and therefore rather full of buck. On
the whole we are rather lucky to have this pair with
us.

Dave finds me at mid-day during the hour dedicated
to rest and refreshment. He has done wonders already,
including a good morning's work. He has found an
estaminet where there is some beer, and leads me gently
by the hand in that direction. He has also thought that
it would be a good scheme to sleep out in the orchard on
fine nights, and having caught Medville in a good mood
has asked and received his permission.

" Next thing," he says, " is to get hold of a couple of
beds."

" Beds ! " I exclaim.

" Oh," says Dave airily, " we shall be able to win a
couple of beds all right if we keep our eyes skinned.
Estaminet's down the hill here. Don't put your head in

the old cow's bedroom. It doesn't half whiff. I wouldn't touch her with a barge-pole, but she's got some daughters, though."

He smacks his lips, winks and adds the one expressive word : "Yum!"

CHAPTER IV

Life in Bavincourt turned out to be idyllic—a long
happy picnic, but it was not until I came to see it in
retrospect that I realised how happy I was. The work
demanded of us was very light, in fact negligible, and our
first bad impression was melted by next morning's sun.
It was what we called a " mike."

Haig duly arrived at the château and a double guard
was mounted. The programme was one day on guard,
the next day free, and the third day very light fatigue
duties. However, not all of us were required for guard
duties, and some of us, Dave and I among others, got
fatigues all the time. These were not worth talking about.
If one got a job which lasted more than an hour one felt
hard done by. Having done it, the obvious thing was to
keep out of the way and avoid being roped in for something else. Thus I never had the honour of presenting
arms to the Commander-in-Chief. Indeed, I only saw
him once, and then in unfortunate circumstances which
I shall describe presently.

Dave " won " his bedsteads all right. He " won "
them from the R.E. dump. What they had been
intended for I don't know, but by the time Dave had got
to work with a saw there were two steel mattresses enclosed in frames. To make legs for them was easy enough,
and even the R.E.'s wouldn't have recognised their
lost property. How they made it good I don't know,
but probably by stealing from some other dump. That

was the way of the Army. If somebody stole something from you, you stole a duplicate article from somebody else. If somebody made a mistake he shouldered the blame on you, and you dumped it in turn on somebody else. So it went on in a wide and vicious circle.

We set our beds under a blossoming apple tree in the orchard, and only occasional rain drove us into the rat-infested barn. We could lie there under the stars and talk for half the night if we chose, and we often did, pausing at intervals to listen to the croaking of the frogs and the shuddering rumble of the guns.

Rations were neither plentiful nor good—but they never were with us. Possibly we had an unskilful Q.M. Civilians have infuriated me by alleging that we got all the food in France. The full ration was barely sufficient for men living and working (I am not now alluding to the work we did in Bavincourt !) in the open air. But if I were to subtract what I had from what I was supposed to have I should find that the Army owed me enough food to keep me for a year. Perhaps that is why the A.S.C. were so popular with the French peasantry.

Still, we could buy plenty of bread and eggs in the village, and it was the shortage of bread which was ordinarily our worst trouble. We were supposed to have half a loaf a day, but I don't think I received this full ration more than twice the whole time I was in France.

I ought to have been very happy, and I was at times, but my flesh was sensitive to the lightest shackles. I could not do just exactly as I liked. Even if my taskmasters were lenient I was still a slave, and none of us knew how long this leniency would last. It used to be said that the Army could do anything to you except put you in the family way—but that was before the W.A.A.C. was founded.

Sometimes when Dave and I lay under our apple tree listening to the drumming of the guns my conscience pricked me. It did not seem fair that we should be living this life of peace and idleness while within walking distance men were living like wild beasts and dying in indescribable agonies. Still, it was our good fortune, not our fault, and it was not for us to grumble. But I felt in my bones that we should pay for it sooner or later.

I had plenty of time for writing and I was thus reasonably well off for pocket money, for my kindly agent was able to send me some besides supplying my people at home. Even then I was able to spend half my days lounging in the woods with Dave Barney or sitting in the little estaminet half way down the hill.

The old woman of the establishment was called Madame Tindrawers. It was not her real name, of course, but she answered to it readily enough. She was a fat, foul-mouthed old hag, dirty in mind and body, and what Dave had said about her bedroom was something less than the truth. As the door, which opened from the living-room, generally stood wide, at least two of one's senses responded to what lay within. I should not think that the bed-linen had been washed or changed within living memory. Stout-hearted fellows used to come and eat the good lady's omelettes, but after having taken one glance at the family frying-pan I preferred to buy my own eggs and cook them myself. I don't know what Monsieur Tindrawers did for a living, as I only saw him occasionally of an evening, when he was generally disposed to chaffer for the virtue of his wife and daughters.

The two girls were quite good-looking, but very different in type. I found out afterwards that they were not really sisters, one of them having been adopted for a consideration. She was probably the result of an accident such as might happen to almost any French lady.

Nearly all the local peasants were genial, dirty and obscene. They had the manners, morals and habits of tame monkeys. They thought nothing of recommending their female friends and relatives for a purpose which, if specifically named, would bring the blush of shame to the cheek of Innocence. They spoke a little broken English, but their vocabularies consisted mainly of the foulest words. That was the fault of the men who had gone before us. It seemed a damnable shame that they should have used dirty language in front of these women. But when one is in Rome one does as the Romans do, and we soon found ourselves doing the same.

Even the smallest children could swear like troopers— or like infantrymen, which is probably worse. Poor little devils, they did not know what they were saying and they thought it funny. I remember one small boy who used to come round with *Answers* and *Tit-Bits* and, of course, the inevitable *Continental Daily Mail*. " Bloody good news for the Ingleese ! " he would shout. " *Ten more ships down ! Bloody* good news for the Ingleese ! "

We used to patronise Madame T. only for beer and wine. When we wanted food or coffee we went to farms or private cottages. Madame T. kept two kinds of beer which she labelled " French " and " English." They were both a pale dandelion colour and held only a faint flavour of real beer. " French " was a penny a glass and " English " was fourpence, but apart from that their own brewer wouldn't have known the difference.

The best house for coffee and bread and butter was a

one room cottage, the home of a widow lady whom we called " Madame Cow." Her name was something like Vache, but it wasn't quite. She was middle-aged and had one small boy. She spoke quite good English, in which she made functional jokes which used to worry the unco' guid quite a lot. One pious youth flamed red in the face and rushed out of the cottage after Madame had prophesied what would happen during the night if he drank any more coffee.

" I put it down to her ignorance," he remarked coldly afterwards.

" You poor ass ! " I said to him. " Don't you see that you're exposing your own ? Haven't you yet realised that these people are about two hundred years behind us in civilisation ? If you could have walked into an English country pub a couple of hundred years ago, the most virtuous landlady would have said things which would have made you wilt at the knees."

As a matter of fact Madame Cow was a very good-living woman and went to Mass every morning.

Another place where the coffee was good and where they had Petit Beurre biscuits for sale was a small farm about ten minutes' walk from our billet. But I never liked the place. In one corner of the room there was a curtained bed, and behind the curtains something living moaned and mouthed and shifted and gurgled. I don't know what kind of horror was behind those curtains, and now I shall never know, but I still sometimes dream of that room.

Yes, those were good days, when we were so near to the war and yet so far from it. Occasionally an enemy aeroplane would come over and twist about like a tiny insect while little fleecy clouds of shrapnel would come bubbling out of the blue sky around it. And once we got a real shock, when the ammunition dump at Gouy went up. We did not know what had happened, and thought at first that the Germans had invented some new and terrible engine of war. We were two miles distant, but the shock of every explosion seemed to go through our vitals.

It was a bad show and a good many were killed and injured, but the touch of comedy which follows upon tragedy in real life, as surely as it does in a drama on the stage, was not absent. In a hut close to the dump an A.S.C. man lay in his bunk with a rheumatic leg. When the dump started going up he rose from his couch and did the two miles into Bavincourt in rather less than twenty minutes, which was fairly good going, having regard for the fact that he had told the M.O. that he was unable to walk at all.

Sometimes at night, when there was a strafe on in the Arras sector, we climbed up into the church tower, and saw roughly the enemy line and ours pricked out in gun-flashes. On Sunday, after Monchy-au-Bois had fallen, we walked over to look at it and saw for the first time the site of a recent battlefield, the shell-holes, the smashed up German trenches and a derelict gun or two. We walked down into deep German dug-outs and found empty German cigarette cartons on a table. But now everything was eerily silent and deserted. There was nobody else about. The war had passed on, and now there was an eloquent silence, as if to say that God had not approved the din and destruction. Only our own voices, and the bees busy among the wild flowers and rank grass which grew around and between the ruined trenches broke the awesome stillness.

The cleaners-up had done wonders, but I stumbled—iterally—over one oversight. He was a German and he had been dead just long enough to be offensive. In my unadventurous life this was the first dead man I had ever seen, save for my father, who had lain smiling in his last sleep after months of weariness and pain. But this man was not smiling. I stumbled away physically and spiritually sick, and began to wonder, since this single poor corpse had turned my stomach, how I was going to face the Real Thing when it came. War, I knew, must be bad enough for a man burdened with his five senses, but it must be hell indeed for any with that sixth which is called " imagination."

Not more than a mile behind this battlefield—we had passed through it on the way there—was a village which had hardly been touched by war. The church and one or two farmhouses had been smashed, but that was all. Why the Germans had almost spared it I don't know. I could understand their smashing the church with its high tower, because I had already learned that churches were not used exclusively as places of worship.

Now, although the tide of battle had scarcely ebbed, peace lay upon the little place like a blessing from the skies, and old folk sat outside their cottages sunning themselves as they do in England. They had stood by their homes all the while, I suppose, in the expectation that at any moment a shell might fling them into eternity among the shattered ruins of their poor belongings. I have much to say against the French peasants—their greed, their physical and moral filth, their cruelty to animals—but I shall be the last to deny their stoical courage. Frankly I don't think our people would have endured what they endured. Later I was to see them

46

clinging to their poor little homes in villages where death and destruction whistled and hissed and crashed all day and all night, until they were actually ordered away. And when they went they left their cottages swept and garnished as if they were about to let them furnished to summer visitors.

Of course they hated us, and that embittered us at the time. But who shall blame them? How would our own rustics like a foreign though friendly army to invade their homes, sit in their chairs, drop their body vermin and make indecent overtures to the women? Generally speaking, the indecent overtures were not resented, but the few pure and fastidious women must have suffered torments.

I don't mean to suggest that the British Army was an army of Huns. Probably it was the best behaved army in the world. The disgraceful stories of the Peninsular War were not repeated. Generally the men paid for what they had, and paid dearly. The chaff, if obscene, was always good-natured. I never heard of a case of rape—that would have been the shortest step to a firing party and a wall. But war has a way of bringing out the wild beast in man, and boys with gentle mothers and sisters, and clean sweethearts waiting for them at home, said and did things which I can only hope they lived to regret.

I wrote home to my mother describing the wreck of Monchy-au-Bois, and was heartily rebuked for mentioning the village by name and made to re-write the letter. This was Medville, our O.C. detachment, who thus exercised his duties as censor. So I wrote another letter in which I said that I mustn't mention the village by name, in case the Germans found out there had been a battle there.

47

The problem of censorship was a very acute one to me. It was well enough to write a short story, but the difficulty was to get it censored. Officers were shy of tackling five thousand words or so, written in indelible pencil. True there were " green envelopes " which could be sent away sealed and were liable only to censorship at the base, but these were only sparingly issued. I solved the problem after a while.

There was in Bavincourt at that time a certain chaplain who took an interest in me because I wrote things, and he it was whom I coaxed into censoring my work. But in order to get him into the necessary good humour I had to sit in his billet by the hour and discuss with him the probable torments of the damned. Never before nor since have I met a man who was so fond of Hell. Directly one mentioned the word, save as an ejaculation, his eyes used to shine. He used to fire off at me barrages of Latin and Greek, which was a little embarrassing to one who had left school from a very low form at seventeen—and would have been superannuated if he hadn't ! However, I pretended to understand, and I also pretended to be very holy. I had to be the " Blue-eyed Boy " in order to get my copy past him.

Our friendship—if I may call it that—ended rather disastrously. One morning, after I had done my day's work, which consisted of pumping water and chloride of lime out of a well for about half an hour, I visited Madame T.'s estaminet, feeling that a little beer was indicated after the labours of the day, and I stayed for perhaps a couple of hours.

Now both the girls were what one might call high-spirited and given to horse-play, particularly the adopted daughter, who was apt to give one back-handers where they were calculated to hurt most. When I got up to go she sprang to the door before me and, to prevent my going out, spreadeagled herself across the threshold, hands and feet against either doorpost.

In order to get past her without using force I tickled her. The girl collapsed, screaming with laughter, and fell out into the road. The resistance having been thus suddenly withdrawn, I too fell, and we lay a laughing and struggling heap. And at that moment the chaplain happened to pass.

This was very embarrassing for me. I felt that my reputation as a very good young man was rather blown on. Moreover, my regiment was very keen on saluting, and there was nothing in the drill book or King's Regulations to say what a soldier ought to do when, in such circumstances, an officer passes. I could not spring to attention because the lady, having found that my hair was too short to permit of a substantial hold, was grasping me rather firmly by one ear and the collar of my tunic.

I did my best to nullify this oversight on the part of the War Office by declining to see the chaplain, but he certainly saw me, and after that I thought it would not be wise to call on him in his billet. However, shortly afterwards I met an A.S.C. lorry driver who had stolen enough green envelopes to last me for the rest of the war ; and since he only wanted two francs for them I was free of the censorship from that day forward.

Dear Bavincourt ! What fun we had there ! The job I " clicked for " nearly every other day was to get water for the R.E.'s, pumping it from a well close by Madame T.'s estaminet. Since I was nearly always the senior man, it generally fell to me to march the party down to the R.E.'s, whose camp was at the bottom of the hill. Nearly every day we met a little French General riding up the hill on horseback. I think he must have been some kind of liaison officer in attendance at our advance G.H.Q. He was probably a fine man, but he was a rotten horseman, and his charger was extremely nervous.

Thus, as we approached him, I would scream at the top of my voice : " *Party will march at atten-shun !* . . . *Party, 'shee-hun !* . . . *Heyes—left.*" At which the horse would behave like an unbroken bronco, and the little Frenchman would bounce like a pea on a shovel and scream angrily at me : " *As it were ! As it were !* " To save the civilian from puzzling over this cryptic word of command, I think he meant to say : " As you were ! " Dear man, I hope he never broke his neck while riding, for he provided me and many others with moments of the purest joy.

I am loath to leave Bavincourt, and before I do I must mention the one incident which singled me out for notoriety as a private soldier.

One morning I had been warned to present myself to the R.A.M.C. for a job, and having tumbled out of my bed in the orchard breakfastless and unshaven at the disgracefully unsoldierly hour of eight o'clock, I went to report in loose dress to the sergeant in the yard beside the château. Another man and I were singled out to sweep the veranda and steps of the château.

Now the Army has the queerest ideas about surface cleanliness. The room which the cleanest housewife in the world would consider spick and span would bring tears of shame and anger to the eyes of the martinet.

I would not for anything be a maid in the household of a really zealous officer. The sight of her shaking a mat out of a window would bring on a paralytic stroke. Her obvious duty would be to take the mat at least half a mile away before shaking it, and then disinfect it with something which made the eyes water and thus impregnate it with one of those very healthy smells which are so difficult to live with. Thus it was no surprise to me when the R.A.M.C. sergeant said to us :

" Now don't go sweepin' this 'ere dust on to the parth. Sweep it up into a neat 'eap on the bottom step, see. And then when you've done that, see, go and find a tin, and sweep it into the tin, see, and take it down to the incinerator, see."

Imagine the steps of a private house being swept in this manner ! Discipline, I suppose. Oh, well !

We swept the veranda and steps of the C.-in-C.'s château quite efficiently, I believe, and the dust was duly gathered into the shape of a small beehive on the bottom step. Now it chanced that morning that I was in the mood, for once, to carry out an order to the letter without being watched—and of course I paid for it. So said to the other man :

"B.O. and find a tin somewhere and I'll wait here and keep the heap tidy."

Off he went, and I hovered over the little pile of dust, tickling it with the broom from time to time when the breeze showed signs of scattering it. I was so engaged when the glass doors flew open and Sir Douglas Haig flew out on to the veranda.

I sprang to attention as well as a man can when he has a broom in his hand, and gazed vacantly nto the distance with that glassy stare which was considered so respectful. Sir Douglas Haig spoke. He said :

"I don't want to see you stand to attention. I want to see you get your work done, not standing about here doing nothing. Go on, man, sweep that dust away and then go ! "

Now he could not have known it, but this was hardly fair. I was carrying out an order, but I could not tell him so. There were some limits to my impertinence and greater limits to my courage. Besides, why should a great man who was concentrating his mind on a war of attrition be worried by such a trifle ? So I swept the dust broadcast on to the drive and ran for my life, privately hoping that Haig would subsequently find my companion lurking on the steps with the tin and waiting for me.

I went and reported back to the sergeant.

"Well," he said, "did you sweep that there dust up into a tin ? "

"No, sergeant," I said meekly. "I swept it on to the drive."

"But didn't I tell you——"

"Yes, sergeant," I said, still more meekly, "but I received another order."

Plainly his dignity was hurt.

"Oh ! " he exclaimed darkly. "'Oo from ? "

"The C.I.C.," I murmured, and enjoyed his facial expression.

"What shall I do now ? " I asked gently, after a pause.

"I think you've done enough for one day," he grunted ; and I thought so too.

The story was all over our detachment by mid-day and I was not popular.

" You bloody fool, you'll get us sent up the line," I was told.

And up the line we certainly went, although whether or not it was owing to me I don't know and now I shall never know.

I deeply regret now that I missed my one opportunity of meeting Earl Haig after the war. It might have amused him had I recalled the incident and pointed out to him the dangers attendant upon carrying out a simple order ! And now that this book can never fall into his hands he will not know how its author, the most un-soldierly soldier in his Army, is proud to have received even a rough word from him.

CHAPTER V

Of course it rained on the day we moved off—but I grow weary of mentioning an almost invariable accompaniment to any move of ours. The battalion was being gathered together from, it seemed, every back area of the British front, and we were to muster at Mont St. Eloi. Not more than fifteen per cent. of our men had been under fire before : what sort of a show were we going to make ? The longer men were kept out of the trenches the less they liked going in. It was like the celebrated dug-out disease from which most of us suffered later. Keep men in open trenches and they will endure shell-fire with equanimity ; but they will emerge from a safe dug-out into a strafe with the air of intelligent dogs who have heard the word " bath."

It is unnecessary to mention the number of the brigade or even of the division to which we were going. It was a hard-bitten fighting crowd, a " stunt " division, with a bad name among the Germans and a good name at G.H.Q. I daresay it was thought that these were the fellows who would make soldiers of us, but our new comrades in the division were not jealous of the honour.

We had a bad time from them at first and were always referred to as the something Blanks. They parodied our voices, and stung themselves to a fine fury at the thought that most of us had joined for the purpose of taking commissions. They thought we held ourselves superior to them, which, as soldiers, God knows we did not. Also

54

we had had a soft time which they, perhaps very naturally, resented. They took a special joy in describing to us the horrors of life in the trenches.

I had a verbal passage of arms with quite an old chap one day. At least, he was about forty, and that seemed old to me then ; and in appearance he might have been Old Bill's tidy brother. At last he asked me what something use we thought we were going to be when we got into the something line, and I answered, " We'll damned soon show you."

Quite to my surprise he put his hand on my shoulder and said very kindly, " That's the way to talk, chum." Perhaps it was, but my heart was in my boots when I said it.

I shall always hate the memory of St. Eloi with its ruined tower standing on the hill which echoed at most hours of the day and night to the angry voices of the guns. The noises made me think of the gnomes playing skittles in *Rip Van Winkle*. The camp itself made me think of the base camps reduced to a small scale, although we had huts to sleep in. There was the same unforgettable stink of incinerators, the same atmosphere of staleness, the indescribable odours of polluted earth where too many men have camped for too long a time.

It was that same earth that became one's friend when one was short of water. One cleaned one's knife and fork by sticking them into the ground and working them up and down. One cleaned out one's mess-tin by scrubbing it with the earthy side of a dab of turf.

Here we became lousy for the first time. It was an unforgettable sensation, that first time when one felt something walking under one's collar and pulled out a hitherto unfamiliar insect. I dropped my first specimen like a hot coal and shook with nausea. Soon we were all swarming, but we got used to it as we got used to every other detail of the pigs' lives we were compelled to lead. I found that the army pants, not being closely woven, provided the enemy with too much cover. Life was too short to spend in going through every square inch of one's pants pulling lice out by their hind legs, so I discarded pants altogether and never wore them at any season of the year.

We seemed to spend most of our spare time going through our clothes, catching lice and cracking them between our thumbnails, and burning their eggs under the seams with cigarette ends. Not that we had much spare time. It was parades, parades, parades all day, bomb-throwing, bayonet-fighting, the musketry range.

One amusing incident is worth recording. A surprise rifle inspection took place in my platoon. Of course no soldier out of the line cleans his rifle more than once a day, and ours had got dusty since the first parade, but as they had then been inspected and passed nothing much could be said.

I stood Number One in the ranks, and the young officer, coming first to me, spent about five minutes in adverse criticism. As I stood working the bolt before ordering arms I wondered how the next man was going to fare and cocked a glance in his direction out of the tail of my eye. The officer began as usual by lifting up his back sight—and a spider ran out.

It is a terrible thing to want to laugh when you dare not. I was not on battalion parade that morning in England when, in full view of all, a small stray dog mistook one of the C.O.'s legs for a street corner ; and I was on leave on another occasion when, mounted, he fell base over apex off his charger while dashing across the parade ground to rebuke some real or imaginary offender. I am glad I missed both. These things are very amusing afterwards, but they hurt too much at the time. I strained all the muscles of my face while the officer skipped like a young mountain goat at the sight of that spider.

As a step nearer the line we moved down to Aubrey Camp, Roclincourt, about two miles on the left flank of Arras.

Who will ever forget Arras who saw her then in the middle days of the war ? The whole rows of houses with their façades torn off so that one could see into every room, as in an architect's sectional drawing ; pictures hanging askew, beds with the clothes dragged aside and left just as when their occupants leaped up and ran for safety, perhaps more than a year since ; open wardrobes and garments still hanging on the pegs ; intimate medical appliances left ruthlessly exposed. Other houses were mere shells, others were a mess of rubble, others had smashed roofs and dropping eaves, others again seemed miraculously to have escaped untouched. Indeed, I found one road with high walls on either side and foliage brushing their tops, and little doors set in them here and there—reminding me of Mr. Wells's famous story—that seemed not to have been touched by the war.

Walking down this strangely quiet street with Dave one evening I could so easily fancy myself in some " genteel " London suburb or in the " residential " part of a quiet English country town on a Sunday night. I half expected to see rise in front of me a young man in blue serge and a bowler hat with his arm around the waist of a girl, sauntering slowly through the shadows.

The cathedral stood, a stricken giant, its steps barricaded by blocks of its own fallen masonry. Opposite was rather a curious sight. Out of an indescribable waste of rubble there soared triumphantly an iron spiral staircase, undamaged and apparently untouched, but leading only into mid-air instead of to a sometime top-floor block of offices.

Arras was a more poignant sight than Ypres. Ypres was a bleeding corpse and Arras still writhing in her death agony.

A few inhabitants still clung to the town, living mostly in cellars. For the most part they sold drinks and chocolate to the troops and mended watches.

Watch-mending was the great game in Arras. You took your watch to be mended and the wizardly old thief who took it from you promised it back by a certain day. On the eve of going up the line you went to get it and found that it wasn't ready. Then, of course, if you happened to get killed or wounded, or panicked off suddenly to another sector—which was always likely to happen—Monsieur stuck to the watch.

The first shell I ever heard and saw burst fell on Arras, which received a daily ration that varied like our own rations of food. We had just arrived at Aubrey Camp when we heard a crescendo whine and saw over Arras a black cloud arise, containing no doubt large quantities of bricks and mortar. After that came the crash of the explosion. We looked uneasily, almost guiltily, at each other. We didn't like it in the least. And yet that shell had fallen nearly two miles away ! Good Lord, what were we going to be like presently if we were jumpy now ?

Aubrey Camp will always be a mystery to me. We

were in tents in the open almost under our own captive balloons. Opposite us, rising above the second of two ridges of hills, were the German "sausages" from which we must have been perfectly visible. German aeroplanes came and went overhead all day, like wasps buzzing in and out of a room. They must have seen us, but they never attacked us. Nor did a single shell ever fall near the camp.

Shells screamed over us at night and crashed on a road just behind the horse lines in our rear. Shrapnel burst accurately over the cross-roads two or three hundred yards away. Three minutes' walk distant along the Arras road was a shell dump ranged between poplar trees and tastefully camouflaged. "Jerry" put that up one night and drove us into dugouts for shelter. But he never shelled the camp, from which we could see the Verey lights rise from his own front line at night.

I have often puzzled over this. Was there, behind that second far ridge of hills, a camp similar to our own ? Was there a tacit understanding to the effect : " All right, you shell our reserves and we'll shell yours ; you leave ours alone and we won't worry yours " ? I suppose there must have been mutual unspoken arrangements of that sort to prevent even war from becoming too impossible.

At the time I thought it rather clever of me to achieve trench fever without having been in the trenches. I felt it coming on for three or four days before we were due to go into the line—that hot-and-cold, miserable, all-overish feeling which one associates with the beginning of influenza or any other feverish condition. However, I did not feel inclined to go sick. It might have looked pretty bad under the circumstances,

59

particularly if the M.O. could find n. thing the matter with me. Going sick out here struck me as being very different from going sick in England.

I had been in this condition for two days when, standing on parade, I reeled and nearly fell. This led to my being sent to the M.O.'s dugout, where an orderly took my temperature and then turned and cursed me.

" Why the hell didn't you go on the sick parade this morning ? " he demanded. " Do you know you're up to over a hundred and three ? "

It ended in my being sent to the Field Ambulance at St. Catherine's on the outskirts of Arras, and made to walk there with rifle and full equipment, if you please. I crawled there somehow, entered a door labelled " Walking Wounded " and flopped.

I think I was about a week at St. Catherine's, in a ward full of lightly wounded men whose hurts were not sufficiently serious for them to be sent further down the line. These bright lads celebrated their temporary absence from the trenches by singing choruses, mostly unprintable, all day and all night. I lived on ordinary Army rations and scarcely slept a wink all the time. No one seemed to take any notice of me until one morning a doctor came round, looked at my temperature chart, and, seeing that I still stood at about a hundred and four, asked me if I felt any better. I told him that I was getting steadily worse, whereupon he had me shot off to a C.C.S. at Aubigny.

There for about a week I was too ill to take much interest in my surroundings, and for nearly a fortnight I lived exclusively on tinned milk. For that reason, perhaps, I have never since been able to endure the taste of it.

The C.C.S. was a home from home. It was constructed of huts, and mine was half empty when I arrived. The occupants of the beds—real beds with sheets—were mostly sick men ; but we heard the wounded being probed and dressed in the other wards. The doctor was a good chap and the nurses were fine.

I cannot express my admiration for these women, most of whom had no more vocation for nursing than most of us had for soldiering. They worked like slaves. They had to sacrifice their modesty—or false modesty, if you will—perform disgusting offices and ask us embarrassing questions about the functioning of our bowels. Thank heaven I could always manage to crawl out to the latrines, although not much further—as I was to learn when I was feeling quite well again and allowed to dress and sit up.

There was a canteen in the C.C.S., and when I heard that some bottled Bass had arrived I made a bee-line for it—and tumbled down in a faint opposite the counter. This, I know, is an excellent testimonial to the Burton brewers, but since this book is anonymous they will not be able to reward the writer with a few cases.

The fellow in the next bed to me also belonged to the Blanks, but he was not in my company. We discovered that not only were we at school together, but ten years since we had sat side by side in the same form. But we did not recognise each other, and it took us a fortnight to find it out. The Padre was another Old Boy. We agreed that it was a pity that we couldn't have a dinner.

Those of us who were convalescent went outside and took our meals in a mess hut. This was a mixed blessing, because the mess hut was next to the operating theatre, and while we were queueing up to go in we could look through the windows and see some practical surgery, while the reek of ether pervaded everything.

Some of our own wounded began to arrive. The battalion had not yet gone into action as a battalion, but parties had been sent into the trenches with other units for instructional purposes. One or two had already been killed. Two chaps had been wounded in the streets of Arras without getting any nearer to the line. One fellow brought into my hut had lost three fingers from his right hand, and seemed very pleased to think that he was out of the war. His description of the trenches was not inviting.

I stayed on at the C.C.S. until I was thoroughly ashamed of myself. I felt perfectly fit, and kept saying so to the M.O. when he asked me, but still he wouldn't let me go, until at last one day he said that he thought I should do. I was issued with a rifle and full kit and told to rejoin my unit at the same old camp near Roclincourt. For some of the way I was able to go by train, but the last five miles had to be walked.

What a strange complaint trench fever was. One got extraordinary temperatures, and it got one down most terribly but I never heard of a man dying of it. I had set out feeling quite well, but that five miles walk in full marching order was too much for me, and I arrived feeling as ill as I had ever felt. It was my duty to report to the M.O. and he took my temperature and cursed heartily.

" What's the use of sending men back like this ? " he demanded. " You've got a temperature of a hundred and two."

I explained to him that I had felt quite well for some time.

" Yes," he said, " but you haven't had a proper con-valescence. The battalion's going into the trenches to-morrow, and you can't possibly go with them. You'd better take a blanket to-night and go on the sick parade to-morrow morning."

But after a good night's rest I felt quite fit again. My temperature came down to normal, and I was marked " Medicine and Duty." I was to go after all. As it chanced, the M.O. did me about the worst possible turn.

CHAPTER VI

Eight days in the front line, eight days in the supports, eight days in reserve—that was to be our programme for many weary weeks. Sixteen days " in " and eight " out," but " out " did not mean going back to Aubrey Camp. It meant going into some lice-ridden dugouts in the railway cutting at Gavrelle, just by where the communication trench began, with our own batteries blazing away around us and German shells for ever seeking them.

It was summer and a so-called " quiet " sector of the line, else no mortal man could have stuck sixteen days of it off the reel. By the word " quiet " it was meant to convey that there had been nothing more than a little friendly shelling on each side, and one or two almost formal calls in the way of raids. Our own people were not meditating anything really dirty, and there was no reason to suppose that Jerry had any dishonourable intentions on a large scale.

We paraded on a hot, sunny afternoon—an afternoon which proved to be much too hot and sunny for me. I have forgotten what a soldier's complete kit was supposed to weigh, but it was something pretty considerable although the weight was scientifically distributed. We found, however, that going into the trenches, or anywhere else that was inaccessible to the transport, there was always something extra to carry—Lewis-gun panniers, bombs, rations in sandbags, rifle ammunition.

I had not gone very far before realising that, despite my temperature having been normal in the morning, I was still a sick man. By the time we reached the railway cutting and the entrance to Ouse Alley, the communication trench, I scarcely knew how to crawl.

Then began a seemingly interminable trek up a winding ditch six and a half feet deep by about four feet wide. Fortunately the trench was dry enough despite its name, but there were hundreds of irritating little obstacles which were for ever making one break his step or bend his back. Every minute the word came down to be passed on, " Wire overhead " or " Wire underfoot." I staggered on, my head splitting, my mouth dry as a kiln and my clothes drenched with the sweat of fever. Some Christian soul, seeing my distress and knowing the cause, had taken my rifle, but it was all that I could do to keep on my legs.

There came a crescendo scream and a ringing crash. Over the parapet we saw rise out of the earth, fifty yards away, a black cloud in the shape of a great chestnut tree, which seemed to hang in the still air a full minute before it began to melt. That was, so far, my closest acquaintanceship with a shell, and I flinched and ducked at the explosion while all the while I wanted to die.

I believe the system of the Army was to make men so tired and miserable by the time they reached the front line as to be entirely indifferent to their lives and destinies. No happy man wants to die. We were very shortly to become victims of this system, and looking back on it dispassionately, as one who has passed through it and is unlikely to do so again, I must freely admit that it was as sound as it was cruel. That I, who should have been in bed once more and living on slops, got about a quadruple dose of this medicine was merely my misfortune and the M.O.'s fault.

I was in the half-company which was to go into the supports for the first eight days. I passed out of one of the circles of Hades and we reached the support line where, thank God, we could take off our packs and ease our aching backs against the walls of the trench. The fellows we were relieving were glad to see us, begged cigarettes of us, and told us that there wasn't much of a war on locally. They hoped it would keep fine for us.

A stretcher party came shoving past us. On the stretcher, completely covered by a blanket, was something that moaned and whimpered. I heard afterwards that he was a sergeant who had had the rod of a trench mortar go clean through him and that he could not possibly live. I was half sorry that the blanket covered him, because I had lately made a resolution.

I was one of those sensitive, nervous men who could not endure the sight of pain or death. I stopped short of fainting at the sight of blood, but I hated to see even so trivial a wound as a cut finger. But since I had somehow to endure the hell into which I was about to be flung, I was determined to know the worst at once—to take a damned good look at the first shattered man, living or dead, that I could find, and get it over.

I had not long to wait. It was a mistake to relieve in the day-time, even in the quietest sector, ye All-Wise Ones on the Staff. Those sausage balloons were not up there for decorative purposes, nor to advertise Dewar's whisky or the *Daily Mail*. There came a series of terrific explosions quite close to us. There is no explosion which, for sheer gut-stabbing ferocity, is quite like that of a *minenwerfer*. The bursting of one close at hand was like one's conception of the end of the world, but although their local effect was terrific they did not do much damage laterally.

A minute or two later I was detailed for a job about ten bays of the trench further on. The parapet was smashed to pieces, and on the opposite wall was a great splash of blood. On the ground lay a man with a grey and witless face, one of his legs hanging by a string from just below the knee. Close to him lay a headless trunk with one leg attached to it. Two out of the three in that bay had been killed. Stretcher-bearers were coming for the man who still lived : our job was to clear up the mess. We picked up unspeakable things with our hands, putting them into sandbags.

Strangely enough the actual experience was not so revolting at the time as it seems in retrospect. I could not have endured it before ; I could not endure it to-day ; but I derived an odd sort of comfort at finding that I could endure it then. At least I knew the worst that my eyes could show me. I was unlikely ever to see anything much more beastly.

I learned afterwards that one of the smashed-up men was an old comrade of mine in England. Poor devil, that was his fate after ten minutes in the line, but perhaps it was a merciful one. He had not to plod on in misery and hardship for months and even years, and he could not have felt even the shock of his soul being jolted out of his body. The only way to live out there was to turn one's face against sentiment and regard human flesh merely as flesh. From that point of view one can see just as unpleasant sights to-day in almost any butcher's shop. For some reason unknown to our philosophy we were fortified against ugly sights by the knowledge that our own bodies might be torn and distorted out of God's image and likeness.

Since I was introspective and had enough egotism for three people, my own psychology interested me enormously. I was horribly afraid, but I was never terrified as I had been on comparatively trivial occasions unconnected with the war. Fear in battle came to me as a deep depression, a black wet blanket of misery which enfolded me, a leaden weight dragging at my heart. Long afterwards I had one nerve-storm when I was alone in a shell-hole, but that, I think, was because my senses had been blasted out of me. At first I was admittedly, and I am afraid obviously, jumpy ; but that was due to my physical weakness and the fever in my blood. I promised myself that after I had had some sleep I would wake again as fresh as I had woken that same morning.

Sleep ! I did not yet know what I was in for. When darkness had fallen and we had " stood down " I was detailed to go on a ration party. We had only brought up with us enough food for the rest of to-day, and to-morrow's had to be fetched. There was no cover for the cooks anywhere near the line, and they remained with the transport in St. Catherine's and sent the stuff up cold. We had to brew our own tea on fiendish contrivances called Tommy Cookers, which took on an average two hours to boil half a pint of water.

The ration dump was in the railway cutting and the rations were pushed up on trucks. Jerry could hear the trucks and he rarely failed to present his compliments in a solid form. He knew exactly when we went to get rations, and having a section of the trench called Brad-ford Alley beautifully " taped " he invariably plastered it with shells at about the time we were going through.

68

Here it was that Trewarren was killed a few nights later, and one of our sergeants, an amateur county cricketer, was picked up with over seventy small wounds from a *minenwerfer*. The miracle is that he played cricket for his county at least once after the war.

To get rations entails that long march through Ouse Alley, and a long wait in the cutting with parties from every other battalion in our sector until our truck arrives. It was here that a very amusing incident once occurred.

Tommy's great delight was to talk to an officer in the dark and pretend not to know his rank. One black night a party of the Artists Rifles was waiting in that cutting, with parties from many other units, for the trucks to come up. There was the usual strafe, and a swift scattering to find cover. When it was over the Artists officer started trying to collect his men, and going up to a fellow who happened to be in the Drake Battalion he asked : " Are you an Artist ? " " No," came the prompt answer from this scandalous marine, " I'm a fornicating comedian."

Getting rations occupied literally the whole of the night. Indeed, dawn was breaking by the time we got back, and it was time to " stand to." I have no recollection of how I got back, laden with my sandbags of rations, but I did it somehow. Thank God that after stand-down and the inspection of rifles I shall be able to get some sleep.

Do I ? I am immediately warned for sentry. This consists of two hours of staring at a scrap of looking-glass inverted on the parados so as to reflect a little area of coarse grass waving in the breeze. I must sleep ! Oh, God, I must sleep ! I shall go mad or die if I don't sleep.

A Good Samaritan has been making my tea for me, and the water has just boiled when I come off sentry. The tea does me good. Now at last, surely, I can sleep, and if they bung over every bit of stuff that ever came out of Krupps they won't wake me.

But not likely ! We are very short of water, and the water-point is where everything else seems to be—at the entrance to Ouse Alley. Three other men and I are each given a brace of petrol cans and told to get them filled. Sobbing under my breath, I start off.

We walk into some desultory shelling, which increases my agony, and crouch for five minutes at the bottom of the trench while earth and stones are rained on us and we get the taste of explosive in our mouths. By the time we have filled the petrol cans I am useless. I am the biggest and perhaps normally the strongest of the four, but I cannot carry the two cans. The others, nearly as tired as I am, curse me heartily, but help me. We get back somehow. Now, sleep ! Oh, sleep !

But there is nowhere to sleep. One can sit on the fire-step. Apart from that there is only the bottom of the trench where one has to risk being walked on. The officers have roughly constructed dugouts and the ser-geants have funk-holes, but we are allowed nothing. The soil is soft, red and sandy, and we are forbidden to make funk-holes for ourselves for fear of bringing down the walls of the trench.

I have always felt that even the platoon commander, who lived with his men, never realised their sufferings. *He* had at least a shelter where he could stretch his legs, comparatively ample food, and —whisky ! I don't mind owning that I would have risked my soul just then for a double Scotch.

Our company officers were the best fellows in the world, with one exception, the one exception being my platoon commander, but I am sure they never quite realised what we were going through. I don't know why my platoon commander had been given a commission in our crowd, because he was not of the same social caste as the earlier members. He had been a village schoolmaster, and was used to browbeating smelly children and telling them that they mustn't go to the lavatory during the spelling lesson. He put on as much edge as if he had been a master at Eton—and I have met some Eton masters, God bless them! This ex-pupil-teacher was a bully, but I bear him no ill-will, for he was a good man in the line. The kind of bully I really loathed was the skunk who crumpled up when there was dirty work about.

An officer's job was a damned hard one. I didn't realise it then as I do now. How to be decent and human to the men, and at the same time keep an iron hand on them, must have been the devil of a problem. A lot of fun has been poked at the Temporary Gentleman, but the fellows who came from shops and offices, with little education and less tradition, did their job somehow and did it well. I hated being jiggered about (we used a slightly different phrase) by people that I considered my inferiors (I don't mean our first batch of officers), but I who was a private, and a bad one at that, freely own that it was the British subaltern who won the war. American papers please copy.

Quite the worst type of officer was the promoted sergeant-major. You could always tell them—vulgar beasts who waxed their moustaches, men with thick apoplectic necks, bulging eyes and a deplorable lack of aspirates. Whatever rank they achieved they were still warrant-officers in spirit. They could never be anything else.

To return to my own troubles, after bringing back the water, I squat on the fire-step, close my eyes, and am sound asleep in a second. This blissful state of unconsciousness lasts for twenty minutes. I am nudged. The Brigade Staff is coming round. The Brigadier, who looks extremely well nourished and well rested, regards us with a well-bred scorn. The sight of a man resting is as hateful to the sight of a Brigadier as a vulgar picture postcard from Margate is hateful to the sight of a refined maiden lady.

" Oh—ah—Captain Perks," he remarks in a rich fruity voice, " Can't you find these men something to do ? "

So we are sent to carry duck-boards to a part of the line where they aren't wanted, and then, of course, we have to bring them back again.

The swine ! Why won't they let us sleep ! Why won't they let us sleep !

The worst of being in a quiet part of the line is that one sees too much of the Staff. They are very bad for one's ego. It is bad to hate people. One cannot conjure up a personal hatred for shells—or for the people who are merely doing their job by sending them over—but it is easy to conceive a hellish hatred for Staff officers.

I have only seen Staff officers twice in places where there was trouble. One, I think, was in the support line through an unfortunate accident which no doubt he regretted ; but the other, an old man, I am bound to confess was a hero and almost made me respect the Brass Hats. He comes later.

Where there was no fighting nor likelihood of fighting, the Staff-birds mooched about the front line and supports to show us how brave they were, and to put a spoke in wheels which were running quite smoothly without them. It was only when things were going badly that we needed these talented gentlemen, and then they were always safe, winning the war by the exercise of their intellects, in farmhouses a dozen or so miles behind the line.

There was something in the demeanour and appearance of these Great Ones which was extremely irritating to us poor slaves. They were much too well groomed, obviously well fed, and had not neglected their beauty sleep. Some of the younger ones we knew to be cowards who had been turfed out of the line because they were unfit to lead men. " He's no good—find him a job on the Staff."

One could have forgiven this and merely envied them their good luck were it not for their behaviour towards us. Suppose the Deity were unjust and unloving, and imagine His attitude towards the lower animals of His own creation and you will have some faint idea of the average Staff officer's regard for the man who carried a rifle. Yet in my battalion there were men better born, better bred and better educated than many of these organ-grinders' monkeys in their primrose-coloured breeches.

I get about three hours sleep in my first three days and nights—bad enough for a fit man, but unspeakably agonising to one in my state. I get partly delirious and begin to " see things." In the morning a sergeant comes round, points to the German observation balloons, the malignant eyes which watch us all day, and says in his high-pitched cultured voice—such a strange voice to belong to a sergeant : "See those bloody sausages ? Well, don't get moving about too much, you chaps, or we shall be in receipt of excrement."

We promise to be good. We don't want to move about. We want to *sleep*. But within an hour the Staff is about and the rich fruity voice says : "Oh—ah—Captain Perks, can't you find these men something to do ?" And so it goes on, and we slog at some back-breaking and perfectly useless task while our sweat irritates the louse bites all over our speckled bodies.

Of course we fall asleep on sentry, but our officers are too decent to make a song about it. A sentry asleep in the line is liable to be court-martialled and shot, but I don't think it was often done. It must stand to reason that a man who can go to sleep *standing up* while his life is in danger must be in a pretty bad way, and even the Army Council cannot alter the laws of nature.

I did it twice, and the first time I was caught by Mr. Cleeves, a short, quiet, kindly " loot " about forty years old. I recognised his type in the elderly lieutenant in *Journey's End*. He tapped me on the shoulder and asked me what I was doing. " I was only blinking, sir," I answered. " Well, don't blink like that again," he said, and passed on. Had I been caught by the excessively military ex-village-schoolmaster there might have been trouble.

The second time I did it thoroughly, and walked in my sleep. This was at night. The rest of my platoon had gone to get rations, and I was left as the one sentry—this was in the supports—until their return. This was practically an all-night job and a pretty tough one. A lance-corporal had been detailed to supervise me, and he very naturally went to sleep. So did I.

74

I woke up in a strange country. To be precise I woke up in the front line on the left flank of the battalion on our left, having walked about two and a half miles through trenches. Trench sentries had been posted to challenge strangers, and thus prevent German spies in British uniforms from prowling about, and I had to run the gauntlet on my way back.

" Why the bloody hell couldn't you answer when I challenged you an hour ago ? Nearly poked my bleedin' bayonet through you, I did." This was the sort of stuff handed out to me at almost regular intervals on my return journey.

I got back just before the ration party to find that the lance-corporal, having woken up and discovered me to be missing, had taken my place on the fire-step, so nothing was known officially about my unconscious exploit.

The following night, when, strangely enough, I was getting a little legitimate sleep, I set off on another ramble, but I had only got through about two bays of the trench when I woke up to find myself talking nonsense to the ex-schoolmaster.

I was not the only somnambulist. We had a sergeant who, by the queerness of his behaviour, showed us one night that he was walking in his sleep. He picked up all our packs and " dressed " them very neatly on top of the parados, while we gathered around him, grinning and nudging, to see what he would do next. Even when one of the packs fell down on his nose, and he swore heartily at it, he did not wake !

After five or six days the fever left me again and life began to be more tolerable. I was still not getting nearly enough food or nearly enough sleep but I lost my jumpiness, and although the shadow of fear always hung over me I felt that I was no longer likely to make an exhibition of myself.

Since we were at some distance from the enemy the front line was more dangerous than the supports. We got the same amount of shelling and there was always the danger of a raid. Moreover the Germans had sent out into the long grass and shell-holes of No Man's Land a number of snipers whose job was to pick out the heads of sentries at night.

I had the misfortune to find myself in a bay of a trench which, owing to the undulations of the land, was capable of being enfiladed by one of these bright lads, and wondered for a long time why I, at the bottom of a deep trench, was conscious of bullets buzzing round my devoted head. Then I happened to notice that the wall of the traverse was pitted with bullet-holes, and I must have had several miraculous escapes. I pointed out these holes to an officer, and we stopped all that nonsense by piling some more sandbags on the parapet of the opposite traverse.

There was not so much work in the front line, and more time for leisure and rest. I was able to do some reading and a little writing. I had taken out with me, Chaucer's *Romaunt of the Rose* and the *Canterbury Tales*, not because I wanted to pose as an intellectual, but because I wanted books which were going to take some time to read. With my limited knowledge of old English it was impossible for me to gallop through Chaucer. I had read the *Canterbury Tales* before and re-read them out there again and again. The *Romaunt of the Rose* I have still to read. I lent it to a corporal who was so careless as to get himself killed while he still had it, so I never saw my copy again.

A fellow in my section had a pocket edition of Robert Browning which I borrowed, and I took a deep delight in re-reading the poems that I already knew by heart. I saw already the necessity for preserving what was left of my soul and not becoming altogether the kind of beast into which the exigencies of our lives were slowly but surely transforming us.

There was no romance, no " fighting." The enemy was as securely hidden from us as we were hidden from him. When shells came over it scarcely occurred to us that a human agency had sent them ; we seemed to be the victims of some eruption of nature, slaves compelled to live precariously and in misery on the brink of a volcano.

Browning helped me to believe that memories of the old comfortable life were not merely the memories of dreams. There were still English homes, and beds, and garden chairs, green lawns and clusters of flowers, food which did not look as if it came out of a pig-trough, ripe-lipped dainty girls, people who did not qualify every noun with a filthy adjective. Some of us would win back to these delights. Surely they could not kill us all.

Here's the garden she walked across
Arm in my arm but a short while since . . .

Thank you, Robert Browning. If in the Great Beyond I have the chance of shaking your spirit hand I shall shake it hard, although, of course, when you tossed your pebbles into the pond, you did not guess how far the ripples were going to spread.

77

CHAPTER VII

Eight days out and sixteen days in. It goes on throughout the rest of the summer. We are becoming acclimatised to trench warfare.

We know by the singing of a shell when it is going to drop near us, when it is politic to duck and when one may treat the sound with contempt. We are becoming soldiers. We know the calibres of the shells which are sent over in search of us. The brute that explodes with a crash like that of much crockery being broken, and afterwards makes a " cheering " noise like the distant echoes of a football match, is a five-point-nine. The very sudden brute that you don't hear until it has passed you, and rushes with the hiss of escaping steam, is a whizz-bang. For a perfect imitation of a whizz-bang, sit by the open window of a railway compartment and wait until an express train passes you at sixty miles an hour.

The funny little chap who goes *tonk-phew-bong* is a little high-velocity shell which doesn't do much harm.

" Minnies " and " flying pigs " which are visible by day and night come sailing over like fat aunts turning slow somersaults in mid-air. Wherever one may be, and wherever they may be going to drop, they always look as if they are going to fall straight on top of one. They are visible at night because they have luminous tails, like comets.

The thing which, without warning, suddenly utters a hissing sneeze behind us is one of our own trench-mortars. The dull bump which follows, and comes from the middle distance out in front, tells us that the ammunition is " dud."

The German shell which arrives with the sound of a woman with a hare-lip trying to whistle, and makes very little sound when it bursts, almost certainly contains gas.

Miles and miles behind us there is a fifteen-inch Naval gun. This is only pooped off about twice a day. We don't hear it fired, but we hear, about seven miles up in the air, the sound of a single railway engine shunting through a station, and afterwards, very far distant, a dull roar. This probably means that some fat Huns, sitting in imagined security in a village well behind their lines, have received a birthday present.

We know when to ignore machine-gun and rifle bullets and when to take an interest in them. A steady *phew-phew-phew* means that they are not dangerously near. When on the other hand we get a sensation of whips being slashed in our ears we know that it is time to seek the embrace of Mother Earth.

We have learned to have an awesome respect and fear of our own artillery and machine-gunners. One of our own eighteen-pounders, firing short, has blown up our front-line latrine. One of our own machine-gunners has drilled a neat hole through the shoulders of a sentry on a front-line fire-step. He fell on top of me, just as I was about to take his place, and complained bitterly.

When we are out at night on working-parties in No Man's Land we learn to fear our own machine-guns as much as we do those of the Boche. Machine-gunners are light-hearted fellows. They make their guns say " *Om-tiddly-om-pom*," and then Brother Boche answers, " *Pom-pom*."

Now this is very amusing, the light-hearted side of war

79

and all that, and just as the editor of *Punch* would like it, but we do wish our chaps would elevate a bit while we are out in front.

We have done wiring parties and we have done raids, and our comrades in the division are slowly ceasing to despise us. Considering the quietness of the front we have had a lot of casualties. Talking of raids, our friend the actor, who was always imitating Mrs. May, has got a Blighty one. The legend, which I have never believed, is that out on a reconnaissance raid one night, he put his head into a German machine-gun post and, in a high falsetto voice, inquired : " Is Mrs. May hin ? " And " Mrs. May " was !

Certain it is that he lay on the lip of a shell-hole all night shamming dead, and ran for it in the morning. It was not until he got back to our trench that this son of Thetis found that he had been shot through the heel—it must have been his only vulnerable spot—and got to England with it, and I don't think he ever came out again.

Yes, ours is a very quiet sector as sectors go. Oppy Wood, haunted if ever a wood were haunted, the Red Line, Gavrelle, the Mayor's Garden. Yet every time we " move to the right in fours " and, swinging on our heels, turn our faces to the north, we know that we are not all coming back. Whose turn is it going to be this time ? Our own, or some other fellow's, who doesn't really matter to us ?

We have become grossly selfish. We think only of our own bellies and our own skins. It has to be that way. Our hearts would break if we shouldered the burdens of others and let our minds dwell on their agonies and deaths. It isn't safe to have a friend. Any moment he may become a mess of human wreckage with a twisted rifle in his hand, and then you've got to look for a new one. When a man is killed we rush to him to see whether he's got any food in his haversack or, that priceless possession, a safety-razor.

I don't see much of Dave in the line. He was never in my platoon, and he has become a stretcher-bearer. Stretcher-bearing is a lovely job when there is nothing doing. There are practically no duties, for the strength of the stretcher-bearer must be preserved in case of emergencies which may occur at any moment. Trust Dave to find a soft job ! When there is real fighting, a regimental stretcher-bearer's life is hell upon earth—as I found out later to my cost.

There is a pretty picture being sold in England, and much in demand among sentimental old maids. It represents a man with a red cross on his arm giving a drink to a wounded man out in No Man's Land, with the shadowy figure of the Saviour looking on approvingly. That picture, we know, is bilge. The men who really rescue and succour the wounded are the regimental stretcher-bearers, who wear on their left arms a brassard marked with the letters S.B. They take their lives in their hands, walking right up to the German wire, if need be, to look for the wounded, and carry them to the Aid Post, which is generally situated far back and in comparative safety. There they are handed over to the tender mercies of the assorted brigands who form the rank and file of the R.A.M.C., to be carried a further stage to the Field Dressing Station, and if they get there with their personal possessions—or get there at all—they're damned lucky.

Dave is having as good a time as any soldier in the

line could expect to have. Every time we meet he utters a catch-phrase which I think was of his own invention— " Never were there such times for the working classes ! " I decide that I too will become a stretcher-bearer if I get the chance, and so get rid of my blasted rifle. I did eventually—but I did it at the wrong time.

My rifle is a curse to me. We are all specialists, and I am a rifle-grenadier. My special job is to fire Mills bombs on rods out of the rifle by means of blank cartridge. Nothing fouls a rifle more than " blank." All we rifle-grenadiers are given bad rifles, and we have to subject them to rough usage, but when there is an inspection our " hipes " are supposed to be as perfect as the next man's, which is quite impossible. This gets me into quite frequent trouble.

Well, as you see, we are slowly becoming real soldiers, although many of us have not yet set eyes on a German at large. Few of us have killed our man, and we are slowly realising that the job of the infantry isn't to kill. It is the artillery and the machine-gun corps who do the killing. We are merely there to be killed. We are the little flags which the General sticks on the war-map to show the position of the front line.

Looking back, I fear there is no place for me in Valhalla. I pooped off a few rounds, but if any Fritz got hit by me he was very unlucky. I have been in a number of so-called bayonet charges, but never saw a bayonet used, nor have I met more than one man who received a bayonet wound. We were either killed in heaps long before we got near the enemy line, or found a few poor shell-shocked devils who were screaming to surrender.

All very unheroic. We find for ourselves the truth we have already been told—that there is no romance in the war. It is an inglorious hotchpotch of misery and dreariness, varied occasionally by short spells of stark dreadfulness. Yet there are moments. Sometimes when we are standing-to, I realise that I—I of all people—am holding my own little bit of the line with rifle and bayonet, standing between England and those fellows in field-grey over yonder. But I have never mentioned it until now, and it was perhaps only an idle thought that blew into an empty mind.

I have been reading an account of the war written by one of those fellows in the opposite trenches, and I am appalled at the dullness of my own narrative. *We* were never barraged in a cemetery and constrained to yank corpses out of coffins and climb into them for cover. Strange how these coffins came out of the ground nice and whole, having been uprooted by shells. Had I found a shell-crater deep enough to blow out a coffin I should have been into that better 'ole—never mind about the coffin—and felt safer than I now feel in crossing the Strand.

In spite of the " funks " we had in the battalion—and I was one—we kept our trousers clean on the inside. I never played cards in a hospital ward while one of the patients was attending to the natural requirements of his wife. I never swam, like Leander, to court a French lady whose virtue was to be had in exchange for a loaf of bread and a pound of sausage. I think the cold water would have damped any ardour that the paucity of Army rations had allowed to remain. Forgive the dullness of this narrative, my masters. I could, if required, write something quite interesting—but it wouldn't be true.

Mr. Bottomley has been in the back areas of our sector.

but has now returned home and is telling the working classes, through the medium of *John Bull*, what the war is really like. The restrained title of the series of articles is " Somewhere in Hell." Only think of it—Mr. Bottomley has been in places where he had to wear a gas-mask ! He also writes, " I have held the hand of the dying "— a most menacing observation. Suppose I am knocked out and, while unable to defend myself, Bottomley comes and holds my hand ! Mr. Bottomley has added a new terror to modern warfare.

We have learned to jest and even boast about our own fears. " By gad, I did have the wind up when those ' minnies ' came over last night." " I bet I had it worse than you, old bean." We have learned too to jest at death, even as very pious men sometimes indulge in light profanity. " *Oh, Death where is thy sting-a-ling-a-ling or Grave thy victor-ee !* " Nothing seems quite the same after it has been ridiculed, and even the King of Terrors can be robbed of some of his grim majesty.

Although we have not been in any heavy engagement so far, we have lost quite a lot of men. A new draft has joined us. We are now nearly half conscripts, and let me say at once that the conscript, having been made to take the plunge,was on the average as good a soldier as the rest. Quite a number of them are fine fellows who, in more fortunate circumstances, would have joined up in August '14. Who expected a man with a wife and family, and a business entirely dependent on his own supervision, to rush into the Army while single young men were dodging the Service and earning good money? Nobody, surely, except the old men who had "given" their sons and the old maids who had "given" their nephews.

84

A bit of good news at last ! A persistent latrine-rumour has actually come true. We are going out of the line for a long rest. There is also an ominous rumour to the effect that this only means that we are only going to be fattened up for a killing on a really big scale. Bitter fighting is going on at Passchendaele. Division after division is being hurled at that plague-spot, which is going to be no damned good to anybody after it is taken. The casualty lists have swollen to three times their normal size at midsummer.

But what does anything matter ? We have learned to live entirely in the present. Each individual feels that something may turn up to save *him* from the slaughter. Meanwhile we are going out to *rest*.

One night's real sleep—seven blissful hours of it—on the outskirts of Arras, and then on a sharp, sunny September morning we fall in and swing along in columns of fours with our backs to the line on the way to our first camping ground. We are brown and lean and hungry, but apart from the nerve-strain which shows in the eyes of some of us we are fighting-fit and almost as happy as if we were going home on leave.

The drums are with us. They have been in St. Catherine's all the time practising martial music and making those fiendish Tommy Cookers. They play marching tunes for us to sing to, which we do with a will, and when they are resting we sing our own songs.

It seems a pity that many of the soldiers' songs, probably because of their obscenity, will in time be lost as irretrievably as those that were sung in the Napoleonic wars. Some were merely foul, but others were quite funny, and one or two showed signs of genuine literary craftsmanship.

" *The lady she was dressing, Dressing for the ball*——"
—what Tommy took this straight from the Decameron
and put it into verse in the true ballad form ? It was very
amusing, admirably executed and, to me, not offensively
dirty ; but no modest pen could quote one single stanza.

I Love my Girl was simply filthy. A bawdy song
ought to be at least partly redeemed by humour.

One of the division's favourites, set to a good marching
tune, consisted only of one verse. I give a Bowdlerized
version of it.

> *I 'aven't seen the Kayser for a 'ell of a time,*
> *I 'aven't seen the Kayser for a 'ell of a time.*
>   *I bin on the Somme to see what 'e's bin doin',*
>   *The —— ——rd Division will be the bastard's ruin.*

> *I 'aven't seen the Kayser for a 'ell of a time,*
>   *'E's the leader of 'is Army—Army,*
>   *'E's the leader of the whizz-bang band,*
> *So damn 'im 'e's no cousin of mine !*

I did not hear *Mademoiselle from Armentières* until
I got back to England, and I think it must have
derived from another song we used to sing which had the
same tune and burden. Having politely altered a few of
the words—which ones the initiated will easily guess—I
can jot down a few of the verses from memory.

> *A German officer crossed the Rhine, parly-voo !*
> *A German officer crossed the Rhine, parly-voo !*
>   *A German officer crossed the Rhine*
>   *To know the women and drink the wine—*
> *Inkey-pinkey-parly-voo.*

86

Oh, landlord, have you a daughter fine? Parly-voo!
Oh, landlord, have you a daughter fine? Parly-voo!
  Oh, landlord have you a daughter fine
  Fit for an officer from the Rhine?
Inkey-pinkey-parly-voo!

My daughter, sir, she's much too young, parly-voo!
My daughter, sir, she's much too young, parly-voo!
  My daughter, sir, she's much too young
  To be messed about by a son of a gun—
Inkey-pinkey-parly-voo!

Oh, father dear, I'm not too young—parly-voo!
Oh, father dear, I'm not too young—parly-voo!
  Oh, father dear, I'm not too young,
  You can go and ask the gardener's son!—
Inkey-pinkey-parly-voo.

Tommy's songs varied extraordinarily. There was the frankly obscene, the mawkishly sentimental, the utterly ridiculous and inconsequent, the humorously funky, and occasionally the good stuff. I am no musical critic, except that I know that anything that appeals to me is pretty sure to be extremely bad. I like Molloy's *Boys of the Old Brigade,* and I don't care who knows I like it. I heard it sung once in an estaminet, and after the usual songs, sung in self-mockery, such as *I Want to go Home* and *Take me Back to Blighty,* this old song swept over us like summer fire over a parched common. We felt like men while we were singing it.

Nobody ever invented more boring and idiotic songs than those about the man and his dog who went to mow a meadow, the grasshopper that jumped over another grasshopper's back, and John Brown's Baby who was afflicted with a pimple on an un-named part of his anatomy. We are wedded by sentiment to *Tipperary*, but was there ever a lousier or more whining tune ?— and the words speak for themselves. I recollect the song before it was famous, when it used to be sung on the music halls by a lady in tights with the largest pair of thighs I have ever yet seen exposed to the simple inhabitants of these islands.

Tommy loved singing songs about how he hated the war, and didn't want to die, and wanted to go home. The psychology of this is simple. We were all more or less " windy," and though we tried to hide it from each other with varying degrees of success, most of such secrets were open secrets. Since we knew each other so well it was better to own to fear and make fun of ourselves than try to run a bluff which wouldn't have deceived a blind infant.

One song was always sung with real feeling. It properly belonged to the Scotch, that hardy race of savages who continued to hate the Boche and lust for battle long after we soft Southerners would willingly have laid down our arms and accepted a *status quo*. Most of us had wives or sweethearts waiting for us at home, and it was very moving to hear a crowd of men whose lives were worth about ninepence in the pound, singing *Loch Lomond*.

> *For I and my true love will never meet again*
> *On the bonny, bonny banks of Loch Lomond.*

I was with some hundreds of men who will never again meet their true loves, unless the all-loving God has provided in the after-world a trysting-place for soldiers and soldiers' lasses.

88

But to-day we are in fine fettle and our songs are absurd and indecent rather than sentimental.

Our heavy boots slog rhythmically along the road. The drums clatter, the fifes wheeze. We pass through inhabited villages, and the inhabitants come out to inspect us with that kind of bovine interest which attracts cows to strange dogs. We have been standing between the enemy and their homes, but they have no enthusiasm for us. Why should they have? They have got used to us. Khaki is as stale a sight to them as it is to us. They are merely hoping that we will halt, and that they will be able to sell us their poisonous white wine at three hundred per cent profit. I did not last until the end of the war, so I never entered a recaptured village linked by the arm to a girl, with her hat dangling from my bayonet. Times like those must have been worth living for.

We come at last to our destination, a little village on the Scarpe, the same narrow, swift, deep river which hurries through Arras. No, I won't tell you the name of the village for one or two reasons which you would never guess. But some day I hope to sit again in an old mill and eat eggs and chips in comfort, without Time hanging over me like a threat and with the knowledge that I haven't to return to a lousy and broken-down barn at nine o'clock to clean my equipment for to-morrow morning's parade.

The village reminds me of Flecker's " Riouperoux " save that there are no high and solemn mountains around it. It is " small and untidy," and " the river drives a mill," and it is set in fairy-like surroundings. It has been untouched by the war and almost unspoilt by the troops. There is ample evidence that troops have been there before us, for their lice and their empty tins

89

of " bully " and " Maconochie " are waiting for us in
the straw of the barns. One lady in an estaminet has a
fine fat baby which she proudly displays with two words
of explanation : " Souvenir—Canadian." But the village has not been a regular camping-place, and the
inhabitants have not yet learned the gentle art of
profiteering.

One buxom woman who keeps an estaminet is a real
dear, and charges us hardly any more than she would
charge her own countrymen. We link arms before her,
dance up to the counter and dance back again, singing
to the tune of " Nuts and May " : " *Est-ce-que vous avez
des œufs, madame ?—œufs, madame ?—œufs, madame ?* "
and the old thing roars with laughter at our clumsy
gambols, charges us very reasonably for her omelettes
and supplies us with wine at about a franc a bottle less
than we have been asked to pay elsewhere.

The officers are billeted in a little white château
standing in a little park. There is a romance about that
château. Three or four pretty girls are living in it, all
by themselves save when officers are billeted on them.
Their mother is dead, their father is with the French
Army. They are standing by to mind the property until
the better days come. They are sweet and demure and
obviously gentlewomen. I don't know what became of
them, but I should like to think that they all married
British officers and lived happy ever after. It would be
nice to think that something romantic and " pretty "
and " out of a story-book " was germinated by the
beastliness of war.

But for me and for one or two others who discover it,
the principal charm of the place is the old mill. The
miller and his wife are two perfectly charming people

who make us very welcome, get meals and coffee for us at any hour, and charge us so little that we are half ashamed to visit them. We do not use any bad language in that house, although probably they would not understand it. They have two sons, fine, strapping, English-looking lads, and they are very worried because, before very long, the elder will reach the age for being called up. We cheer them up as best we can, telling them that the war isn't so bad after all, and anyhow it will soon be over. There was some way to go yet, but I hope those lads got through.

I always felt with those people that I was sitting and talking with friends, despite the barriers raised by my own very bad French and their (if possible) worse English. Some day I hope to sit in their kitchen again and eat fried eggs, if the old mill still stands and the miller and his wife be there. For no reason at all I am sure that they remember me as I remember them.

The people at the farm where my company is billeted are not too pleasant, but we get our own back. Possibly they are still discussing the Great Cow Mystery. Their cow provides milk in the afternoon, because we are then on parade, but it is always dry in the morning. This is because Dave rises even earlier than the farmer, and although a Londoner with no previous experience of country life, he has learned to milk that cow.

Dave and I are in the same billet, and sometimes when it isn't raining or too cold we sleep out under a haystack, for the barn stinks horribly. When off duty we amble forth together in search of food and drink. Occasionally we separate, because when I have had some wine or beer I prefer going to the mill for food, and Dave prefers the Rabelaisian atmosphere of the estaminet kept by the lady with the Canadian Souvenir. He is not averse to the prospect of providing her with an English one.

It would be like Bavincourt over again, but subtle changes have taken place in us since those days. We have seen a little of the raw stuff of war. We have memories, expectations and forebodings that clog and ache. For better or worse our minds will never be quite the same again. We are perambulating Stomachs, thinking only of filling ourselves and keeping warm.

Our ambitions are quite pathetic, seen now in retrospect. We discuss the chances of getting back to England not too painfully wounded. After the war we arrange to meet in a little pub in Epping Forest—about as far out of London as Dave could be persuaded to go—and get gloriously zig-zag while discussing these bad old times. That's all we ask of the future—just safety, just comfort and enough to eat and drink. If only we can come through alive we will never, never grumble at the petty annoyances of life which civilians know no better than to call misfortunes and even tragedies.

Dave is a widower and I often wonder what he was like before he lost his wife. He has no respect for women, whom he regards as suitable for only one purpose, yet he loved this wife of his with the imagination of a poet. So much I learned from him under the stars and appleblossom in the orchard at Bavincourt, for men can say things to each other in the dark which they could not say in the light.

I have still some ideals—or I had before they made a beast of me—but only at odd moments now does the ghost of my dead soul rise to haunt me. I struggle hard to preserve some of my own mental decencies and write a little verse. It is correct verse, but probably very bad poetry. Still it comforts me to know that I am still capable of evolving a decent thought, and it doesn't do harm to anybody else.

Evidently there is soon going to be dirty work at the cross-roads, for we are having an orgy of bomb-throwing and bayonet-fighting, and every day we practise " the battalion in attack." Nearly every day we are being harried by the Brigade Staff—or rather our poor old C.O. is being harried.

I am sorry for our C.O., an elderly, decent, gentle, good sort, but as hopelessly inefficient as I should be in his place. He was an amateur soldier before the war, knows little more about the business than most of us, and now finds himself burdened with the responsibility for all our lives. Probably he could do an executive job out of the line extremely well.

He takes us out to practise an attack and loses two of his companies. Some of us are hiding behind a hedge laughing, while he and Captain Penny, the adjutant, are riding about in search of us. Menacing mounted figures appear on the hill-top ; the Brigade Staff is bearing down on him. " Penny, Penny," he groans frenziedly, " where's the battalion ? "

" Penny, Penny, where's the battalion ? " becomes a catch-phrase with us, but I think most of us are sorry for the poor C.O. We know what it is to be bullied, and *he* has never bullied us.

It is not his fate to lead us into the shambles. I remember so well a morning when we paraded on a farm in Flanders before climbing on to the old London 'buses —the sure precursors of imminent trouble—when he said good-bye to us with the tears running down his cheeks. Poor old chap, he would have liked to die with his men.

Well, we are having quite a good time in spite of being worked rather hard, but the omens are not propitious. The cold weather is beginning, and we are faced with the prospect of a winter campaign. Dave bathes in the Scarpe, but I am not so Spartan, and cannot face the prospect of drying myself afterwards on a very inadequate towel.

One day we get the inevitable sad news. We are going to leave this fairy village. And when next day we move off we march towards Flanders—and Flanders means Passchendaele.

CHAPTER VIII

We are sorry to leave the little village on the Scarpe, but we march away in good spirits. The next may be as good. I think we all prefer a day's march to a day's work. Certainly I do. Nothing is more boring or soul-destroying than practising the drill we already know by heart, throwing dummy bombs, range-finding and making mechanical gestures with rifle and bayonet.

But marching on a good road in crisp weather is a sheer joy, so long as we are not dragged on to the point beyond which weariness becomes agony. When the order has come to " march easy " and rifles are slung, and we find an easy swinging rhythm for our feet and talk or sing or smoke, we begin to feel like free men. There is a pleasant sense of irresponsibility. All our belongings are on our own backs. The cookers are coming up behind to supply us with the necessities of life. We don't know our destination but, anyhow, somebody else is responsible for getting us to it.

We are supposed to be on our way to " do a stunt," but why worry ? Thinking for myself, I may be left with the " nucleus " in the transport lines. I may in the mean-while develop some highly desirable ailment and get sent back to England. The powers that be may change their minds and call off the attack in which we are supposed to be taking part. We may even be going to Italy where, we are given to understand, the war is being conducted in a spirit of gentlemanly moderation. In a word, I have learned the art of living in the present.

This is yellow talk, is it not ? Well, I don't apologise. I am only speaking of myself, but I am willing to lay long odds that there wasn't one in a hundred of us who, if he could have crawled home with a shred of honour left, wouldn't have taken the opportunity. On the other hand we knew that the war had to be fought out and that somebody had to do the fighting. But had we been asked the plain question : " Will you go on, or will you let Germany win ? " I don't think there was more than one in a hundred of us who would have thrown in his hand.

This sounds contradictory, but it is really quite simple. There was the personal equation and the national emergency. Most individuals thought : " If I can only get out of this, somebody else will come and take my place—and good luck to him, poor devil ! " There was always somebody else, and one wanted the somebody else to do the job. If, by some impossible circumstance, there had come the plain alternative, " Either you must die or Germany must win," I hope and honestly believe that most of us would have swallowed voluntarily the Darker Draught.

Most of us were cowards—I was certainly one—but there are as many degrees of cowardice as there are shades of a primary colour. I could respect my own brand of cowardice, and that of others like me, because we laughed at it and owned to it and didn't expect anybody else to take any interest in our own personal reactions. But the really repulsive coward—apart from the officer or N.C.O. whose fear got the better of his temper and made him a bully—was the complete egotist who felt that his skin was too precious to be punctured, and expected the next man—also in the same boat—to sympathise with him. I was extremely interested in my own skin, but I felt that I couldn't be expected to take a great deal of interest in the skins of people who were only casual acquaintances.

There were three really horrible worms in my crowd, and two of them had come out on the last draft. One of them was a second class county cricketer who had surprisingly failed to get a commission in a safe branch of the A.S.C. He poured out his troubles to me *ad nauseam*. He was a single man with plenty of money, and he used to wail to me and others of the tragedy of his precious life being endangered.

Another beauty, also a single man without responsibilities, used to scent himself—which was at least considerate—and talk about his " fioncy." This stout fellow was almost tearful when discussing the sanctity of his person. He was always trying to get a commission in the R.M.A. because he had a theory that all their guns were " heavies " and that he would thus be kept well behind the line.

There was another suburban hero quite as unpleasant as the last mentioned. He was very young, which asks for consideration. Thank God I hadn't to face the job at his age. He had been " combed out " of a Government office, and he must have been the most disgusting bit of work that ever darkened the doorstep. God had provided this human scarecrow with huge staring eyes —which later stood him in good stead—and he used to whimper to me and ask me if I thought it was any use for him to sham madness. I think he had tried every other complaint on the M.O. except leprosy and womb trouble.

I believe these three swine are still alive—unfortunately—and I hope they will read these lines and recognise themselves. As I have owned to funking it myself all this may seem a little uncalled for. But in my code there was a difference between *wanting* to get out and *scheming* to get out ; and why the blazes should they have supposed that anybody else took an interest in *their* precious lives ?

The last draft had provided us with several curiosities, among them a youngster who had been given a commission in a county regiment at the outbreak of war. For quite obvious reasons he had never been sent overseas in the capacity of an officer, and he was an even worse parade-ground soldier than myself. His old regiment seemed to have stuck him pretty well, all things considered, but at last, owing to his habit of coming on parade with only one puttee, and his obstinate refusal to learn anything remotely connected with the drill-book, they made him resign. He came out to us as a private and seemed not in the least sorry for himself. I couldn't believe that he had any brains until, poor devil, I saw them for myself a few months later.

I am going to call him Rumbold, because I must mention him again. Poor Rumbold had arranged a code with his mother so that when he wrote to her she would know what part of the front he was on, without the censor of his letters knowing that this information was being illicitly imparted. The code was simplicity itself. His mother would know by the initials he put before her name on the face of the envelope exactly where he was at the time of writing.

This would have worked admirably, but unfortunately poor Rumbold had invented no code letters for Passchendaele. When he approached that delightful area he boldly addressed a letter home to Mrs. Passchendaele Rumbold. Even the blindest censor couldn't stand for that, and poor Rumbold fell into water of a very uncomfortable temperature.

It was while we were moving towards Ypres that we were compelled to swallow about two hundred men who had been combed out of the Motor Transport. Many of these chaps were drawing six shillings a day. They had signed on at that rate of pay and King's Regulations permitted them to go on receiving it. But as our pay was sixpence or a shilling—according to whether we had arranged for a separation allowance—there was naturally a little jealousy. This was due to that highly ridiculous system in the Army which ordained that the further you kept away from the line and the less risk you took, the more pay you received.

These A.S.C. fellows didn't mingle very well with us at first. They didn't want to come to us and we didn't want them to come. A few of them were men with a certain amount of education, but the bulk were of the genus Gor Blimey. There was one whom I will call M'Cracken, who came into my section, and we hated each other on sight and became the bane of each other's lives until, right at the end of my period of active service, we began to like each other.

Several times we were near coming to blows, but neither of us really wanted to. Life was wretched enough as it was, without going about with bunged up eyes and cut lips. I am glad we didn't because I am sure I should have had the worst of it, and because M'Cracken

99

afterwards saved my life through a gift which is called second sight in the land of his forebears.

M'Cracken was a Scotch Canadian with a nasal twang which would have startled even a New Yorker. He was not uneducated, however, and, if what he told me were true, had been apprenticed to an American doctor. He used to talk about me in his sleep, restlessly muttering : " Ah never knew such a bloudie man."

Another curio was a fellow we called Mr. Binks, who was very short and had a comic-paper face. Mr. Binks was an acrobat and a contortionist, and had been on the music halls in a celebrated troupe. Mr. Binks, walking along a road, would salute a strange officer with the utmost precision. Then he would look absent-minded, stand on one foot, and scratch the back of his head with the heel of the other. The effect was nearly always tremendous.

Mr. Binks was at his best on " physical jerks." One of the games was to make two men come out, each hopping on one foot, and try to barge each other over. On these occasions Mr. Binks invariably drew his jack-knife and assumed an expression which would have daunted any of Mr. Edgar Wallace's characters.

Since Mr. Binks was a little *difficile* on parade, and apt to destroy the gravity of even the R.S.M., he was made a sanitary man. Now this was all very well, but nobody felt very happy using a latrine which had been constructed by Mr. Binks. There was always the danger of becoming the victim of some really dreadful practical joke.

In his capacity of sanitary man Mr. Binks was not supposed to go " over the top." But when long afterwards we went over at Cambrai he went with us, and loosed off every round he'd got, the funny, brave little devil. He got through all right, too, for in 1919 I met him in the Strand, when some kind friends of mine had hoaxed me to meet a girl—who wasn't really there at all—at the Strand Palace. I couldn't stay and talk to him for more than a minute because of the " appointment." I didn't mind the hoax, but I should have liked to ask Mr. Binks to dinner and an evening out which might have ended in Vine Street.

I was rather sorry for these A.S.C. drivers. They had joined early without knowing that their job would be comparatively safe—the A.S.C. had had a very sticky time in the Boer War—and having been allowed to get used to this feeling of security they were made to learn the work of infantrymen and then bunged into the line. Their places were supposed to be taken by men who, while physically unfit for the trenches, were sound enough to drive a lorry.

Theoretically the policy was excellent, but I don't know that it paid in practice. It was at about this time that we began to notice the number of " ditched " lorries beside the road, which suggested that the new drivers were not so skilful as the old. The comb-out should have taken place in England and no Class A man should have been allowed to join a non-combatant unit. Yet in 1916–17 the finest Rugby football side in England was the A.S.C., consisting mainly of officers on home service. Rugger is a game for the young and the very fit. Further comment is needless. Splendid fellows !

We march by fairly easy stages, sometimes sleeping under canvas and sometimes in byres and barns. They don't over-work us ; they are conserving our strength.

But it would be a good policy to give us a little more to eat, although the people in England seem to think we are getting all the food. White bread—think of it ! But what's the use of white bread if your day's ration consists of barely enough for breakfast ?

One evening we camp at a spot half a mile beyond where I have seen, and mentally noted for future reference, an A.S.C. ration dump. When we are dismissed I try to get hold of Dave but can't find him, and there is no time to be lost, for plenty of others have probably noticed that dump. Rumbold and I race together for it, and arrive there and beg like two starving tramps on an English roadside.

The chap in charge is decent and sympathetic and gives us two plates of dinner to eat then and there, and a loaf to take away. A good fellow, bless him ! and I hate to tell how his kindness was requited. I find Dave in an estaminet half an hour later and tell him about the feed I have had. Dave immediately sets out to pay his respects to the A.S.C., but his call is no formal one. Nobody seems to be about and he forgets to leave his card. But he returns with two hams and as much bread as he can carry.

Now the chap there has been very good to me, and I don't know how he is going to account for the loss of this provender, but my tender conscience does not prevent me from sharing the spoils. The tragedy, however, is that the hams are raw, and we daren't give them to the cooks. But it is not hard to do a deal with the lady of the estaminet who seizes the hams with a glad cry, straining them to her bosom and crooning over them as if they were her twin babies which have just been restored to her after having been lost for days.

On the strength of the hams we eat omelettes containing an incredible number of eggs, drink much red and white wine, and bear away with us many packets of chocolate.

At one village where we stay for the night there is a rather good-looking hotel, but it is for officers only, and there is nothing else which begins to look like an estaminet. So Dave and I, on the same old quest for food and drink, knock at a likely-looking cottage. The door is opened to us by a middle-aged woman who is obviously a lady, and who addresses us in perfect English.

This is rather embarrassing, and I stammer something and try to get away, but with a rather fine dignity she invites us in. We are conducted into a little salon, not too badly furnished, and are gravely presented to two other middle-aged mesdemoiselles, both of whom also speak English as well as ourselves. We suddenly find ourselves plunged into an atmosphere which is terribly alien because, a few months since, it would have been so home-like.

These three old maid sisters treat us, private soldiers and intruders as we are, as gentlemen and visitors. The British ! Ah, what do they not owe to the British ? They have to thank the British for their lives and the preservation of their virtue. They are refugees from Ypres. Yes, Belgians. And they tell us, with faint blushes, how they had to escape in their night-dresses when their home was smashed by a shell. They have private means, enough to live on without hardship. There are many refugees so much worse off. They have a great deal for which they must thank God.

We take coffee and cakes with them and I am strangely mistrustful of my manners, feeling at twenty-eight a gauche and sensitive boy. I don't think Dave is at all worried. If he were to be presented to the Pope he would wink at him and suggest that there must be ladies hidden somewhere about the Vatican. We leave only just in time to rush back to the broken-down byre, which is our billet, and get our rum ration.

The effect of this small experience on me is indescribable. I have been somewhere and back on a magic carpet. I forget the name of these ladies and the name of the village, but by this time they are probably back in their beloved Ypres. Dave, going through his shirt, and causing much inconvenience to his uninvited guests with the burning end of a cigarette, expresses the hope that we didn't leave them any " souvenirs." Poor, dear, kind old creatures, I too hope we didn't !

We find plenty of refugees as we draw near to the Belgian frontier which we eventually reach. They live mostly in little wooden huts and enter into competition with the local natives by selling things to us, which does not make the poor devils too popular. Quite the most picturesque of all the folk on view are the Chinese Labour Companies. British officers and N.C.O.'s who have superintended the alleged activities of the Chink tell me that he is a good worker. It may be so, but I never catch him at it. We are for ever passing large numbers of Chinks in picturesque blue overalls who are supposed to be at work on the roads. They are always standing quite still in blissful idleness with happy smiles on their bright faces, while dixies of rice boil at regular intervals, watching us poor mugs slog past. " You makee fight ; we catchee money." And a very good scheme, too. The coolie is not so simple as he looks.

We strike the Belgian frontier at Houtkerque, but our

camping ground is on the French side, on a swamp of a field belonging to a picturesque old Flemish farm. We are to stay here for nearly a fortnight and do some more training. It is now the middle of October and the weather is mainly wet and cold. We sleep on the wet ground in overcrowded tents, but we enjoy the luxury of a blanket each and we don't mind the over-crowding because it makes a fug which keeps us decently warm.

Every morning the drums play us out of " bed " as soon as réveillé has sounded. They play three tunes, the first being, ironically enough, Harry Lauder's song, *It's Nice to Get Up in the Morning.* The second is *Never Let your Braces Dangle,* and the third is always *I 'aven't Seen the Kayser.* There is a duck-pond with water like half-dried ink which we use for washing and shaving, but, as most of us are suffering from a sort of barber's rash and are used to saving the last few drops of our tea for shaving water and ablutions, this is comparative luxury.

Rations are still bad and short. We know that if there is porridge for breakfast we shall get no rice for dinner with our stewed bully and one potato. In civilised life I hate porridge, but such is my desire to fill myself " over there " that I walk three miles one night to a Salvation Army hut where I have heard hot porridge may be bought. They refuse to serve me when I get there, because a company of R.A.M.C. who are going up the line—as they are pleased to call it—are about to hold a prayer-meeting in the hut.

Just beyond Houtkerque and a few yards beyond the Belgian frontier some genius has erected what authority is pleased to call a " Russian bath." If such baths really existed in Russia, and the proletariat were compelled by the tyranny of Czar or Soviet to make use of them I do not wonder at the spirit of sadness and discontent which has always permeated that unhappy nation.

But a bath is a bath, and we are overjoyed when we are paraded and told we are going to have one. We are marched off in drenching rain, and are not quite so pleased when we are told that we must strip outside and leave our clothes in the wet. We are then marched into a pitch-dark chamber full of steam, and about as hot as we can stand it. Dante would have liked that place. The only way out is through another chamber, not quite so dark, where showers of icy water are playing in all directions.

Afterwards we stand naked outside while the heavy rain easily defeats all efforts to get ourselves moderately dry with our small wet towels. We then march back to camp, feeling no cleaner than before, and a great deal colder, damper and more miserable.

Lice are becoming a still more difficult problem. We try hanging our shirts outside our tents at night in the cold and wet, hoping that the exposure will kill our live-stock. But it does nothing of the sort. It only improves their appetites !

CHAPTER IX

I have been in worse camps than the one near Houtkerque, but it is miserable enough. The latrines are a
disgrace. We are compelled to squat on them in the open
in full view of women passing to and from the farm. The
Old Tabbies in England would have something to say
about it if they knew—and for once the Old Tabbies
would be right. There is no need to makes beasts of us
for the sake of sparing a few yards of canvas. It is almost
time the papers stopped yapping about the coarseness
and indecency of the Germans. This propaganda on
both sides is all a game of pots and kettles, and it is
costing hundreds of lives.

Each side reads that the other murders its prisoners,
and then begins a game of reprisals which is played out
to the end—thanks to a few lies invented by civilians in
Fleet Street and Berlin. There are quite a few thousand
wives, parents and sweethearts who may thank my
brethren of the pen for the loss of their men-folk. The
theory of war, which even the almighty Staff sometimes
forgets, is not necessarily to *kill* your enemy, but to
incapacitate him. Men are frankly threatened with a
shortage of rations if they take too many prisoners.

Do you forget, some of you fools with red tabs, that
some of these ignorant men to whom you speak will
survive even your plans of attack and become private
citizens again? And what kind of private citizens are
they going to make when they have been taught by you

to weigh a human life against half a tin of Frey Bentos ?
There will be quite a good crop of murders in England
when the war is over !

The instructions given to stretcher-bearers are rather
harsh. " If you find two men wounded, and can take only
one away, take away the one more likely to make a fit
soldier again." Therefore the one more urgently in need
of attention must be left to die, because he would walk
with a limp and would never again be able to carry a
pack. Sound business, of course, but just a little hard.
Meanwhile we may read the papers sent out to us and
thank God that Our Side insists on conducting the war
in a thoroughly sporting and gentlemanly spirit.

We are told that we are going to make an attack on
Passchendaele, alongside a Canadian division, north of
Poelcapelle. Our brilliant Staff has got every move in
the game worked out twenty-four hours ahead. Our
jumping-off place is already assigned to us, and we are
to advance about five hundred yards, crossing a stream
called the Paddebeeke. We are shown a clay model of
the landscape, including the roads which are no longer
there. We practise the method of attack every morning,
and every afternoon the specialists split up into sections
and try out their own respective murder tools. You see
little groups around Lewis guns—which invariably jam
—lines of men twenty yards or so apart bowling dummy
bombs at each other, men firing dummy grenades out
of rifles. We all learn each other's jobs in case of an
emergency, but I admit that the Lewis gun defeated me
every time. I rather liked bomb-throwing, though. I
found that, having played a bit of cricket, I could very
easily bowl " googlies " with my dummy bombs—which
was horribly bad for the shins of my opposite number.

The countryside is stiff with troops who, like ourselves, are on their way up to " do a stunt " or are on their way down, having done one, to rest and wait for fresh drafts. The reports of those who have already sampled Passchendaele are not reassuring. From what we hear a battalion is lucky to lose only fifty per cent. in casualties. This seems to make it an affair of " heads " or " tails." On form we have each of us an even money chance.

I am not unduly depressed by this thought. The war looks like going on indefinitely and sooner or later I am bound to become a casualty. Well, the sooner the better. If I survive the coming slaughter I shall only be fattened up for another, and then perhaps another, and so on until the destined end. Life is sweet, but not this sort of life. Both Dave and I are willing to " give 'em a leg and call it square." But my trouble is that I am one of those cowards who can't endure pain. I would stick months of slow torture rather than hand myself over to a dentist. The thought of meeting a slow and agonising death or getting some unspeakable but not fatal wound hangs over me like a cloud. I have heard men having their wounds dressed—fine, strong, hard-bitten men with enviable decorations. I want a straight one between the eyes and good-night all, or a clean one through the arm or the leg which won't have to be probed or messed about with. But unfortunately one is not allowed to choose, and only the late Mr. Henley claimed to be master of his fate.

But our evenings, when we can drink a little and forget, are not so bad. We have the choice of visiting two small towns which are about equi-distant—Houtkerque in France or Wateau in Belgium. Dave and I much prefer

Wateau. In Houtkerque the estaminets are comparatively dull, but there are two on the town square at
Wateau that old Falstaff would have loved.

Each contains a piano which is rather over-worked,
and in the larger house of the two we pass some really
amusing evenings. There is a Mrs. Quickly and a Doll
Tearsheet on the premises, and I hope they don't
understand the words of some of the songs that are sung,
for even their Shakespearean prototypes would have
registered a protest.

The place is crowded with men from all sorts of units
and always there is an impromptu concert. The man
at the piano is rather a wonder. He can always improvise
some sort of an accompaniment, even if he has never
heard the song before. The vocalist walks over to him,
hums something in his ear, and both are ready to make
a start.

First, let us say, a lance-corporal in the Worcesters
gets up and sings a long and truly awful—though polite
—ballad about a blind organist. I have always thought
that blindness was too good for that organist, and that
he ought to have been provided with some worse
affliction. However, it goes down very well with the
uncultured ninety per cent. of the audience which likes
its sentiment hot and sweet and thickly spread.

Then comes a little stumpy round-faced villain of a
sapper who sings an unprintable ditty about a family
with extraordinary and repulsive habits. It begins, " *The
gong it was sounded for breakfast, By the butler so stately
and stout.*" I am ashamed to own that it always makes
me laugh.

Afterwards one of our fellows gets up and sings
Private Michael Cassidy which always goes well, and

provides us with a chorus to sing and a chance to bang the table.

> *Cassidy, Private Michael Cassidy,*
> *He's of Irish nationali-tee,*
> *He's a lad of wonderful audacity—*
> *Private Michael Cassidy—*(crash)*—V.C.*

Follows a gunner, who has obviously been a farm-labourer, and I should like to know what part of the country he is from, but can never get near him to ask. He sings a version of *Lillibulero*—of all things ! Not the *Lillibulero* which laughed James II off his throne, but a bawdy ditty rendered almost respectable by its antiquity. It is mentioned in *Peregrine Pickle,* and begins :

> *Little pig sits with his [back] to the wall,*
> *Lillibulero and pig.*

The refrain consists of obscene porcine noises very difficult to imitate, but which the performer manages with the utmost skill. I should like to know how this song has come down to him intact through the generations. It can never have been printed !

Next somebody gets up and bores me stiff with an excruciating ballad about a caged skylark in a mining-camp. Seemingly this inspired bird softened its rough audience by the sweetness of its singing, and made them think of their mothers (why ?), so that they all led better lives, shot the local prostitute, and stopped playing poker, shooting each other, and being unkind to Indians. If caged skylarks really do have this effect on miners, what about sending a few to South Wales during an industrial crisis ?

Another obscene ditty follows in this bright and varied programme, sung with intense gusto by a cheerful young scoundrel in another unit of our division. It is of the narrative sort, sung in the first person, and concerns the harsh fate of a gentleman who was so ill-advised as to interfere in an unconventional love affair between his daughter and a soldier. The song is of such a nature that not three consecutive words can be quoted, and even the title is unmentionable ; thus, so far as this modest pen is concerned, it must go down into oblivion.

Then Dave gets up and, after a whispered conversation with the pianist, sings *Songs of Araby*. He has an untrained but very pleasing tenor voice. I half close my eyes and go back across the sea, and through a year or two of mis-spent life to a young girl in a white frock and a Kentish cherry orchard when the blossom is out. " And all my soul shall strive to wake sweet wonder in thine eyes." Well, we have all felt like that about some girl or another, I suppose, and the great art of living is to go on feeling it.

Then back go Dave and I through the darkness and mire to the camp, perhaps calling, if there is time and money, at a cottage quite close to our destination in the hope that Madame may have something for us to eat.

Not until now have I mentioned this Madame. I forget her name, or the name by which we called her, but she comes into the tale. She is a youngish woman, living alone, for her husband is serving in a non-combatant unit of the French Army. She was a good sort who got us food and coffee without robbing us. Dave and I were very careful at first not to be seen entering or leaving the premises, not for the sake of the proprieties, but because Madame could get only a limited supply of food and we wanted to keep the place to ourselves. Others, however, soon found her out, and there was generally a full house.

She spoke a little English, but, like that of all French peasants who had taken lessons from the troops, it was English of the unprintable sort. Even apart from that there was no false modesty about the lady. When her husband had been home on leave for one night only she regaled us with details of his short visit which, if said elsewhere or in any other circumstances, would have been highly embarrassing.

She and Dave indulge in some very heavy badinage in which Dave does not always come off best. Dave accuses her of having an affair with a sergeant, which always infuriates her, for she has quite a reasonable and proper hatred for sergeants. She gives her opinion of this particular sergeant in words which would cost forty shillings or one month if uttered aloud in any public place in England.

But she was one of the best, and actually straight as a die and fond of all of us in a sisterly sort of way. More than a month later when a few of us came back to that camp, Madame knew me at once and recognised our badges, but all the faces of the men who wore them were strange to her except just two. She asked me what had become of " *Camerades* " and when I told her in the pidgin French we talked, " *Camerades* all *tues*," she burst out crying. She would not take any money for her coffee that night, and all the while fresh tears were glistening on her eyelashes.

Dear Madame, I could find my way to your cottage

at this moment of writing, and some day I shall, and hope to find you there still with your husband safely restored to you. Then we will all three crack a bottle of wine together and talk in a weird mixture of our respective languages of the bad old days, when your cottage with its light and the warmth of its little stove gave us so much comfort before we went back to sleep in the mud three fields away.

On one of my rare excursions into Houtkerque I met a man I had known in England. He was a private in another London Territorial battalion, and he had got very drunk on champagne. This he could well afford, for he was worth about £80,000. He had been up to Passchendaele and was going again. I think he would have given every penny of his fortune to be safely out of the Army. I have not seen him since and I am afraid he went under.

Another odd encounter was with the son of a Huntingdonshire farmer who had allowed me and a small friend to make a cricket pitch in one of his fields when I was quite a little boy. I had not the money to buy him a drink and he insisted on my sponging on him quite shamelessly, perhaps because I knew his native village, and the Great Ouse, and the roach swim close to the ferry, and the " Pike and Eel Inn " up at Over, where —according to Rupert Brooke—" they fling oaths at one." It was odd to recall those names and places in our present surroundings, and our conversation was baffled by a Zouave, complete in red bags, who insisted on attaching himself to us and telling us, with businesslike gestures with a knife, what he was going to do to somebody who had absconded with his young woman.

I could write a great deal about that camp. In retrospect it seems to me that we were there for months, and yet I know by comparing the date of our leaving Arras with the date of our going into action that we were there for less than a fortnight.

There came the inevitable morning when the camp had to be cleaned up early and left tidy for our successors, and when the blankets, ten to a bundle, had to be delivered over to the transport. There was a battalion parade, and our poor old colonel who was leaving us made his last speech and wished us God speed. Most of the fellows were rather caustic about him, but I saw the tears in the old chap's eyes and I knew he would have given his life to come with us. I was sorry for him, but when you've enough troubles of your own you haven't much pity to spare for anybody else.

We have no colonel now. The senior major is our C.O., a man so elderly that one would have thought he ought to be sitting comfortably in a London club, boasting about the sons he had " given." But then he would have been wasted. Major Eagle, tall, lean, grey as a badger, and sixty-odd if a day, is one of the best and stoutest-hearted of the whole crowd.

In a sense I am in luck's way. Medville has got his captaincy and is going to take our company over. Captain Perks is away on a course, which is excellent for his sake and ours. Moreover the horrid elementary schoolmaster is now commanding another platoon, and my platoon commander for the time being is a tall, dark chap named Jackson. I didn't know him very well, and I regret to say that he didn't live long enough for me to better the acquaintance.

At Passchendaele, owing to the mud and the absence of ordinary trenches and even established lines, it is impossible for even a platoon commander to have entire control of his men. Section commanders with two stripes, or one, have more than the usual responsibilities thrust on them, and even we numskulled privates are told that, up to a point, we must use our own initiative.

This is rare and refreshing fruit. Hitherto, if we obeyed an order to the letter, and the result was unfortunate and unexpected, we were asked : " Why couldn't you *think* ? " So next time we did the commonsense thing, and were asked : " Who told *you* to think ? "

Our N.C.O.'s are mostly good fellows with just a few exceptions. The funks were nearly always bullies and the bullies nearly always funks. The most disgusting specimen I can remember had no right in our unit at all, and had got in through some strawberry-skinned old fool at the War Office. This splendid fellow, having joined another regiment in England and finding himself in danger of active service, had applied for a commission and been transferred to our reserve battalion for that purpose. Once there he had moved heaven and earth to avoid getting one. Now that he was compelled to go into the line they had made him a sergeant. He was a vulgar little beast with eyes like unripe gooseberries and in civil life he was connected with what he called the " tylerin' tryde." One wouldn't have minded him if he hadn't been a four-letter man.

I am afraid he got through safely. While I am writing about him he is probably measuring one of his betters for a pair of trousers, with a pencil behind one ear, a bit of chalk behind the other, and a yard measure in his hand. As 'somebody said in *Evan Harrington* he is " in perpetual contemplation of gentlemen's legs." Well, most of us survivors have got back to our own niches in life.

But I have digressed, and here we are paraded and ready to move off. We march into Houtkerque and find the old London 'buses waiting for us. Even if we hadn't known that we were going over the top the 'buses would have given it away. The older soldiers regarded them much as about-to-be victims of premature burial must have regarded hearses. We go on a joy-ride through a bit of Belgium which looks staler, flatter, muddier and more war-worn at every mile.

Every village is crazier and dingier than the last, and deep craters are visible beside the road in numbers which become more and more distressing. We know that these are the results of bombs dropped from the air. We arrive at last at a camp of huts beside a road a foot deep in mud and water, which lorries are for ever ploughing up full and other lorries are for ever slushing down empty. There is nothing to see anywhere but a few bare trees, mud-flats, horses and mules, splashing lorries and earth-stained men.

Next morning we are on the march again along a road made of sleepers. We pass Canal Bank, where the Labour Corps is working like a hive of dingy bees. They live in rat-holes in the bank, and although their expectations of life are a great deal higher than ours their guts is being sweated out of them, poor devils. Even their officers look meaner and worse cared-for than our privates. They are either too old or unfit to fight, they are worked to death with perpetual navvying, they get rotten rations, and they are nobody's babies. Nobody is proud of being in the Labour Corps. Somebody should tell the tale of the work these fellows did and the miseries they endured.

How different were the "Oirish gintilmin" I found working in " civvies " in a very safe place miles behind

Arras. They explained to me how they were there. They were too proud to wear the khaki of the Oppressors (and take a shilling a day), but they weren't too proud to help the Oppressors win the war by working at trade union rates in a place of safety.

The point of view was not new to me. I had rarely met a fat Irishman with a good job in England who failed to curse the country which was supporting him after no stingy fashion. Had I been an Irishman who felt that way about England I should have had the pride to remain in the country of the Dear Little Shamrock. (Och, thank God, thank God !)

We entered Ypres in search of billets. Oddly enough, I didn't know at the time that it *was* Ypres. All smashed-up towns looked very much alike. Anyhow, we didn't stay. There were no billets for us, and we were marched off to a delightful resort called Irish Farm, where the greater part of us had to bivouac.

A bivouac, as distinct from a tent, is a long low canvas shelter with an entrance like that of a dog kennel, and in which it is impossible even to kneel upright. You have to enter on your hands and knees and, if your bed-place is at the far end, crawl over the fellows who are already in possession.

Irish Farm is a multitudinous collection of canvas dwellings set in a waste of mud reminiscent of Southend at low tide. All residents of the Essex mud-side resort who arrived at Irish Farm must have been deeply moved and dreamed sentimentally of home. All that is lacking are some automatic machines and a few whelk-stalls.

But there are other drawbacks instead. The drawbacks consist mainly of air-raids. While Mr. Lloyd George is assuring a credulous civil population at home that our Air Force is in supreme command of the air and that no enemy 'plane dares come over our lines, life in Irish Farm consists of one perpetual air-raid.

The average Boche airman in these parts must be very industrious. He works at least eighteen hours a day. He comes over and drops what he's got, goes back, snatches a hasty meal, and comes back with some more bombs. And so *ad infinitum*. Nor is he ineffectual. Hasty interments are going on all day, and any chaplain in the camp who doesn't know the Burial Service by heart and backwards ought to be reported to an Ecclesiastical Commission for mental deficiency.

It was here that I found the old hero in the Y.M.C.A. tent who, after having had to blow out his one candle about ten times in thirty minutes, found that most of his stock was gone.

We had one night in this health resort, and on the following morning I was reminded that I hadn't yet made my will. I hardly knew if it would be worth while leaving anything that had to be prefixed by the sign which denotes a bad word or a minus quantity, but I gravely went through the motions in my pay-book with an indelible pencil, making (without his permission) a friend of mine who was an officer in the reserve battalion at home my literary executor. After all, something that I had written might sell posthumously. I hadn't much sense of humour, with which to mystify and annoy women readers, so there was just the chance that I had already produced a best-seller. (I hadn't.)

We are paraded late in the afternoon and march off to the real business. A nucleus of about a hundred and twenty men is being left behind as a peg on which to hang a new battalion if we should be completely chawed up. I imagined the married men with the longest families would be on the nucleus, but not a bit of it. The lucky ones were probably picked out with a pin, and one or two really shameful mistakes were made.

There were in my company twin brothers who were only sons. Surely it would have been only fair to keep one of them back. There was also a fellow who had been out in '14 with a commission in a crack regiment which he had lost through being found drunk in the line by his colonel who was a great deal drunker still. The colonel, when he became sober, tried to stop the machinery which he had set in motion, but it was too late and the poor chap was cashiered.

He had joined us to get back his commission. His father was squire of a village in the north of England and he couldn't return home as a private. This fellow's papers were expected to come through from day to day. One would have thought that, in the circumstances, he should have been left behind.

He and the twin brothers were all three killed. But the ex-officer died an officer, for his papers came through while he was breathing his last in a casualty clearing station.

The march up to the shell-holes—I can't say trenches—on that drizzling mid-autumn evening is still one of my favourite nightmares. Everything was grey and wet and beastly, and death lay everywhere beside the muddy tracks which had once been roads. Dead horse, dead mule, dead man, a whole stretcher party blotted out—they lay in an almost monotonous rotation as we slushed past them. And our way was lit by the flashes of our own guns, already beginning to growl the threat which we were supposed to fulfil.

I had been talking to a gunner at Irish Farm. " Well, chum," he said, " we've got six thousand guns to see you over with." This, of course, was an absurd exaggeration, but I never saw such a display of ordnance. Our guns stood literally wheel to wheel, and when we got on to the very necessary duckboard track and began to wind our way among them we half expected to have our heads blown off from behind, while the noise was deafening. Even an eighteen-pounder going off just behind you and firing over your head can make you jump.

In spite of the terrific din going on there is a curious, dream-like sense of unreality about it all. We are proceeding now in single file, but of course the wretched Rumbold, from whom I can't escape, is within conversational distance of me. He is much too brainless to be awed by this inferno of noise and lights and has a soul-destroying taste in fatuous conversation. He is the bone-headed type of P. G. Wodehouse characters, and he oughtn't to be here at all. He should be in the Drones' Club, listening to the love affairs of a fellow member, and longing to escape to the Albany and Jeeves.

It was during this ghastly trek that I had a moment of prescience. I am not one of those people who call themselves psychic, for which I am grateful, for it must be highly painful always to be aware of the unpleasant things that are about to happen. But there have been moments in my life—perhaps not more than three or four—when I honestly believe that I have seen through the Dark Glass. But I will own—to save the sceptic from pouncing on me—that this was certainly the time and place to inspire one of them.

We had halted for a brief rest and were sitting on the edge of the duckboards. I had made some futile remark intended to be funny, which raised a little laugh. My platoon commander, 2nd Lieut. Jackson, who was passing at the time, heard it and smiled at me, and as he smiled I saw Death looking at me out of his eyes, and I knew that his number was up. I can't describe what I saw. It was just Death, and it made me afraid in a ghastly, shuddering way which was foreign to my present way of being afraid. The momentary transfiguration was just as unpleasant as if his features had melted into the bones of a death's head. He was killed in the first few minutes of the attack.

The " Job's comforters " who had already trodden those duckboards had warned us that getting into the line and coming out again were precarious adventures. The reason for this was obvious. The Germans must have known what the duckboards were for, and as they were being attacked every other day they must have known that reliefs were frequent. Accordingly at night they cast their bread upon the waters—or their shells upon the duckboards—with prodigality and distressing accuracy. Shells began to burst in front of us and behind us and all round us, and we ran the gauntlet through showers of mud. The new men were jumpy, and communicated their jumpiness to some of us—certainly to me. But luck was with us up to this point. I think we got into the line without a casualty.

After much weariness of the flesh and spirit we had to leave the duckboard track. Then we knew what mud really was. We progressed at the rate of about half a mile an hour, sometimes sinking thigh deep and helping each other out.

I hope to see in the modernised geography books for the use of schools : " Flanders is noted for its mud."

CHAPTER X

My company goes into the supports where we are perhaps lucky in not having to live in a string of shell-holes. There is a breastwork about five feet high in front of us which, while it affords a certain amount of protection, attracts too much attention.

We relieve a battalion of marines, and we haven't been in ten minutes when the gentlemen over yonder proceed to let us have it. We receive generous samples of pretty well everything that was made by Krupps. It is impossible to stand upright because swarms of machine-gun and rifle bullets sizz just over our heads. We crouch down and hope for the best.

I get a dig in the ribs. The awful man Rumbold is crouching beside me. " I say ! " he exclaims heartily and chattily. " I say ! "

" What's the matter ? " I grunt. " You been hit ? "

On occasions when things were not going too well I was always a man of few words. I had no time for bright and airy conversation. I liked to crowd myself into the smallest possible space and have a nice think. It was not so with Rumbold.

" Oh," he said quite equably, " I haven't been hit. But—ah—would you considah that we are undah fire ? "

It was his first time in action, and he wanted to write home and tell his mother that he had been under fire, but was conscientious about using this time-honoured phrase before its exact technical meaning had been made

clear to him. I did not at the time understand the psychology which had prompted the question. Since
everything around us seemed to be going up in the air
and descending again in the form of stones and showers
of liquid mud, accompanied by the noises of whining
nose-caps and the mosquito-like hum of roving splinters,
the question seemed to me to be utterly uncalled-for and
in very bad taste.

"You stick your bloody fool's head up and you'll
bloody soon see," I said.

Rumbold subsided quite satisfied. He *was* under fire.

When the worst of it was over—and the worst didn't
last for more than half an hour—the Cuthbert from the
Admiralty came plunging past us. He was the lad with
the staring eyes who had tried to sham madness.

"That's the kind of wound to get," he said, and held
out his right index finger across which was a small cut
such as one might get in sharpening a pencil.

"Well, don't drip your stinking blood all over me," I
said. "Do you think you're going to get away with
that?"

"Captain Medville's sent me down to the Aid Post to
get an anti-tetanus inoculation," he answered, and
pushed on.

The queer thing was that he *did* get away with it. He
went to the Bedfords' Aid Post instead of ours. There the
M.O. didn't know him, and by virtue of his staring eyes
and some indifferent acting he got sent down the line
with shell-shock, eventually reached England, and never
came out again. By this time he is probably married,
living at Purley or somewhere worse, propagating his
awful species, and sustaining the reputation of a hero.
I myself have precious little to boast about, but—ugh!

There are no working-parties, thank God, and we get some sleep. A patrol goes out, but it doesn't concern me because I am not on it. In the morning we get some comforting news. Our officers hardly know where we are. The lie of the land, which we have all been studying, is useless to us. Our proposed jumping-off place hasn't yet been taken by our predecessors, and nobody seems to know what our objective is going to be. There is no learned member of the Staff to advise us. In *that* place ! Not bloody likely !

We are not due to go over the top on the following morning. Zero is at six minutes to six on the morning after. Dawn reveals to us a sight which nobody could visualise without having actually seen it. We can stand up and see the round of the horizon. It is like being on the sea, but our sea is a sea of mud. There is not a blade of grass visible nor a spot of colour anywhere.

Only the least undulations tend to relieve the monotony of complete flatness. In the middle distance there is something which might by exaggeration be called a "hill." We imagine that this must be the celebrated Passchendaele Ridge. Just before us our front is hidden for some distance by a fold of the ground which conceals the bed of the Paddebeeke. And the mud is pitted with craters of various sizes and depths, most of them half full of water, and set as close together as the pockets of a bagatelle table. It used to be said that no two shells fell in the same place, and this was generally true. The Somme and Passchendaele provided the exceptions. In both these favoured districts there were shell-holes within shell-holes within shell-holes.

We have a fairly quiet day, but in the afternoon I click for a rather rotten job. There is no telephone communication with battalion headquarters about two miles back, and most of the runners have either been knocked out or are already engaged. So four of us are sent with messages to B.H.Q. It is the same message, of course, but Medville sends four of us in the hope that one will survive and get there, for we must use the duckboard track which the German gunners have " taped," and they have a nasty habit of sending over " presents from Potsdam " when anybody is seen using the track in broad daylight.

We walked at intervals of fifty yards and got there and back without the least inconvenience. It was only while we were actually in B.H.Q. and partly sheltered that some shells came over near enough to encourage our determination to lead better lives in future. I heard afterwards from an officer in the reserve battalion that we were all mentioned in despatches for carrying out the order, for the disobeying of which we should have been shot. If this were so, I haven't yet received any of those bits of paper from the War Office, but at this moment of writing it is only twelve years ago, so there is plenty of time yet. My three companions, I am sorry to say, were all killed on the following morning.

Everything at Passchendaele was unique. The arrangement of our equipments—" battle order " it used to be called—was all different from that of former and future occasions. We had to go over with our packs on. This was because we had to carry with us three days' rations, it being impossible for supplies to be sent up. We wore our entrenching tools in front instead of behind, to protect a part of the anatomy which it would be indelicate to mention. When we attacked every man carried a spade stuck down his back between his pack and equipment, so that he could consolidate any position in which he happened to find himself. Moreover, each of us carried a hundred and eighty rounds of extra ammunition hung round our necks, and I—being a rifle-grenadier—had to carry twelve grenades in an extra haversack, perforated at the bottom to allow the rods to stick through.

A Mills grenade, if I remember rightly, weighs about five pounds, three hundred cartridges weigh a bit, and there was one's rifle and the usual accoutrements, so obviously one was not quite a feather-weight. Yet, burdened like pack-horses, we were expected to fight for our lives with the bayonet if the occasion arose. No wonder that Haig afterwards said that no troops in the whole history of war had ever fought under such conditions ; and the square-headed Hindenburg smugly observed that " the British Army broke its teeth on Passchendaele Ridge." It may be added that we had to wade through mud of various depths and of consistencies varied between that of raw Bovril and weak cocoa.

We are to go over from tapes laid by the Engineers. The whole thing must be done with mathematical precision, for we are to follow a creeping barrage which is to play for four minutes only a hundred yards in front of the first " ripple " of our first " wave." I am in the second " ripple " fifty yards behind the first. The first " ripple " is to go over in extended order, four paces apart, the second " ripple " is to start in artillery formation—sections in single file at a given distance apart—changing to extended order after having covered two hundred yards. It is of the utmost importance that we should keep as close as possible to our own barrage and even risk becoming casualties from it. Well, if we know our own gunners we haven't much doubt about the risk !

The lance-corporal in charge of my section is a man named Edmonds, much junior in service but considerably older than I am, and quite rightly promoted over my head. He is a conscript, a teetotaler, a non-smoker, a non-swearer, a hater of smutty stories, but a damned fine fellow. He is the father of a family and the owner of a one-man business which has gone west. He has been dragged into the Army with a real grievance, and shows himself to be one of the stoutest-hearted fellows in the whole crowd.

The mentality of Edmonds, with his pluck and his queer Nonconformist conscience, is of some professional interest to me. He tells me that he hates stories relating to the deed of kind because he thinks there is " something sacred " in it. This shows that he is a sensualist, although he hasn't the brains to see it, because when a man considers that something is sacred he does quite a lot of thinking about it. My bawdy talk, which annoys him very much, is just the scum on the surface of my mind, but having spoken I don't go on thinking.

Edmonds doesn't take his rum ration, which is all the better for the rest of us. But he disapproves of rum. He has our ration in an extra water-bottle, but won't issue it overnight because he says we may need it in the morning. In the morning he gets wounded—and so the poor dogs have none !

We do not move up to the tapes until midnight, but crouch fidgeting behind our breastwork. Plenty of stuff comes over. Jerry treats us to quite a lot of petrol shells—containing liquid fire—but they don't do much harm and, in fact, provide us with a really beautiful firework display. They remind Edmonds of the Crystal Palace in the days of his youth. He must have gone there often, for a firework show was about the only kind of entertainment which wasn't considered immoral in the quaint creed in which he was reared.

D Company, in reserve, come up and dig in just behind us, and immediately they start they are plastered with shells, for all the world as if Jerry can see them. Then things quieten down and the other fellows in my section, wanting something to occupy their minds and remembering that I am a professional writer, ask me to tell them stories.

" Not your usual ones," says Edmonds, who does not want anything to upset his elaborate preparations to meet his Maker.

So I tell them, in my poor way, two of the finest stories in the language—Quiller-Couch's " The Roll Call of the Reef " and Barry Pain's " A Lock of Hair." The former is of course well-known and highly esteemed, but Barry Pain's tale deserves to be taken out of its present obscurity. It is to be found in one of his books called *Curiosities*.

At midnight we move up to the tapes amid heavy shell-fire. Each section digs for itself a little pit in which to crouch. It is called intensive digging. Each man in turn digs like fury until he is fagged out and flops, the others meanwhile lying on their bellies and waiting their turn to seize the spade. In this way quite a big hole, like a small section of a trench, can be dug in a very few minutes.

All the while shells are screaming over our heads, throwing up great geysers of mud all around us and further mutilating the ruined landscape. Our better 'ole is about big enough to accommodate us when there is a cry for help. The section which includes Dave Barney

has been buried by a shell. Dave has given up stretcher-
bearing for the time being and is a rifleman or bomber—
I forget which. We dig them out again, swear at them
heartily, and get back to our own slot in the ground. Ten
minutes later they are all blown up and buried again,
with worse results than before. Dave is the only one of
them left alive, and he is entirely unscathed but badly
shaken and inclined to think that war is an over-rated
pastime. I want some rest, and beg him not to make a
hobby of getting himself buried. One could always say
light-hearted and stupid things even when one was
frightened to death.

We went back to our little slot in the wet earth and
I crouched down and proceeded to sleep like a hog. It
would have been rather amusing if everybody had slept
as I did, for there wouldn't have been any attack. I
don't think that even the barrage, terrific as it was,
would have wakened me. And at the same time I was
already the victim of tragedy.

While doing my share of intensive digging I heard an
ominous snick behind me. When you are batting, and
miss a ball, and hear that snick, you know that a bail has
gone. In this instance I knew that it was my rear trousers
button, the survivor of two. Only men with very strong
chins, such as "Sapper's" heroes, can keep their
trousers up by will-power alone. My braces were now a
useless and invisible decoration, and I had to improvise
a belt out of pack straps. This was very unsatisfactory,
since there were no loops on the trousers to keep the belt
in its place.

I was not allowed to sleep peacefully through the
attack. Edmonds woke me at about a quarter to six by
sticking an elbow into my ribs and we went forward to

the tape. Ghostly figures ranged up on either side of us, and a dead silence was broken by mutterings and whisperings and the *snap! snap! snap!* of men jerking their bayonets on to their rifles. When one is in imminent peril some impressions are confused while others burn their way into one's consciousness. The first pale fingers of dawn were in the sky, just beginning to show above the horizon. Having regard to what I imagined to be our front, I had supposed that the sun would rise somewhere on my right. But evidently it intended to rise in front of me and half-left. This was very mysterious, and I haven't solved the problem to this day. Two thoughts occupied my mind while I waited for zero—the sun was rising in the wrong place and my trousers were in danger of leaving me—from at least one angle—naked to mine enemies.

I salute the artillery. At ten minutes to six, hundreds, perhaps thousands, of guns behind us went off like one gun. All the inhabitants of hell seemed to have been let loose and to be screaming and raving in the sky overhead. The darkness just in front of us was rent and sundered. Blinding flashes in a long and accurate line blazed and vanished and blazed and vanished, while the guns which had at first roared in unison now drummed and bellowed and thumped and crashed in their own time. Their din was half drowned by the variegated noises of the exploding shells. No maniac ever dreamed anything like it.

Matters didn't improve. The German was not asleep, and within a minute his own barrage had multiplied the inferno by two, while machine-guns broke out with the rattling of a thousand typewriters. I stood dazed by the din and didn't notice that our own barrage had lifted until somebody shouted, " Come on ! "

I must say, without meaning to praise myself, that it was a good show. Nobody hesitated or looked back. I was simply a sheep and I went with the flock. We moved forward as if we were on the parade ground.

But it didn't last long. With shell-holes and impassable morasses we had to pick our way. It was no use looking for " dressing " to the section on the left or right, which was either in the same predicament or had already been blotted out. Led by Edmonds my section made a detour, turning a little to the left and heading for some higher and drier ground. Unfortunately most of the battalion were compelled to do this.

I was in the rear of the section, and, through no fault of my own, kept ten yards behind the man in front of me. My burden of rifle-grenades pulled me lop-sided and I had to keep on hitching at my trousers. Edmonds kept on turning and waving me on, with the heroic gestures of a cavalry leader in the Napoleonic wars. I cursed him heartily, although he could not hear. Did the damned fool think I was funking it ? No, my trousers were coming down.

My trousers seemed a positive curse to me, but I believe they were a blessing in disguise. They may have saved me from an extremity of terror. The human mind is not capable of concentrating on many things at once, and mine just then was principally concerned with my trousers. We fell into mud and writhed out again like wasps crawling out of plums, we passed a pill-box (which we thought was in British hands), we staggered between a few shell-blasted trees, passed another pill-box and came out on to a little plateau of about the size of a small suburban back garden. From there the ground sloped down to the bed of the Paddebeeke, but there was no stream left. It had been shelled into a bog. The Germans had left one long single plank bridge, and we should have known what was certain to happen if we attempted to cross it. But we went on to the edge of the plateau—and it was perhaps as well for us that we did— until Edmonds noticed that nobody else was standing up. Then he signalled to us to take cover. We flopped into a shell-hole, lying around the lip, for there was about six feet of water in the middle.

We had already seen what had happened to the first " ripple." They had all made for that spot of higher and drier ground, and the Germans, having retired over it, knew exactly what must happen, and the sky rained shells upon it. Shrapnel was bursting not much more than face high, and the liquid mud from ground shells was going up in clouds and coming down in rain.

The first " ripple " was blotted out. The dead and wounded were piled on each others' backs, and the second wave, coming up behind and being compelled to cluster like a flock of sheep, were knocked over in their tracks and lay in heaving mounds. The wounded tried to mark their places, so as to be found by stretcher-bearers, by sticking their bayonets into the ground, thus leaving their rifles upright with the butts pointing at the sky. There was a forest of rifles until they were uprooted by shell-bursts or knocked down by bullets like so many skittles.

The wounded who couldn't crawl into the dubious shelter of shell-holes were all doomed. They had to ie where they were until a stray bullet found them or they were blown to pieces. Their heartrending cries pierced the incessant din of explosions. The stretcher-bearers, such as still survived, could do nothing as yet.

Well, I found myself in a shell-hole with the rest of the section, strangely intact. I had lost merely a bit of skin from the bridge of my nose. I had been stung by something a minute after we started to advance and, having applied the back of my hand, found blood on it. This was a close shave, but a miss was as good as a mile. But a tragedy worse than the precariousness of my trousers had befallen me. I had lost my rations.

While crossing the plateau it had seemed to me that somebody had given the pack on my back a good hard shove, and I had looked all round but there was nobody near. Then I was aware of things falling behind me. A piece of shell about the size of a dumb-bell had gone through my pack, and all my kit and food were dropping out. I didn't stop to pick anything up.

How my section had so far remained intact is a mystery which I shall never solve in this world. After a minute or two of stupor we discovered that we were all as thickly coated with mud from the shell-bursts as the icing on a Christmas cake. Our rifles were all clogged, and directly we tried to clean them more mud descended. If the Germans had counter-attacked we had nothing but our bayonets. In the whole battalion only one Lewis gun was got into action, and I don't think that more than half a dozen men in the three attacking companies were able to use their rifles during the first few hours.

We saw Germans rise out of the ground and bolt like rabbits, and we had to let them bolt. They had been able to keep their rifles covered and clean, but we had bayonets on ours. Moreover their artillery knew just where we were, and our own gunners were now firing speculatively. We were getting the shells and the rain of mud and the German wasn't. Good soldier that he was, he soon took advantage of this, and we began to suffer from the most hellish sniping.

The mud which was our enemy was also our friend. But for the mud none of us could have survived. A shell burrowed some way before it exploded and that considerably decreased its killing power.

Edmonds decided that our shell-hole was over-crowded and told me to get into the next one. I didn't like exposing myself even for a second, but it was only like rolling out of one twin bed into another, and besides I wanted to get away from the awful man Rumbold who was quite likely, at any moment, to ask me if we were under fire. Half a dozen bullets spat at me in the one second it took to make the change.

There were two men in my new temporary abode, a fellow who was in the Bedfords—on our left—who had got himself lost, and a chap in my company, but not in my section. I knew his company by the red square on his shoulder.

This man lay with his rifle at his shoulder in the attitude of one about to fire. I spoke to him and he didn't answer. Then I shoved him. Then I noticed that there was a jagged hole at the back of his tin hat and a thin trickle of blood down his neck. He had got it right through the head, and this—if I had needed it—was a warning to keep mine down. I addressed myself to the Bedford.

" Well," I said, " we're in a pretty nasty mess. Are we going to get out of it alive, do you think ? " I did not say this lightly : I am trying to make it quite clear that I was no hero, and I was just then one of the most hot-and-bothered men in the universe.

The Bedford rolled his eyes.

" I put my trust in Almighty God," he said.

The remark infuriated me. I prayed for myself—as I shall tell later—but I never " trusted " in God in the sense that I expected as a right that He should do as I asked. To beg for something is one thing ; to " trust " you are going to get it is another. Thousands of us had to be killed, and it was damnably presumptuous of this fellow to say that he trusted in God to save his own wretched life.

I pointed to the shambles behind us where half a million pounds worth of education was already beginning to rot.

" You bloody fool ! " I said. " Do you think some of those fellows didn't put their trust in God, too ! He isn't up there just to look after *you*."

The Bedford thought I was blasphemous—God knows I wasn't—and obviously didn't like my company, for he presently braved the hell which was raging outside the shell-hole and went off to find his own people. I hope he did, but he was probably dead in less than a minute. Anyhow he would probably have been killed if he had stayed, for I don't think two men in the same shell-hole could have survived the narrow squeak which came to me immediately afterwards.

There was still a tornado of shells raging around us, and one must have landed in the same shell-hole with me. I didn't hear it come, and I didn't hear it burst, but I suddenly found myself in the air, all arms and legs. It seemed to me that I rose to about the height of St. Paul's Cathedral, but probably I only went up about a couple of feet. The experience was not in the least rough, and I can't understand why it disturbed me so little. I think that by this time I was so mentally numb

that even fear was atrophied. It was like being lifted by
an unexpected wave when one is swimming in the sea.
I landed on all fours in the shell-hole which Edmonds
had told me to leave, sprawling across the backs of the
rest of the section.

" And now," I said firmly, " I'm going to stop."

Edmonds didn't demur, and I asked him what about
some rum. The Nonconformist conscience prevailed, and
he said that we might need it presently. Merciful
heavens, didn't I need it now ! We lit cigarettes and I
began trying to think. I wondered if I could smile, and,
still having control of my face muscles, found that I could.

After all, I was not very much afraid in that shell-hole,
but I knew that I daren't move out of it. I dared not go
out and try to do anything for the wounded—coward
and hound that I was. After all I wasn't a stretcher-
bearer. A damned good excuse !

Nothing had stood up and lived on the space of ground
between ourselves and the pill-box a hundred and fifty
yards away. I saw a stretcher-bearer, his face a mask of
blood, bending over a living corpse. He shouted to
somebody and beckoned, and on the instant he crumpled
and fell and went to meet his God. To do the enemy
justice, I don't suppose for one moment that he was
recognised as a stretcher-bearer.

Another man, obviously off his head, wandered aim-
lessly for perhaps ninety seconds. Then his tin hat was
tossed into the air like a spun coin, and down he went.
You could always tell when a man was shot dead. A
wounded man always tried to break his own fall. A
dead man generally fell forward, his balance tending in
that direction, and he bent simultaneously at the knees,
waist, neck and ankles.

Several of our men, most of whom had first been wounded, were drowned in the mud and water. One very religious lad with pale blue watery eyes died the most appalling death. He was shot through the lower entrails, tumbled into the water of a deep shell-hole, and drowned by inches while the coldness of the water added further torture to his wound. Thank God I didn't see him. But our C. of E. chaplain—who went over the top with us, the fine chap !—was killed while trying to haul him out.

I don't subscribe to the creed of the Church of England. The cognoscenti of my Church—when they can be got to speak frankly—are dubious about the post-mortem fate of heretics and less than dubious about the fate of heretic clergy. But I am very sure, if I am to believe in anything at all, that our dear Padre is in one of the Many Mansions. I like to think of him feasting with Nelson and Drake, Philip Sidney, Richard of the Lion Heart, Grenville, Wolfe and Don John of Austria. And perhaps when these have dallied a little over their wine they go to join the ladies—such ladies as Joan of Arc, Grace Darling, Florence Nightingale and Edith Cavell. *Requiescat*—but he needs no prayers from a bad soldier and a worse sinner.

Edmonds and I held a sort of council of war. If we were counter-attacked in our present circumstances we hadn't the chance of mice against cats. My theory was that we ought to make a bolt for the pill-box behind us, clean our rifles once we were inside, and thus have a defensive position and a chance to fight for our lives if Jerry decided that the bit of ground we had won was worth re-taking.

Edmonds agreed with me, but was loath to retire. I

daresay he thought that an extra hundred yards or so of mud was going to make a material difference to the result of the war. If he had had a Union Jack with him I think he would have stuck it in the ground as a kind of announcement that we were there. He wouldn't go back on his own initiative and at last told me to go and find company headquarters and get an order from Captain Medville.

Company headquarters was any shell-hole that Captain Medville might be in if he happened to be still alive. I didn't want to wander about in an area in which nobody had been seen to stand up for much more than a minute, so I told Edmonds I didn't know where to look. He saw by my eyes that I was afraid to go, and before I could summon a little more resolution and stop him, he went himself.

By a miracle or an accident he found Medville, who seemed to have agreed with my suggestion. Edmonds came lumbering back and waved us towards the pill-box, himself starting in that direction. But he hadn't gone ten yards before he rolled over, clutching at one of his thighs. I saw him crawl into a shell-hole, and I am glad to be able to say that eventually he got back to safety.

That left me in command of the section.

CHAPTER XI

I was the senior private and I suppose by strict Army law the others were compelled to obey me. But not having the authority of even a single stripe, and knowing that whatever I decided was most likely to be wrong, I said that each of us ought to please himself as to what he did. I gave a brief harangue (without any " hear, hears ") and of course I don't remember exactly what I said, but the gist of it was this :

" Here we are, being shelled to Sodom and Gomorrah. If a small boy came over armed with a catapult he could pinch or murder the whole bloody lot of us. We've been directed to retire to the pill-box but we haven't had an actual order. Once there we shall be fairly safe, but it's the getting there. I think now it's every man for himself, but what are you going to do ? "

The general opinion, after a long argument, was that we should make for the pill-box one at a time. The next question that had to be decided was who should go first. Having Lance-corporal Edmonds's wound on my conscience, I said that I would. I don't know if the others attempted to follow me or not. I saw only one of them again, and that was, of course, the awful man Rumbold, who was unable to give a coherent account of what had happened. I dumped everything except my rifle and the extra ammunition hanging around my neck and made a dash for it.

I ran and ducked and dodged like an international

three-quarter, slipping, falling, rising and plunging, and getting somehow over the mud and the dead bodies and between the shell-holes. It amuses me now to think that during this mad dash it is quite possible that not a single shot was fired at me. Probably the spectators in field-grey were laughing too heartily to begin to take aim. It used to amuse us to see some poor devil of a German dodging about like a stoned rat, and their humour was at least as grim as ours.

The little concrete blockhouse was approached by a sort of slide leading to its only entrance. I skidded on the seat of my trousers down a muddy incline and into a pool of water which swam in an open doorway not much higher or wider than the entrance to a dog's kennel. I saw at once that the place was uninhabitable so far as I was concerned. There was about three feet of water inside, and the dead bodies of the late German garrison were floating about. I did not then know that it was in German hands when we passed it in the morning, that we owed a great many of our casualties to the machine-gun crew who were now safely dead, and that we had to thank our own C Company for a really magnificent deed of arms. Since I was not in C Company and wasn't even aware that this phase of the fight was going on, I can tell of it without being accused of boasting.

Thanks to our magnificent Staff—God bless them !— we had gone over from a jumping-off place which we knew nothing about. The two pill-boxes in front of us were supposed to have been vacated by the Germans. Nobody had orders to take them. C Company on our extreme left became painfully aware that one of them was in German hands but thought that the job of obliterating it belonged to the Bedfords—on *their* left—

since they had had no orders. When the true state of affairs became known C Company went back and got that pill-box. It could only be got by being surrounded and by somebody heaving a few bombs through the kennel-like door. This was done. When C Company came out of the line it was twelve strong and led by a lance-corporal. The dead were found by a burial party—from the R.M.L.I., I think—in an accurate circle around that pill-box.

I was fairly safe in the half-fathom of water into which I had slid, but I could not stay there and I was feeling rather homeless. I scrambled up again and dodged round to the other side of the premises where there was a certain amount of cover. To my surprise I found a sort of family gathering. All the wounded who had managed to crawl so far were congregated there, and I was delighted to find that three of my old friends had " Blighty " ones.

One of them a very old man of nearly forty and a Boer War veteran, had been shot sideways through the seat of the trousers. He was in considerable pain but responded quite happily to badinage. I told him that he couldn't possibly show his honourable scars to his lady friends and that he might find it difficult to convince the pretty nurses that he was facing the right direction when the bullet found him. I pulled his leg to buck him up, not to annoy him, and the brave fellow, who was lying on his stomach, laughed quite happily. I hate to record that his wound turned septic and that he died very shortly afterwards in a C.C.S.

Tim's Irish pal, who attributed all his misfortunes to the machinations of Protestants, had a bloody bandage around one arm instead of a sleeve. He couldn't very well blame the followers of that strange but business-like bookseller, Mr. Kensit, for what had happened to him, but I believe that even to this day he is sure that it was a Lutheran Prussian who shot him.

The boy with the almond eyes, who used to put me to bed in England when the bed revolved or miraculously multiplied itself, had one through the shoulder, and seemed not to be in very much pain. They were all waiting to be carried away, or for nightfall and the chance of crawling out on their own legs.

Captain Medville had evidently thought that my suggestion to make for the pill-box was a pretty sound one, for I found him already there. He had been wounded in the process of arriving, but not badly enough to necessitate his going down the line. He was calm but looked very worried and was, I suppose, being baffled by the problem of how to get together what remained of his company. I asked him what I should do and where I should go, and he told me to go and join D Company which had been in reserve to the other three companies and was now strung out in a long line of shell-holes on either side of the rear pill-box. This was obviously to be our line of defence in the event of Jerry seeking to regain his lost ground.

D Company was lucky. It had lost only about half its men. I faded away in the direction indicated and found a D Company sergeant who was pained because I hadn't shaved. He told me to get into a shell-hole—any one would do—clean my rifle and shoot any one who couldn't properly pronounce the consonant "W." Like a fool, I got into a shell-hole just in front of the pill-box.

It was now about two in the afternoon. Time is supposed to drag when one is in misery. This is generally so, but to me the past eight hours seemed to have gone

in one. I settled down alone in my shell-hole and proceeded to have my " bad time," which, thank God,
nobody witnessed.

The Germans started a really appalling bombardment, quite as bad as the one we had endured in the
early hours of the morning. Shells fell around me like
acorns dropping from a tree and the shock of every
explosion was like a punch over the solar plexus. I had
been through a great deal already, and now I felt that I
couldn't bear it. I crouched shivering and whimpering
in my extremity, and cried out on God. I don't think it
was altogether funk ; I think my wits were being blasted
out of me. I didn't realise at the time that the Germans
were shelling the pill-box and that I, being just in front,
was getting the exclusive attention of a few batteries of
field artillery.

I crouched, moaning, " Oh, Christ, make it stop ! Oh,
Jesus, make it stop ! It *must* stop because I can't bear it
any more ! I can't bear it ! "

It was the only time in my life when, so far as I can be
sure, I had a direct answer to prayer. I don't mean that
the shelling stopped : that would have proved nothing to
me, and besides the shelling hadn't. I may never again
enter a branch of my infallible Church, and try to follow
the Mass and go to Confession and Holy Communion.
I can't quite believe in a lot of it. I wish I could, for I
should be a better and happier man. But I do believe in
God, and I do know that God, the Father of us all, hears
us and answers with a father's gentleness when we cry
out to Him in our last extremity.

I begged God to spare me for my mother's sake, while
all the while I knew that I was only praying for the
preservation of my own dirty hide. I made Him promises

of the saintly life I would lead if I got through—promises which I didn't keep, and He knew that I wasn't going to keep them. But He was merciful, and His mercy came to me like a sudden shaft of sunlight.

It happened all in a moment—a sudden change to peace and calm and perfect confidence. It was like a miracle and perhaps it was one. All in a moment I was changed from a raving, gibbering idiot to a calm and serene man, utterly fearless for the time being, and quite confident that I was safe. A five-point-nine crashed down not more than five yards away, drenching me with mud, but I did not mind it. I knew that God was going to save me.

This, having regard to what I had said to the Bedford a few hours since, may seem paradoxical. But I only " trusted " God after He seemed to have spoken to me. I did not say in effect : " Well, I've prayed to You, and now it's up to You to get me out of this. Fair's fair." Believers and unbelievers may make what they like out of this. Snuffy little short-sighted doctors who attribute every malaise and cure of the mind to sex would probably give me some quite astounding explanation. I only know that if an angel had come and taken me by the hand I could not have been more assured of my present safety.

I don't mean that I was never afterwards afraid. I merely knew that just for the present I was safe. Physically I was still wretched enough, starving, mud-drenched and tortured by lice. My improvised belt kept slipping, and every time I moved, lying on the incline of the shell-hole, my trousers, slack at the waist, scooped up mud which ran down cold along my belly and thighs.

Strangely enough I thought of a girl I had loved as

finely as I knew how some two or three years since. Wisely, she had not cared for me and was now married to another man. I had stopped loving her but I revered her, as I still do. I felt that if she saw me now, filthy and verminous as I was, she could not but put her arms around me in compassion.

After this excursion into sticky sentiment I thought I had better find some grub. There were plenty of fresh corpses lying about with food in their packs or haversacks. However, I hadn't to rob the dead for I had no sooner started on my food-hunt when I found two D Company fellows in a shell-hole only a few yards away who had plenty to eat. The shelling had died down a bit, but I jumped into their shell-hole to dodge one which seemed to be coming uncomfortably close, and landed almost on top of them.

I didn't know them but they were decent chaps who shared their food with me. Also they provided me with human society, which I needed more than food and drink. They seemed to think they had had a pretty rough time, and were horrified when I told them that I didn't think there were fifty officers and men left out of the three companies which had made the attack. Mine was a pretty good guess. When we eventually mustered we numbered forty-nine. My company (A) was eighteen strong, including two officers, there were nineteen of B, and twelve of C.

Just before nightfall I saw Lloyd threading his way towards us, and hailed him. Lloyd was a signaller in my company, a little rosy-cheeked Welsh boy aged about nineteen who had joined the Army straight from school. I asked him what had become of the rest of the company, and he told me that, so far as he knew, we were the only

two who had not become casualties ; and he looked at
me out of the haggard eyes of an old man.

Lloyd and I both decided that it would be a good idea
to spend the night in the pill-box a stone's throw away
if it happened to be dry enough inside. It would be safer
in there, and there would be shelter of a sort from the
rather threatening weather. Since there were no shells
coming over at the moment we went and prospected.
It was beautifully dry inside, but a number of wounded
had crawled there, and the place stank of blood worse
than a slaughter-house. Still, we should have put up
with that, but the loathly person Goatly (the ex-village-
schoolmaster officer) was in possession, and meant to
spend the night there himself, so he turfed us out although
there was plenty of room. I hated this vulgar and domi-
neering person, but I heard that he had behaved with
the utmost gallantry, so all is now forgiven. He didn't
worry us much longer for he got a series of soft jobs and
became, I believe, a chronic "town major." If he reads
these lines in the intervals between teaching the Third
Standard long division and how to control its water
there is not the least chance that he will recognise himself, so he will not require my blood in a bottle. I salute
him as the bravest cad with whom I ever had to be
associated.

Lloyd and I began by camping in a shell-hole. I think
it was the one in which I had had my " sticky time." We
fired questions at each other, trying to get news, but
neither of us seemed to know much. Then Lloyd
answered unconsciously the question I had been afraid
to ask. He told me that Dave had been killed.

That was the last straw. I was still pretty badly rattled,
and I began to cry like a baby. A damned funny sight

I must have looked. Oh, Dave, are you really gone ?
Shall we have no more meals and drinks together ?
Shan't I ever hear you sing *Songs of Araby* again ?
No more women for you ? No more love—as you understand love since that wife of yours was taken from you ?
Did God at the last moment stretch out His hand to you
and re-unite you with her ? Or are you wallowing somewhere in a worse hell than this ? Whatever the change,
you have gone somewhere else, and here am I, a filthy
oaf, with the tears running down my dirty cheeks
because of you.

Owing to the conditions something like seventy per
cent. of the casualties could be marked down as
killed. Lloyd and I knew that it must be so. Nearly
everybody that we knew and liked seemed to have gone
west.

We did not find the slope of the shell-hole conducive to
slumber so we decided to sleep in the open if we could
find a dry spot. We found a corrugated iron arch called
a " baby elephant " and used for the support of shallow
funk-holes and dugouts. We crawled under this, and
with no protection against the cold of a night which
ushered in the month of November, except the clothes
in which we lay—without even our overcoats—we slept
like hogs until a red sun winked in our eyes and finally
woke us.

Only twice did these mud-sodden, overgrown Babes
in the Wood wake during the night. Once we were
roused by the screams of a wounded man who was being
carried to the pill-box. He kept shrieking, " Oh, God !
Oh, Christ ! "—the same words over and over again. We
were sorry for him, of course, but for our own sakes we
wished he wouldn't do it. On the second occasion Lloyd

nudged me and complained of the cold and asked me to lie closer.

The pill-box presented a queer sight in the morning. We went in to see if we could do anything for the wounded and found others trying to improvise a breakfast for them. Medville was feeding his own batman like a baby. The poor fellow had been badly hit and he died shortly afterwards. There was still that terrible stink of raw blood which smote our nostrils pretty hard as we came in from the fresh air.

The regimental Aid Post was a mile or so back, and it took time to get the wounded there. Our M.O.— whom I didn't particularly like—had worked like a slave, and when we passed the shelter on our way out that night there was a pyramid of shorn limbs standing outside. He had been busy with the casualties of other units besides our own, and had been rather a mark for stretcher-bearers because of the dimensions of the Red Cross flag which floated above.

There were quite a lot of field guns near that Aid Post. Query : were the guns too near the Aid Post or was the Aid Post too near the guns ?

Lloyd and I began to think rather wistfully about breakfast, but we hadn't so much as a crumb between us or a drop of water. I don't know what had happened to Lloyd's rations. However, he had a Tommy Cooker and a tin of coffee cubes, so we decided to risk making coffee with shell-hole water. Lloyd went out with our mess-tins to find the cleanest looking shell-hole and came back with them full, and quaking like one about to vomit. He had found half a well-preserved Highlander lying just outside the shell-hole from which he had drawn the water, and had had a good look at him and wished he hadn't. He kept on saying, " I wish I hadn't looked at that damned Scotsman." It wasn't until after we had drunk the coffee that the horrid thought occurred to us that the other half of the Highlander might be in the shell-hole from which Lloyd had drawn the water. This was probably not so, for we suffered no after-effects.

Soon after we had had our coffee Lloyd was sent for. There was a job of some sort for him. I remained in lonely glory for some hours. A few shells came over, and during this period a terrible scarecrow came running and dodging towards me. The face seemed to me to consist entirely of gold-rimmed spectacles and teeth. It was the awful man Rumbold.

I kept my head down, but with the unerring instinct of the bore who has scented his victim from afar, he came straight to me, flopped down beside me and said cheerfully : " Hullo, is that you ? "

I didn't tell him it wasn't, because he wouldn't have believed me, and he would have stayed all the same.

He didn't seem to know where he had been during the past twenty-four hours, what he had been doing, or what had happened to anybody else. Indeed, he was magnificently unconcerned with these things. Suddenly and quite chattily he asked me : " I say, X, what do you think of Lloyd George ? "

Now how could I tell him what I thought of Lloyd George ? I didn't want to use such language. I might be killed at any moment and I wanted to die in a state of grace.

I suggested that there was another shell-hole over there which looked awfully comfortable, but of course I couldn't get rid of him. He stuck to me closer than a brother until we were relieved at night by a battalion of marines.

We learned during the day that the Canadians on our right, advancing at the same time as ourselves on the higher and drier ground, had taken their objectives. Subsequently we were told " unofficially " that we were not expected to get very far through the swamp and that we were merely being used to draw fire while the Canadians did the job. Well, it wasn't the last time that I was used as cannon-fodder.

The papers were loud in praise of the Canadians but had practically nothing to say about us—except in the casualty lists. Officially we were told that we were " too brave " and had gone too far ; but Sir Arthur Conan Doyle, in his *History of the War*, dismissed us with the remark that we " seemed to find some difficulty in getting forward." The difficulty consisted mainly of being killed in heaps.

Now I love Sir Arthur Conan Doyle without ever having met him. His stories delighted my youth, and he sent a charming letter to me—a practically unknown man—complimenting me on one of mine. But he should have left the war alone. I should go to him if I wanted a really authentic photograph of a fairy or a trunk call through to one of my sleeping ancestors. But he should have left the war to the soldiers. You cannot write about the war by merely reading newspaper reports and looking at maps.

The remnants of us crawled out dead-beat along the eternal duckboard track. Some of us would have collapsed if we hadn't met a water-cart on the way. We got to Irish Farm and were greeted by a really hearty air-raid—as if we hadn't been through enough already.

When it was over and we started looking for the tents allotted to us I was struck by the kindness of the fellows who had remained behind. Our Q.M.S., whom I had always found rather military, met us and carried my rifle for me.

" You've had a hell of a time," he said with a catch in his voice.

" Pretty bad," I agreed, " but it might have been worse."

" Worse ! " he gasped.

" Yes," I said. " We didn't see any of the bloody Staff."

That at least made him laugh.

They had rationed for about five times the number of men that actually returned, so for a change I got enough to eat. The Q.M.S. then gave me three-quarters of a mess-tin full of rum—neat, and proof spirit at that. It would have killed a man who didn't really need it. But I drank it and slept like a little child for six hours.

There was a crowd of ignorant, dirty-nosed Bible-thumpers in England who were trying to stop our rum issue. If they had succeeded I should by this time have founded a society for the wholesale slaughter of village grocers.

Funnily enough, it isn't the doctor who wants to stop me from having a drink. I don't know a teetotal doctor. But the Nonconformist ex-elementary-schoolboy grocer of course knows more than the medical faculty, and, if he makes it a matter of ethics, I don't know how he gets over the miracle at the Marriage Feast at Cana. Perhaps he tries to persuade himself, his sour-visaged consort and his awful offspring, that Christ turned the water into lemon squash (" which I keep in my shop ").

On Sundays he offers up much praise to the Lord under corrugated iron—which is just as well, because when he is safe in chapel he can't be swindling anybody. His young are apt to pilfer anything that isn't nailed down, and apart from that they have the morals of over-sexed rabbits. I have had some opportunities of studying the breed, which produced rather more than a fair percentage of conscientious objectors. If this breed existed in the time of Bloody Queen Mary, all I can say is that she scamped her job.

CHAPTER XII

On the following morning we go down to Poperinghe in trucks on a light railway, which we board somewhere close to Irish Farm. " Pop " is a civilised town with real shops and houses all standing intact. We are billeted in some Nissen huts on the town square.

We were there for about three days and I made my acquaintanceship with Talbot House. Toc H was an institution which deserves to be perpetuated. It was the only club which the private soldier could enter and find himself in civilised surroundings. It was a real joy to find comfortable chairs and see books and magazines lying invitingly about.

I am afraid I pinched Masefield's *Everlasting Mercy* from the library, but I didn't mean to. I took it out and lent it to another fellow, who lost it.

While we were in " Pop " Captain Medville disappeared and, I think, went home sick, but Captain Perks returned from a course and took charge of the remnants of the company. The change was not a welcome one, for Perks was entirely lacking in imagination and had no tact in handling his men. He seemed quite oblivious of the fact that we had been going through a pretty thick time while he was in safe and comfortable surroundings.

He celebrated his return by giving me six days extra duties for being absent from a rifle inspection which we had not been warned was to take place. It was on a

Sunday, and I had gone to Mass at the parish church. Coming out I made one of those strange coincidental acquaintances, for, seeing a little dried-up man who was in the Munsters, I asked if he knew Mr. O'Rorke who was killed just before Christmas in 1914. Poor Jimmy O'Rorke and I had been friends at school, but he had gone almost straight to India after leaving Sandhurst and I had only seen him once since. By a freak of chance this fellow had been his batman and was beside him when he got a bullet straight between the eyes.

I had money enough to buy him and myself a meal, so I didn't return to camp but got some writing materials and polished off half a short story in Toc H. It was a great relief to me to write when it was at all possible—to sit down and lose myself in the pleasant old world I used to know and pretend to myself that there never had been a war. Some of my editors seemed of the opinion that we were not suffering from one now. One dear old chap, since dead, who controlled one of the leading fiction magazines, used to write to me saying, " Couldn't you let me have one of your light, charming love stories of country house life by next Thursday." I would get these letters in the trenches during the usual " morning hate " when my fingers were too numb to hold a pencil, when I was worn out with work and sleeplessness, and when I was extremely doubtful if there would ever be another Thursday so far as I was concerned.

But I was sorry I took the day off for more than one reason. A well-known painter whom I had known and liked in England, and who had just been made an official war artist, having heard that I was in " Pop," came round to see me and, of course, I missed him.

One of the tragic incidents of our days in " Pop " was

the division of the food in the parcels sent out to the men who were already dead. The officers had first pick—a rather tactless mistake on their part, I think—and what was left was thrown to us rabble. It wasn't too pleasant to think that one was eating cake which a mother had made for her son who was lying disembowelled in the mud, but one ate it all the same.

My own parcels were few and far between. My mother was too poor to afford to send me anything, and I gave her to understand that we had all the food we wanted. Some well-meaning friends of my family, however, having heard all about the lice, kept me regularly supplied with all sorts of preparations guaranteed to discourage, dismay, and destroy them. Whenever I got a parcel everybody knew what it contained, and it became a joke against me.

Strange and wonderful were the chemists' preparations which were supposed to aid us in our battles with our most intimate enemies. About the least successful was a belt supposed to be worn next the skin, and manufactured by a firm of multiple cash chemists. According to the manufacturers lice couldn't live within a mile of it and they retired from one's person in disorder and settled on the next fellow.

As a fact I found that lice loved that belt. They used it as home, nuptial chamber, incubator and nursery. They went for walks on it, mated on it, laid their eggs on it, and brought up their offspring on it. Until some of them met with a sudden death at my hands they hardly left it except to draw rations. It would embarrass me if the manufacturers should ask me to write them a testimonial.

After a few days in " Pop " we moved to a camp some

two miles distant called Dirty Bucket Camp. It was aptly named. It was a canvas camp with the tents standing like a dingy flotilla of fishing boats riding at anchor in a sea of Flanders mud.

There, where we were supposed to be " resting," we went through the same old " training." Much button and buckle polishing and rifle cleaning were followed by eight or nine hours of physical jerks, squad drill, bayonet fighting, bomb throwing, and the whole dreary round of it which we knew by heart to the point of sickness. We had had a pretty rotten time, and a little real rest might have healed our shattered spirits ; but the Brass Hats wouldn't have felt they were doing their job properly unless they found unnecessary work for the men.

But we got the usual hour or two off in the evening and there was an inhabited village close handy where one could get omelettes, French beer and the usual two wines of different colours and indeterminate origins.

But it's a dull world without Dave, and young Lloyd is away on a course. The loss of so many of our companions is like a ton's weight of misery lying on us. We survivors have been lucky : next time we can scarcely hope for luck. There is no sign of the war ending and the official voices of every government concerned are still making bombastic utterances. Certainly we are in for another winter campaign. As soon as some more poor devils have been sent out to make us up to about two-thirds our proper strength, up we shall go again to flounder in that unspeakable mud, and die horribly with the mire soaking into our raw wounds.

Captain Perks, who has yet to encounter war at its best and bloodiest, notices this air of depression and lectures us about it. He says he has lost more friends than any of us. How does he know that? Could any-body—except Captain Perks—utter a more fatuous remark?

But our spirits soon revive, even in the grey, raw November weather, although we have nothing to hope for but a wound or a quick and merciful death.

One mid-day I get a great piece of news. *Dave wasn't killed after all!* Moreover he is back with us from the Corps Rest Station where he had a few days' treatment for shell-shock. As I have described, he was blown up and buried twice on the night preceding the attack. It seems now that he was blown up and buried again during the attack—planted in the ground like an onion with his head just protruding—and he would be there now if another shell hadn't blown him out again. And not a scratch!

Of course I am delighted beyond words, but in some odd way I am a little cross with him. I am conscious of having wasted a lot of emotion on the old devil, and I have now got used to the idea of his being dead. Besides, young Lloyd will probably tell him that I blubbed about him. He is the only " Missing, believed killed," who has turned up again. So, glad as I am, I can't help feeling that he might have had the decency to remain dead. I am yet to see *Mary Rose* and learn that I am not the only human being with this queer kink in its nature.

Dave and I rush together and shake hands when we meet. He is as deaf as an adder—and serve him right! —and he has just arrived in the nick of time to save me from posting a letter to his father, saying that he died quite painlessly and quoting some very noble " last words " which I had invented for the occasion. They were very fine " last words," and much better than Dave could have spoken for himself. I am sure that Dave *in articulo mortis* would shock an unconverted charabanc driver.

Naturally the world suddenly becomes a much brighter place for me, and we have an evening out together. Our conversation, however, is restricted by the fact of my having temporarily lost my voice through a cold, and Dave is so deaf that he can only hear " What are you going to have ? " I notice that shell-shock has not interfered with his infinite capacity for loving. Having remarked to me that the girl who is cooking omelettes for us is a bit too young, he asks her if she hasn't a big sister. Morally this is a bad sign, but from the purely physical point of view it is perfectly splendid.

Apart from our restricted conversation it is a great evening. We have each of us a little money, enough to buy omelettes of many eggs and sufficient of the wine of the country to let us forget the hell from which we have come and the purgatory in which we remain. We get back to our respective tents warm, cheery and ready for sleep.

In my tent there is a funny little rosy-cheeked corporal whom we call Jacko. He is very amusing at my expense.

" They can't kill *you*," he says, " and they never will, blast you ! What's the use of my lecturing the chaps and telling them that it's the quickest man to jump up and the quickest to lie down that has the best chance ? You're the slowest blighter I ever set eyes on, but still they can't kill you."

We had a lot of fun in the tent on a rather grim subject. Most of us had the addresses of one another's people in order to write the usual letter in case the worst happened to one or any of us. I had not given my mother's address for, if I became too intimate with some high explosive, I wanted the news to be broken to her a little more gently. So Jacko had the name and address of a lady who was the mother of a girl in whom I was interested, and who had promised to call on my poor mother and break the news, if any news had to be broken.

To Jacko's amusement I pictured the scene. The lady would do it so tactfully ! She would call and have tea and suddenly say : " What a nice fellow your son was." " Not *was—is*," my mother would reply. " No, not *is— was* ! " the other lady would exclaim.

There will be those who think this a perfectly heart-less joke. Yet we found ourselves in that frame of mind. We had to regard the prospect of our own respective violent deaths as something natural and probable, and in defence of the weakness of our own natures we treated the subject as lightly as possible.

It was while we were in Dirty Bucket Camp that we lost our old M.O., who went away sick. In the course of a day or two the glad rumour went round that there was a new American M.O. who believed everything you told him.

We were not slow to take advantage of this example of trans-Atlantic innocence, so all that was left of the battalion paraded sick in the hope of getting light duty instead of the soul-destroying parades.

All of us were a little loose in the bowels, so like one man we said we were suffering from diarrhœa. A doctor cannot tell if you haven't got diarrhœa unless he watches over you like a " nannie."

I had a rather unfortunate experience with this doctor, for I was in the middle of the queue and I didn't know what colossal lies the other fellows had been telling him. Dave, who preceded me, went into the tent and had the nerve to tell him that he had been compelled to visit the latrines twenty-six times in the previous twenty-four hours.

" Gee ! " exclaimed the astonished doctor, and gave him some medicine and three days light duty.

Then I went in and he said : " Waal, I suppose you've got diarrhœa too ? I'm going to call this regiment the Charley's Aunts."

This, I believe, was a delicate allusion to the fact that " Charley's Aunt " was " still running." He then asked me how often I had responded to the call of nature in the past day and night, and I told him seven or eight times. After the tall stories he had been hearing from the other men this brought to his face a look of blank astonishment.

" Gee, man," he exclaimed, " you're bound ! If you come here tellin' me any more stories like that I shall have to give you some opening medicine."

But he gave me a day's light duty, and I went out mystified—and remained so until I heard what the other liars had been saying.

This American doctor soon learned what " swinging the lead " meant, and he turned out to be a thoroughly decent chap, humane, kindly and decently polite. Too many doctors out there were brutal and tyrannical to men whom, for the sake of their own livings, they would have been very civil to in private practice. Strange how the bedside manner vanished out there, where the patient hadn't to pay. I regret to say that we lost our kindly American M.O., who was killed or captured— I have never found out which—on the March retreat.

His successor was also an American, but no use to man or beast. Americans seem to vary a lot, just like the rest of us.

After a few days at Dirty Bucket Camp we were marched by easy stages further back until we reached a village near Bolezeele, which was to be our home for a week or two. It was an uninteresting village set in a landscape as flat as a stale joke. Along one side of a road, and at regular intervals, were farmhouses as exactly alike as so many suburban villas. Each company was billeted on a different farm, and we bedded down in barns on immemorial straw in which we found, if we were rash enough to dig into it, the meat-tins, cigarette cartons, and other relics of our predecessors.

The accommodation was miserable enough, but the walls of my barn were intact and most of the roof still remained. With a blanket besides an overcoat one felt in luck's way. Indeed, a Staff officer who came round remarked to Captain Perks that it was too comfortable for the men and more suitable for the horses. This could only have been meant as a joke, but it wasn't in the best of taste.

On our farm there was a poor wretch of a dog who spent his life in a cage when he wasn't on a sort of tread-mill which turned a churn. On cold dismal mornings I used to go out and try to fondle him through the wire. It was horrible to me to think that there was a poor dumb animal whose life was as wretched as my own. The French and Flemish peasants ought not to be allowed to keep dogs. As Dave remarked, " they treat them as badly as our people treat their soldiers." This dog and I had something in common in that we both wished we were dead.

There were one or two bright spots but, generally speaking, I had a pretty miserable time in that district. It rained nearly all the while, and we did a lot of training in order that our spirits might not be allowed to droop. If anything ever got me down it was button-polishing and general cleaning up. After a spell of " rest " it took me about a fortnight of comparative peace in the trenches to get my nerves right again.

Just at this time we had to keep our bayonets particularly bright and I had a couple of specks of rust on mine which no amount of elbow grease or glass-paper could remove. This got me into trouble at every inspection, because of course you can't hope to win a war if you've got a speck of rust on your bayonet that won't come off. This threw me into collision with Mr. Dutch, my new platoon commander, who proved to be as nice a man and as fine a soldier as ever drew breath. When he saw that I was utterly fed up and that it was of no use to bullyrag me he treated me with great kindness and used to " nurse " me on parade. Long after the war he wrote to me, congratulating me on having outlasted most other members of the battalion and saying, " I never knew a man who was so handicapped in every way as you were, and yet plodded on as cheerfully and doggedly as you did." So, rotten soldier as I was, he must have seen that I was doing my best.

As a fact, before I got to England " for keeps " I believe I was the only front-line man in the battalion who had been in every " stunt " with it. This was rather wonderful luck, and if I haven't had much since I can't complain. And since this book won't bear my name, and I am being quite frank about my own attacks of funk, I can hardly be accused of boasting.

CHAPTER XIII

Dave and I had always been pally with little Lloyd, so it was natural that we should make friends with Lloyd's pal, Denton. Denton was in the Bank of England, a tall, lean, melancholy chap, a little older than me but younger than Dave. He disliked the war if possible even a little more than I did, and had taken to stretcher-bearing in the same spirit that a bereaved mother takes to looking after other women's children.

" If I've got to be killed," he used to say, " I'd sooner go out trying to do a bit of good instead of trying to poke out somebody else's guts with my bayonet."

The four of us went together quite a lot, and we called ourselves the Three Must-get-beers and D'Artagnan. Young Lloyd was D'Artagnan, because he wasn't a Must-get-beer, having joined the Army straight from an unfashionable public school—so unfashionable that he was practically without vices. Denton had more money than the rest of us, and I am afraid he paid rather more than his share. He was a single man without dependants and drew his salary just the same as if he were sitting down and scribbling " R.D." on cheques.

About this time we had a new colonel. He was a regular from a crack corps, and he looked a gentleman and a good soldier. I never had occasion to speak to him and spent half my life making sure that he had no occasion to speak to me. I think he was only lent to pull us into shape, for he didn't stay with us very long.

He was billeted in the last of the row of farms, where we soon found that we could get the best meal—in the kitchen just behind his quarters. The old Madame was very decent to us, and when we had ordered a chicken for dinner—as we did occasionally when times were bright —she used to give us our choice of two birds, the rejected one being for the colonel's table. I have often wondered what the old man would have said if he knew.

Meanwhile we were being fed with drafts of all ranks and were up to fighting strength again. One of these drafts contained two unique characters in Chester and Stribling, both of whom came to my company. Stribling (this of course was not his real name) was—and is—one of the foremost cartoonists of the day. He had been a sergeant in England and had only dropped one stripe on landing in France. More of him anon.

Chester was a second lieutenant, a huge dark, saturnine man who wore a perpetual scowl and was never seen to smile. I think he would have considered it detrimental to his dignity if he had relaxed his face or spoken kindly even off parade to a private soldier—and he was a private himself not so long since. We hated him pretty cordially, but I saw him go unflinching to certain death and say ungrudgingly that he must have been a fine fellow.

Only once did I know him to unbend. I was sitting in the barn on a wet evening trying to earn an honest penny by the light of one candle, with a bit of indelible pencil and a writing-block, when, for some reason or other, Dutch and Chester came in. I rose and stood to attention, and Dutch promptly told me to stand easy and sit down again. He added :

" I read a very charming story in this month's *Windsor Magazine* by somebody of your name. Any relation ? "

" I expect it was mine, sir," I said. " I write for the *Windsor*. I'm trying to do another for them now."

As they were going out I heard Chester say, " Poor devil ! " but I never learned if he were sorry for a writer who had to ply his trade under such conditions or if he pitied the intellect which had produced that particular tale. I expect it was a bit of both.

At the end of the month we are destined to leave the district, and we aren't too sorry. We are a bit unhappy, though, to be marched back by stages to the old camp at Houtkerque. This must mean Passchendaele again. Probably not another " stunt," for the Ridge and village have since been taken, but the very name is anathema to us. I find myself in the same tent as Stribling. He is a most delightful fellow, always making comic drawings to amuse us, and about to go into action for the first time with the lightest heart of any man I ever knew.

Dave and I and some others go out on the first evening and visit the Madame on the road to Wateau. I have already told of her distress when she learned that Dave and I were the only two left of all her old friends who used to come and visit her. We went on to the estaminet in Wateau where other men were now singing other songs. It was only five or six weeks since we were last there, but it seemed years. Dave sang *Songs of Araby*. But when I left I carried a heavy heart, as if something were whispering to me that nothing would ever be quite the same again.

But we are often laughing when we aren't crying. One of the new arrivals is the only man I ever met who knew by heart a complete version of *She was Poor but she was Honest*. This was not a marching song but a parody on the dirges once beloved of street singers. It was not obscene, for the singer was for ever pretending to pick up coppers and when he reached some apparently inevitable word he would check himself and say " Thank you kindly, lydy." I had known this terrible ballad since my schooldays, but only in the form of odd verses, and it was amusing to find a fellow who knew them all.

Our stay at Houtkerque was not a long one on this occasion, because they rang the church bells in London a little too soon over the great victory at Cambrai. The German gentlemen decided that they had better re-take their lost ground, which they did, and in doing so they created a panic in that sector which was only exceeded by their subsequent effort in March.

The Guards, among others, were rushed up to stop the rot, and we followed the Guards. This at least saved us from returning to the land of mud, water and innumerable shell-holes.

It was the fashion to sneer at the Guards because of their fine discipline and excellent parade-ground work. They had their faults, as I was to find later. Most of their N.C.O'.s would do anything, including murder, for half a crown (or eighteenpence, if you could convince them that you hadn't any more). They were the most corrupt lot of blighters that ever levied small blackmail, but they were fine soldiers magnificently officered. You could sleep very peacefully in reserve if you knew that you had the Guards in front of you.

From what I heard, the Guards made a short job of this one, and drove the Germans back beyond the Hindenburg line. By the time we arrived the Guards were going, and all was quiet on the Western Front— much too quiet to be really safe.

We went by train to some place on the Somme—

Mirraumont, I think—and got out of the cattle trucks to find ourselves in an altered world. We had come from a wet and muggy part of the country to find snow a foot deep lying everywhere except on the trampled, traffic-beaten roads. We set out in the direction of Cambrai and spent three or four nights on the road, mostly under canvas.

It was at this time that Stribling the cartoonist began to look rather blue about the gills. He told me that he felt feverish and generally rotten, but didn't like to report sick because it would look as if he funked going into the line. I guessed he'd got trench fever coming on, and his case was very similar to mine. The two or three million people who enjoy Stribling's cartoons to-day may thank me for saving his life, for I advised him to eat as much bully beef and hard biscuit as he could get hold of. This I knew would make him worse and at least ensure his being sent right down the line. As it happened he collapsed when he had been in the trenches a few hours, got to England, and never came out again.

The next time I saw him was in the Y.M.C.A. hut in the camp attached to the reserve battalion at home, just before the Armistice. He had a crowd of recruits around him and he was telling them all about the horrors of war. My appearance on the scene rather baffled him, because he knew that I knew that not more than a couple of shells had fallen near our bit of the line while he was there.

A lot of fellows were going sick at this time, owing to the rigours of the climate. Our old friend " Duckboard Bill " vanished for good. The awful man Rumbold faded away, but he didn't get far and he returned after about a month, poor devil. He missed one nasty engagement, but his name was already written in the Book.

One of our company cooks developed a temperature which remained obstinately in the neighbourhood of a hundred and three. He was a fellow who, through too much association with the smoke from the field kitchens, had very red rims to his eyes and looked like a blood-hound. When he disappeared Dave, with his powerful sense of smell for a soft job, put in for the vacancy and got it.

I had long felt that I should be happier without my rifle and the bayonet with the two ineradicable specks of rust on it, so I put in for a job at stretcher-bearing. I was told that I could be an assistant stretcher-bearer and fill the first vacancy in the company as soon as it occurred. It required no cynic to tell me that I shouldn't have long to wait. The snag was that M'Cracken was a stretcher-bearer already, and I should be drawn into closer association with that terrible Scottish Canadian—who turned out to be not such a bad fellow after all.

Our entry into the line on that sector did not seem promising of much enjoyment. We went up from Metz— the Metz which is close by Havrincourt Wood—and we were taken about seven miles out of our way, owing to Somebody not being able to read a map and Somebody Else mistaking Venus for the Pole Star. Everything was frozen hard and very white, except the new shell-holes which were blackened around the rims and remained so until a fresh fall of snow hid the ugliness of the scars.

The trenches were like glass under foot, and in the first few yards I must have fallen down more times than a comedy tramp cyclist in a twenty minutes' turn at a music hall.

At first there seemed to be no cover for us at all. Captain Perks said that we had better make ourselves as comfortable as we could. It was kind of him to think of our comfort, but when you are expected to pass the night in an ice-bound ditch—and heaven only knew how many subsequent nights—you can't do very much for yourself.

We had not taken over from any other unit. There was in that part of the line a tremendous trench-system, German made, and most of it was untenanted. Fortunately we hadn't been there many minutes before we discovered some really beautiful German dugouts about as deep as the Hampstead Tube Station. The ration, bomb, and ammunition dumps were on the road not more than fifty yards away, so most of us were allowed to get some sleep that night. I was rather unlucky to begin with, because I had to sleep on the steps, but with my hands in my pockets and other men behind me to keep off the draught, I managed to snooze a little.

Next morning, after stand-to, some of us whose fate had been to sit on the steps, went prospecting for more comfortable quarters, and a fellow named Brighton showed me the way to a most astonishing piece of luck. We found that our trench was already inhabited after all, although not by men whose present duty took them to the fire-step. At the bottom of the dug-out, screened by a blanket until Brighton thrust it aside, quite a happy family party was squatting on boxes around a brazier—a brazier with a real wood fire burning in it, and mess-tins steaming, and filling this queer, man-made cavern with delicious warmth and not a little smoke. The party consisted of a young officer, a corporal, and four or five men. We apologised to the officer and prepared to bolt, but the officer smiled and asked us what we were looking for ; so we told him.

" Well," he said, " there are some spare bunks here,

and if your people don't mind you're welcome to come down here and sleep when you're not on duty. Could you do with some hot cocoa ? "

Could we do with it ! I have thought before and since the war that cocoa was the filthiest drink ever foisted upon suffering mankind, but just then it was as if he had asked us if we could do with some Napoleon brandy.

" Got any rum, Corporal Jarvis ? " was this great man's next query ; and behold Corporal Jarvis had rum. However, we hesitated to accept this, for rum, especially during a prolonged spell of frost, was far more precious than rubies.

But when you really want something and are pressed to take it you generally succumb. The corporal poured out for us two lavish tots, and we wondered into what strange delighful company we had fallen, everybody being so " matey " and happy.

We soon learned that the party belonged to the bomb dump of a brigade other than our own, the advance dump being on the road a few yards distant, and the reserve dump in Villerspluich. It was better fun being on the advance dump than on the reserve, as I discovered later, for in the line there was little to do, while just behind the men had to work hard and dangerously. The Brigade Bombing Officer spent most of his time at the other dump, and I saw him only a few times while I enjoyed the hospitality of his men.

The dugout ended in a wooden partition with another dugout beyond. To make matters easier for Brighton and me our platoon sergeant and a few other fellows had taken up their quarters in the other dugout, and since we could hear each other speak quite easily through the partition, it was quite simple for them to give us a shout when we were required up aloft. There we acquired the well-known dugout disease. It was really unpleasant to leave the complete safety of that underground haven for the open trench where a shell was likely to pitch at any moment.

It was a rather strange sector. We were in a salient, and although my company, then in reserve, were in a trench, the supports, between us and the front line, lived in dug-outs in the open. Our front was quite a distance away, but owing to the curve of the line our right flank seemed quite close to Fritz, so that even in Villerspluich, a mile or two back, one often came under machine-gun fire. I think the 2nd Division were then on our right, and holding the flank of the salient, but our disposition puzzles me to this day, for being a private soldier I had no access to maps ; nor have I looked at a map to refresh my memory in writing these recollections. It is better for me to say that I forget the name of a place than to look at a map, say that such and such must have happened here, and perhaps make some ridiculous mistake. If I have mis-spelt the names of certain towns and villages the reader must please smile and forgive me.

I hadn't at all a bad time in the Hindenburg line, thanks mainly to the chaps on the bomb-dump. We did working parties, but they didn't work us too long or too hard. We were supposed to dig a support trench from the long communication trench called Central Avenue. We went out by day at first, until we got spotted by German " sausages " which gave a very accurate range to their artillery, and we bolted for our lives, taking three casualties along with us.

Afterwards the bulk of the work was done—or at-tempted—at night, but in the dugout day and night were one, and sometimes we hardly knew if it were night or morning, and used to have long arguments as to the date and the day of the week.

The work on the trench didn't proceed very quickly. The ground was like rock, and we did twenty times as much work with the pick as we did with the spade. We were like so many clumsy sculptors hacking at marble.

One excellent device was adopted by our people. Had we left the newly-turned earth visible against the snow, the Boche, as the light enabled him to see, would have realised that parties were at work there, and would have sent over some unwelcome presents on the night following. So before leaving we were ordered to gather handfuls of grass and strew them over the bare brown earth. Thus the white frost caught the grass and coloured it to match the surrounding snow-fields.

I shall never forget the atmosphere of that dugout where I spent all my time off duty, the friendliness of everybody, the warmth and comparative comfort, and the strange air of domesticity which all of us seemed to breathe. When a man came down off duty, shook the snow off his feet and spread his hands over the brazier, the rest of us always seemed to me like children welcoming " Father " home after a hard day's work. It was hard for me to realise that there wasn't some homely woman looking after us all.

Our principal hardship was lack of light. There was a shortage of candles, which were sparsely rationed, so little reading or writing could be done. We made do by improvising little lamps which burned string dipped in rifle oil, but these only just saved us from pitch darkness when the brazier was out.

This shortage of light led us to talk more than would

otherwise have been the case, and we soon knew one another's histories. I forget most of them now, and I don't suppose any was particularly interesting, although they all seemed so at the time. Corporal Jarvis, however, I shall never forget, for he was the central character of one of the most delightful incidents that came my way during the war.

Jarvis was a Londoner and he had been a carman in civil life. Since he was married and had been home on leave a year since, it was not remarkable that he should have a baby son three months old whom he had never seen. He was hoping for more leave almost from day to day, but it was long in coming.

One night within a week of Christmas the normal quiet of the sector was broken by a sudden half-hearted demonstration from the German artillery. It didn't affect us in the dugout, for we heard only muffled thuds and felt the place shake gently from time to time as if at a mild earthquake shock. We were just heating some cocoa for a nightcap before turning in, when a runner came down, his eyes still weeping from recent contact with lachrymatory gas. Corporal Jarvis was required by the bombing officer down at the reserve dump in Villerspluich.

Corporal Jarvis swore, put on his overcoat, fitted his equipment over it, and picked up his rifle.

" I don't suppose I'll be more'n an hour," he said.

" All right, old man," said one of his subordinates, " we'll keep your cocoa 'ot for you."

" What's it like outside ? " I asked the runner.

" He's bumping the road a bit," the runner answered, " and there's a sniff of gas about. Nothing very much, though."

So Corporal Jarvis picked up his rifle and went, and I never saw him again. An hour passed, two hours, three, and he did not return. Deep down underground we heard the muffled " *v'rmmm, v'rmmm* " of bursting shells. I went to get some more wood—we used to scrounge duckboards for our fires—and was glad to get down again. It was getting so bad that I was afraid we should be ordered to stand to.

" There's a war on to-night," I reported to the others.

We were all thinking about Corporal Jarvis, and wouldn't tell each other what we were thinking and fearing. We all liked him, and in the dugout we shared a sort of family intimacy which I never experienced in tents or huts. I for one was thinking of the new baby and wondering if it would ever see its father.

Even in peace-time it is no uncommon thing to feel anxious because of the absence of an expected friend. Out there this kind of anxiety—on the rare occasions when one felt anxiety for another's sake—was many times multiplied. Yet no one spoke the thought which each knew was haunting all of us. Indeed, half the night had passed before one fellow ventured to remark that Jarvis had been gone rather a long hour.

We all agreed that Jarvis had probably found more work than he had expected, and then, as another hour or two passed, we decided that the officer had probably kept him there for the night. Then we began to tell one another, in tones which threatened to defy contradiction, that old Jarvis was safe enough. Nothing was ever likely to happen to *him*. If he found it too hot on the road he'd take cover and wait until the strafing had stopped. It was ridiculous to think that something could have happened to old Jarvis. The very last fellow ! So we kept up our own and one another's spirits, but we sat up all night feeding the fire and waiting for the man who did not come.

At dawn or just before I had to go up for stand to, and when I returned an hour or so later with my break-fast ration and a mug of tea there was serious news. A message had come up from the reserve bomb dump. Corporal Jarvis had not arrived.

A deep gloom hung over us for two days and nights, until I was on the eve of bidding my new friends good-bye and going up with the rest of my half company into the supports. But that last night there was glorious news. The bombing officer looked into the dugout to tell us that he had heard what had happened to Jarvis. He had been slightly wounded on his way down, and was by that time probably on his way to England with a nice easy "Blighty" one.

The effect of this piece of news on us was quite extra-ordinary. We began to behave quite childishly. We laughed like a parcel of boys and shook hands with one another. One of the best of good fellows had found a way out of the prison that enclosed us all. He had achieved the ambition of most soldiers, a nice easy wound. Now he would be safe for weeks, months, perhaps even for that indefinite period of time which we all called "the duration." And he would see that new child of his, and the wife of whom he had so often spoken. Why, damn it, when things like that could happen it wasn't such a bad world after all !

Then one of the men who had a mouth organ suddenly remembered that it wanted but a day or two to Christ-mas. "Why, jiggered if we don't 'ave a carol !" he said (only he didn't say "jiggered"). And so we did. We had three and might have had more if the fellows on the other side of the partition hadn't set up a tolerable imitation of dogs howling and cats fighting as a form of protest.

Next day I said good-bye to the members of this strange but happy family, and went up into the supports. I never saw any of them again, and I might to-day rub shoulders in the street with any one of them and not know him. But I hope with all my heart that they all came through.

CHAPTER XIV

I don't think we had a casualty the whole time we were in the supports, but I have been in warmer places which I much preferred. We were in dugouts in the open snow-fields—the trench we were chipping at not being yet habitable—and we seemed to be visible to one or two gentlemen on our right flank who specialised in sniping.

Every time one put his head out of a dugout he heard the spit of a bullet followed by the distant report of a rifle. But we were too far from Fritz to allow him to be effective with the rifle, and I daresay the snow made the range deceptive.

We suffered a certain amount of shelling which did no damage. Indeed, just as were taking over, and I was on the point of entering one of the dugouts, the unmentionable Hun planted three whizz-bangs behind me all at once, and blew me down the shaft on top of Mr. Dutch, who, for the first moment or two, failed to see the humorous side of the situation. As in the reserve trench we did working parties, and life would have been very much the same if I had not missed the cheery company I had just left.

Dave was still a cook, and I saw little of him. He spent most of his time at the bottom of a deep pit, designed by the simple German as a trap for tanks, and drawing shell-fire on our devoted heads by sending up occasional clouds of smoke from the fuel which he and his fellow conspirators used a little too freely at times. Lloyd was a signaller and inhabited another dugout. Denton went home on leave on Christmas Eve, and I did not see him again until I walked into the Bank of England in 1920 and asked for him. Incidentally, the Bank produced five Dentons (remember that was not the real name) before I got the right one.

I was one of the ration party that saw Denton off. There were a lot of machine-gun bullets fizzing about, and poor old Denton was horribly nervous—not that he disliked such things any more than the rest of us, but he was just the kind of pessimist who always expected to be knocked out on the eve of going home, and I am sure it would have given him a great deal of melancholy satisfaction to say, " Just my luck ! " with his last breath.

Anyhow, I saw him climb safely on to a limber and go jolting away, and he chanced to be one of the very lucky ones, for he was taken ill in England and never came out again.

I had explored the rest of my company for possible friendships, and although there were more fellows that I liked rather than not I found myself once more rather short of pals. And one rather wants pals at Christmas time, even if one happens to be living like a half-frozen pig.

Christmas Day in the supports at Cambrai was certainly not " the day of all the year." There was the usual strong latrine-rumour that there was to be an unofficial armistice, and that the stinking old fox of Potsdam, wallowing in seasonable sentiment, had decreed that his men should not fire a shot. Strange the tales that Tommy was glad to swallow ! Imagine the All Highest turning sentimental ! The Peace Child and robin redbreasts and

—oh, dear! oh, dear! It is a pity Mr. Lloyd George did not keep his promise to hang the swine, who ran away from the people he had led to disaster. But Mr. Lloyd George is so apt to change his mind, is he not?

On Christmas morning we went on a working party into the front line to repair a damaged trench. Things were very quiet at first, so that the rumour gained credence among the sort of fellows who in happier circumstances would be glad to give real money to men with three cards and an umbrella. But directly we were spotted at work, over came the " *Pax hominibus*," and our gunners promptly retorted with some " *Bonae voluntatis*." We had only four casualties, but it was a pretty bad imitation of a truce.

Our Christmas dinner, eaten in the candle-lit gloom of the dugout, was not a great success. We had a few extras, it is true. A friend of mine, who was an officer in the reserve battalion in England, and had charge of the Christmas Comforts Fund, had written to ask me what I thought the men would like, and I had suggested some real butter as a change from the awful though illiberal rations of margarine. This duly arrived and was appreci- ated. The officers stood us an extra dollop of jam, and the Army presented us each with a small portion of Christ- mas pudding. Apart from these delights we had bully stew as usual and a loaf between four to last all day. However, one fellow who had a parcel gave me some nuts, so that I knew that it was really Christmas Day. Christmas Day without nuts, to any properly constituted child who never intends entirely to grow up, is quite unthinkable.

While on the subject of Christmas I am moved to say a few kind words about the people at home who subscribed to send us tobacco and cigarettes, and the pigs of contractors who exploited their generosity. Round about Christmas there were bags of cigarettes being handed round, and inside the packages were the cards of the donors, so that we might know whom to thank. They were all people with good addresses who had evidently spent a lot of money on these presents to " the boys," and my gratitude to them is not in the least diminished by the melancholy fact that the cigarettes were utterly unsmokable. They were of no known breed, the tobacco was green, and they tasted and smelt like bad seaweed. No doubt these kind folk had paid the price of ordinary " Gaspers," and the contractors had sent this filth out to us instead. Still, it would be a pretty poor sort of war if nobody made anything out of it.

There's not much war going on just now at Cambrai, but I for one am getting into a queer state of mind. There is nothing to see but the darkness of the dugouts and the waste of snow outside. We move up into the front line a day or so after Christmas, and there everything is just the same. I get into that dream-like state in which I find it almost impossible to believe that I once lived in a place called England, that my body was once clean and warm, that I slept between sheets, sat in armchairs, and did not regard being maimed for life as the height of my ambition. Life has become two alternating nightmares of snow and darkness. Even the letters I get from England seem unreal, It is hard to believe that any human agency is responsible for them, still more so to believe that I once knew the people who wrote them. This of course is only a mood into which I sink in idle and lonely moments. Two minutes later, perhaps, I am chatting to a grinning companion and listening to, or telling, a story which is more amusing than proper. The truth is that although there is no more fighting going on than there is at Surbiton we are being kept too long in the line.

Some fellows have been lucky, and have been taken back to Metz for a few hours for a bath and a semi-clean change. (No, not the fortress, the Metz of the Franco-Prussian War, but the village in the Cambrai sector). But I am not one of the lucky ones. I have not undressed for three weeks, nor taken off more than my boots, socks and tunic, and I am now lousy beyond all dreams of lousiness. You can't undress in the snow when you're supposed to be on duty, and you can't catch lice in the dark when you're in a dugout. Still, nature is kind, and I have lost so much self-respect that dirt and lice don't seem to matter so much.

One of our worst hardships is a shortage of water. It is brought up in petrol cans from the dump close by where I lived with Corporal Jarvis and Co., but there is never enough. Nor do I like the petrol cans. In dugouts they are used as bedroom utensils, and when sent down the line again I doubt if they are properly cleansed. Even if they are, well . . .

We try our hands at boiling snow and make the extraordinary scientific discovery that while snow will melt away in a few minutes under a mild sun it takes hours to melt over a hot fire and then runs to nothing.

When we are really short, parties of us are sent to get water from the cellar in the ruined château beyond what is left of the railway track. I go there twice, and am caught by the romance of the place. It is a small château which was evidently once a shooting box. The well in the cellar is labelled with Teutonic thoroughness : "*Font-brunnen, 40, Gruppe Cambrai.*" It is almost incredible to think that only a year or two ago eccentrically clad French sportsmen hung up Tyrolese hats with enormous feathers in them, and came to gossip and gesticulate in the gunroom ; and that men and women in evening dress sat out on the terrace and flirted more or less discreetly under the same stars that still shine upon us. They could no more have imagined this change than we can visualise the end of the world.

Later I wrote a story around this château, and it wasn't a bad one, though I says it as shouldn't. I sold it through my agent to an editor, a man of my own age, who had prudently avoided the opportunity of seeing the place for himself. He was so ill-advised as to have it set up in print before inquiring the very modest price demanded, when he became infuriated, but had to pay it. He had the nerve to tell me that " anybody could have written that story whether he'd been there or not." That was not true ; but as this gentleman's contribution to the common weal consisted of writing an alleged poem about what he would do for England, and (until he got the sack) taking a pension for being " faithful to the firm " (by sneaking out of the Services) I thought the criticism prejudiced and was not unduly disturbed. At this present time he is now trying to make a living by writing stories. I expect many of them are war stories.

Any ex-soldier who wants a really hearty laugh has only to pick up the magazines which were published during the war, and read some of the war stories. Lord love me and forgive me, I did some of them myself before I got out there, and mine were probably as funny as anybody else's.

After a few cold, miserable and quite uneventful days we went back to reserve, where I met with a disappointment. My old friends on the bomb dump were gone, and another brigade had taken over the premises.

I should have mentioned that at about this time we were " mucking in," as we chose to call it, with a battalion of a regiment which I shall call the Westshires. These fellows constituted the remains of a pre-war Territorial battalion which had been out East since 1914 until a short while since. They were a good crowd. Many of the rank and file were men of education. I daresay in ordinary circumstances they would have been as good as any troops in France, but they could not stand the sudden change of climate, and it was cruel to send them from a hot country straight into a winter campaign on the Western Front. Whenever our brigade was on the march the roadside, after the first mile, was dotted with Westshires who had fallen out. Since we were below strength, and they had lost so many men through sickness, they were merged with us for the time being.

It was here in the Hindenburg line at about this time that I saw and heard something really funny. We were close to the road where all the dumps were situated, and although the trench was wide enough for two men to pass with comparative ease, three was rather a crush. The trodden snow was still as slippery as an ice rink, and falls were frequent.

One evening when we were standing to, a party from the Hawke Battalion in the front line, which had been to get rations, came crowding past us. It was led by a little undersized middle-aged man who carried two petrol cans of water and two sandbags of rations slung round his neck. He fell down heavily about twice in every three yards to the accompaniment of much blasphemy and a loud rattling of tins.

Imagine the chaos that ensued when a party of R.E.'s came down the line trailing much barbed wire, and tried to crowd past us and the party from the Hawkes. The unfortunate little man, sprawling for the twentieth time, now got himself entangled in the wire. I am sure he had no intention to be funny, but spoke out of his heart when he picked himself up and said : " If ever I catch that bleedin' nipper of mine playing soldiers, I won't 'arf kick the little barstard's backside for 'im ! "

On the eve of December 30th we went out on a trench digging or rock chipping job, and got back to our dug-outs just before dawn. It was a beautiful night with the stars burning frostily, and everything as quiet as the countryside at home. But we were hardly in our bunks before ominous sounds from the outer world reminded us that the millennium was not yet. The timbers of the dugout rocked, and shell after shell came crashing down overhead. " It's only wind up," we said, but the wish was father to the thought.

After about twenty minutes a jaded sergeant came blundering down the steps, his face white and drawn and his eyes afraid.

" Stand to immediately," he said. " Battle order."

We stood staring in undisguised dismay. It wasn't so bad to do a job when we'd had ample warning that we had to do it, but to be taken by surprise when we were worn out and about to sleep, to be dragged from a drowsy stupor to meet some unknown terror, was war at its worst.

" What's the matter ? " we asked the sergeant.

" I don't know," he answered impatiently, and added :
" Christ ! it's bloody awful up there ! "

On the whole I think this was an adequate description.
Along with the others I dragged my load of depression
up the steps and came out into one of the fiercest barrages
I remember. Shells seemed to be coming from every
direction, screaming over and bursting on either side
the trench, on the road behind and on " Central
Avenue." The next I knew was a German officer with a
white smock over his uniform being led grinning down
the line. Then the news leaked out. Jerry had crept over
in the snow, camouflaged in white, and taken part of the
front line. Had he chosen to come on instead of giving
himself away by plastering us with shells he could have
walked through.

We were out of touch with our artillery, the telephone
lines having been severed by shell-fire, and our guns, not
knowing where we were, did not reply. Jerry had it all to
himself for a long while. I found myself standing next to
a gunner officer, who I suppose had been on forward
O.P. when the show started. He was a nice boy who
grinned at me amiably and remarked that he'd just been
doing a new job—been leading a platoon of infantry.

While we were talking there was a sudden call for
stretcher-bearers, and since I was in a sense apprenticed
to the business I went with M'Cracken. Just on the
corner where our trench ran into " Central Avenue "
some boxes of bombs were piled on top. A party of men
had been sent to get them down and a shell had caught
them. There was only one casualty, the poor chap who
would have been the last to get down, and he was just
breathing his last as we bent over him. I felt a cowardly
and selfish sense of relief that we hadn't to linger there

and get him down. We lost no time in scrambling into the
comparative cover of " Central Avenue," and as we did
so we heard a voice shouting : " I'll shoot you ! You get
another rifle at once or I'll shoot you ! "

Then we beheld our Captain Perks, his eyes protruding
like a prawn's, covering a cowering lad with a revolver.
This fellow was one of the party that had been on top,
and the shell had blown his rifle out of his hands and
bent it to the shape of a boomerang. Captain Perks was
blaming the poor devil for this ! I thought to myself :
" God help the Company if this silly sod's going to lead
us this morning." Captain Perks may have been quite a
brave man, but in an emergency he was about as useful
as half a rice pudding. Thank Heaven we had Mr.
Dutch and Mr. Chester.

The order came to move, and we ran the gauntlet of
" Central Avenue " under a steady downpour of shells.
The trench was hideously smashed, great boulders
making obstacles for us in every other bay. There were
some bodies lying about too, sickening wrecks of men
disembowelled or lacking heads and limbs. We moved
forward cowering, with our heads down. Suddenly the
order was passed down : " About turn ! " We didn't stop
to think where it came from ; we were only too glad to
hear it. But we had not taken many steps when we ran
into the tall and saturnine Mr. Chester, swinging a stick
and walking as upright as a tower.

" Where are you coming ? " he shouted. " I know of
no such order. Get on, get on ! "

And he was right. Some bloody coward in the middle of
the company had invented the order.

Presently we were halted. The Boche, it seemed, were
over on our flank, and we were to counter-attack from

187

near the top of Central Avenue. I found myself in the same bay with M'Cracken. We crouched side by side, huddling under the wall of the trench.

" I don't like this bay," M'Cracken kept saying. " Let's go into the next."

" They're all the same," I answered. " What's the difference."

But M'Cracken kept up his parrot cry, and at last to keep him quiet I followed him into the next bay. We had not been there two minutes when a Staff officer and Captain Perks came running down. I don't know how the Staff bird got there but evidently he didn't mean to stay. " The Blanks will attack at eleven fifteen," he shouted. " It is now eleven eleven."

Perks moved M'Cracken and me into the bay we had just left, and there M'Cracken was proved to have been justified. During our absence a shell had pitched right inside. Second sight, I wonder, or merely luck ?

We scrambled over somehow when the whistle went, and it was a relief if anything to get out of that dreadful pelting of shells. The air now was stung with all the queer and variegated sounds of bullets. In the middle distance we saw the heads of our enemies, and a German officer standing up as large as life directing fire. Perks soon got one in the leg, which was about the best thing that could have happened from everybody's point of view. Poor Chester hadn't a chance. Such a big man who was so obviously an officer was a certain target. He fell dead while he was waving us on with his little cane. He was unpopular with us but he was a fine brave fellow. I wish to heaven I could have liked him.

Of course we hadn't a chance. We were the small cards in a game of bluff. The handful of us—A and B

Companies—were tossed at the enemy as a tacit way of saying : " We can counter-attack, you see. We've got plenty of men. Don't you dare come any further."

We had thinned out terribly by the time I fell into a sort of gully. All our officers were gone, Dutch too having been wounded. I suppose I should have gone on, not knowing what else to do, if a sergeant hadn't motioned to me to stay. The counter-attack had broken down.

I crouched where I was for what seemed hours, not daring to show my head and suffering agonies of terror lest the Boche should walk over and murder what remained of us. But eventually a runner came crawling along and told us to retire, so we crept down the gully and out into a sunken road which was then part of our front line.

There were some unpleasant scenes in that road, notably an officer sitting bolt upright and stone dead with a handkerchief over his face. It was the handkerchief which intensified the horror. Somebody said to me, " That fellow's been foully murdered." It certainly looked like it. I heard afterwards that his face and head had been bashed in by a German officer's knobkerry.

I spent the rest of the day doing what I could for the wounded without, I own, taking any risks, and knowing now that I was about to become a regular stretcher-bearer. That was precisely what did happen to me. It was the last day that I ever carried a rifle.

The M.O. and his staff worked like horses, sweating their guts out in a dugout in the sunken road. It was the only time I ever saw an Aid Post in the front line. The percentage of wounded among the casualties was, thank heaven, far higher than it had been at Passchendaele, but things were bad enough. My company, apart from the leavening of Westshires, now numbered sixteen. There were five left of B. Little Lloyd the signaller and I found ourselves the only two left in the company who had also been through Passchendaele.

That day I had my first experience of dressing wounds, and I was surprised to see how little a man bleeds from a bullet. There was generally just a little bluish puncture and no more than a spot or two of blood. I dressed one poor lad who had been shot through both thighs and was crying his eyes out because he was sure he was dying and would never see home again. Most fellows, however, were extraordinarily plucky, although I don't think they felt as much at the time as they did later.

Among the survivors of B Company was a corporal, a younger brother of the painter who came to see me in Poperinghe. He was expecting to go home on leave, and when I last saw him he was badly shaken and blackened all over with explosive. He went on leave and never came back. There was a telegram waiting for him at Folkestone—the lucky dog !—telling him to report at the War Office. From that day he was an official war artist.

At nightfall I clicked for a rather good job. The M.O. ordered me to conduct six or seven walking wounded down the line to the Field Dressing Station at Villers-pluich and hand them over to the Red Cross Brigands. The war in our sector, which had blazed up so fiercely in the morning, now seemed to have burned itself out for the time being. I don't know why the wounded weren't told to find their own way down, but I was only too glad to get out of the line for a bit, so I didn't grumble. As it happened it was just as well that they had somebody with them, for one poor chap who had been hit in the face started bleeding again rather badly, and I was able to patch him up for the time being.

It was a very quiet night, but everybody was still on edge, notably the transport people whom I found at the dump on the road close by where I had lived with Corporal Jarvis and his merry men. I found one transport officer about to go, told him I had some wounded, and asked if he would mind giving us a lift down on his limbers. He said, " Yes, certainly," and it was quite an exciting ride. The transport men had been acutely conscious of the noise they had made coming up the road, and they had expected to be bumped all the time they were waiting. Now that the time had come to go they drove their horses like fury at a gallop, the limbers rocked like small boats on a heavy sea, and the snow-covered valley literally roared with echoes. But we got into Villerspluich without the least misadventure, and I decanted my wounded safely at the dressing station and started walking back. A few machine-gun bullets swished across the road, causing me to hug the bank, but on the whole the night continued quiet.

As I walked I realised how tired I was, and suddenly recollected that I had had no sleep for forty-eight hours and nothing to eat or drink for twenty-four. It also occurred to me that there would be no food waiting when I got back, for we had been so badly knocked about that they couldn't afford to deplete the handful of survivors by sending a ration party down to the dump. On such occasions it is each man for himself, and I didn't intend to starve if I could help it. Close to the dump and that sector of the old Hindenburg line there were deep German dugouts cut under the bank and opening up into the road. The mouth of one of these was dimly illuminated and I called down to ask who was there.

A voice replied : " R.E.'s taking cover, sir." I said,
" All right," and walked away. Having been addressed
as "sir" I knew that it would have been foolish to walk
straight down, because they would have wanted to
murder me when they found that I was a full private.
But I came back five minutes later, walked down and
found quite a crowd there. So I begged for a drop of tea
and a bite of food.

Rather to my astonishment I was treated with the
utmost sympathy and consideration, and it wasn't for
some little while that I discovered the reason. I was not
yet wearing a stretcher-bearer's brassard, and the man
who had been hit in the face had bled copiously all over
my gas-mask and the front of my tunic. They therefore
took me for a walking casualty on the way down the
line, and presented me with tea, cigarettes and lashings
of bread and butter and jam. I knew that I should find
myself in a rough house if I failed to play up, so I played
my part with, I think, considerable skill.

One elderly sapper, known to his intimates as Joe,
came and brooded over me sorrowfully.

" You've 'ad a rotten packet, chum," he said.

" Yes, pretty bad," I agreed.

" 'Ad it dressed ? "

" Oh, yes," I said, very hastily.

But I had let myself in for something all the same.
Having had a hearty peck at these good fellows' rations
I tried to go—but not a bit of it. Joe was coming with
me to the dressing station in case I fainted on the way.
He did too, for I couldn't shake him off. So he conducted
me on a weary trek down the road to the dressing
station whither I had already conducted the party of

wounded, and I had a job to prevent him from coming inside with me. I hid in the entrance to the dugout until I felt that Joe had about five hundred yards start, and then once more I started up the road. I was thoroughly sick of that road before the night was over.

When I got back to the company, I was thoroughly cursed by M'Cracken who called me all the sons of bitches he could lay his tongue to. He had been out all night in No Man's Land gathering in the wounded, with Fritz, who couldn't recognise stretcher-bearers in the dark, attempting to perforate his tender parts with bullets. I pointed out to him that it was my good fortune and not my fault that I had clicked for a soft job, but it was a long time before this sweet reason could penetrate the solid ivory of his skull. " Ah never knew such a bloudie man " was all that he could say for hours afterwards. Later, I am glad to say, when he came to realise that a man who spoke the King's English was not necessarily a skunk, we came to a better understanding.

On the following morning we got another barrage which threatened to rival its predecessor, and it looked as if Jerry meditated another attack. However, we were in touch with our guns once more, and Jerry received in exchange a really appalling bombardment. It was one of the rare occasions when we really hated the enemy, and our fellows cheered the shells which came screaming over us, and shouted : " There, you bastards, hold those and see how you like 'em ! " So hot did our guns make it for Jerry that he voluntarily evacuated the bit of trench he had taken. Thus ended an inconsiderable affair which had been pretty bloodsome for us but which was of so little importance that it was not worth more than a couple of lines in the papers.

Just after this unpleasant breach of the peace I had a rather eerie experience, and it came about through my exploring forbidden country. Part of our front line was a sunken road called " Camouflage Road." A trench branched out of it, and the road ran on into the German lines. One could walk up it for a short distance, and then the way was blocked by a huge tangle of barbed wire with green " camouflage " netting on the top, in order to discourage Jerry from paying us any unannounced visits from that direction. However, since his front line was about a kilometre distant, and I found a way of squeezing past the barbed wire, I explored the road for a short distance and made a discovery.

Just on the other side of the barbed wire there was an enormous system of dugouts thirty or forty feet deep approached by shafts let into the banks beside the road. The place had of course been made by the Germans. There were at least half a dozen shafts and at least twenty chambers, and altogether there was almost enough room to shelter a battalion.

I went down and found traces which proved that some infantry officers of another division had made this place their home and had had to clear out in a hurry. One of the traces, which also proved the hurried retirement, was a whisky bottle containing nearly a quarter of its original contents. It was the nearest I ever came to finding hidden treasure. I could hardly believe my senses. I smelt the stuff cautiously and it smelt like whisky. I tasted it and it *was* whisky. So of course I necked it.

Now our cooks, Dave Barney and Co., who were in the line with us, had had much difficulty in finding suitable accommodation and I thought this place would suit them very well. Moreover they were short of water and I found a lot of full petrol cans. So I brought them along and they made a fire and started boiling one of the petrol cans. What the petrol can contained need not be recorded here, but it certainly was not drinking water. After an hour or two the cooks were made to depart from this haven, and it was put out of bounds as being unsafe.

Still I believed it to be safe enough, and as we were short of dugout accommodation and I hadn't a bunk to call my own I decided to sleep in the place. Now that I was a stretcher-bearer I hadn't to go on at stand to or take my turn as a sentry. Indeed I had practically no duties and nobody wanted to see my nice kind face unless there was dirty work about, so that it didn't matter where I slept. There were some nice wire bunks in the chambers of this dugout, so I made it my home— for one night only.

There were doorways without doors to these underground rooms, and I was settling down to try to sleep when I heard somebody coming down one of the shafts, and saw the reflection of an electric torch winking on the wall which I was facing. I thought at first that it was one of our officers on patrol who might see me and turf me out, so I lay quite still. Within a few seconds I was lying quite still for a very different reason. The visitor, whoever he was, *had come down from the German end.*

I was unarmed, but had the intruder been a German who happened to see me he would probably have shot me first and investigated afterwards. However, the visitor happened not to see me. I lay sweating like a bull while he tramped straight past and mounted the staircase of the shaft nearest our line. I don't know to this day if he were friend or foe, but he certainly spoilt my nerve for sleeping in that place and I never tried it again.

After we had been in the line for an unbroken spell of at least three weeks we were relieved for a few days' rest by a Lancashire regiment, the rank and file of which averaged about five feet two in height and had horrid accents. Jerry seemed to know that we were being relieved, for while there was a double quantity of men in the trench his gunners started being rough with us. I wedged myself in the mouth of company headquarters dugout, where an officer of the relieving company was taking over from ours. One of his subalterns shouted down : " Skipper ! Skipper ! Hadn't you better come up ? Suppose they're coming over ? " But the skipper, like the one on the *Hesperus* who was bored to death by the infuriating questions of his little daughter, " answered never a word."

Soon there were yells for stretcher-bearers, so M'Cracken and I went to see what was the trouble. The first man we found seemed to be pretty badly smashed up, but as we were quite close to the Aid Post, already taken over by the relieving M.O., we did not bandage him but carried him straight away. He was a great, long, lean loon and plaguey heavy. He had only just come out to us and we hardly knew him, but I learned afterwards that he was the son of a Buckinghamshire parson. We carried him feet foremost, M'Cracken leading, so that his head was between my hands.

Unfortunately for the patient neither M'Cracken nor I could keep our feet on the frozen surface. First M'Cracken would fall base over apex and the end of the stretcher would tilt down on him, and I would curse him. Then I would do the same thing, and the other end of the stretcher would cant down on me, so that it would be M'Cracken's turn to curse. We must have been giving hell to the poor devil on the stretcher, and I kept on saying to him : " I'm awfully sorry, old dear, but we can't help it."

After a while I heard a muttering come up from the head which was more or less on the same level as my waist, and bent to listen. I thought I was going to hear something to this effect : " You great big bloody clumsy cow, why can't you stand up on your great big bloody something feet ? " I was used to hearing this sort of thing from tortured men whom I had been compelled to shake. Instead I heard : " Into Thy Hands, O Lord, I commend my spirit. Lord Jesus receive my soul." He died not many minutes later.

We also carried to the Aid Post, among others, a little corporal with his foot blown off. I heard afterwards that the humane M.O. of the relieving battalion had said that it was impossible to do anything for him and had ordered him to be carried out to die in the snow. I only hope it wasn't true, but I am afraid it was. I have put a very good conditional curse on him which, if he deserves its fulfilment, will make him think that the Holy Office in sixteenth-century Seville consisted of sloppy senti-mentalists.

CHAPTER XV

This book, before it is finished, is going to be terribly lop-sided. I have skipped a great deal already, and I must skip a great deal more. For my own sake rather than that of the reader—who after all is not compelled to wade all the way through it—I must keep the tale inside a reasonable length. After all, trench warfare when there was nothing much happening was boring enough to endure, and since I do not wish this tale to have the same effect on the reader as a strong bromide I am going to gloss over the next two months in very few words.

Briefly, we remained in the same sector and had a very quiet time. About this time drastic changes were made. A battalion was taken out of each brigade, and we lost our old friends the Westshires who were split up and went heaven knows where. In turn we absorbed half a battalion of a London Territorial regiment which I will call the Chelsea Rifles, and at first they hated coming to us almost as much as we hated their coming, but we soon mucked in quite comfortably together. They completely outnumbered us, for we had already been receiving drafts recruited to this unit—boys who were sent out immediately they achieved the age of eighteen years and nine months, poor little devils.

These youngsters were nearly all unspeakably bad soldiers. Among the very young the best soldiers were public school boys and working-class lads. Boy clerks of the Alf, Bert and Sid variety were terribly deficient in guts. One in ten would be a real hero, but the rest had better stayed at home. I'm not carping at them : thank God I hadn't to endure the same beastliness when I was nineteen.

There are several incidents which I should like to record in detail, but the dimensions of the book must be considered. I should like to describe fully how we went out of the line on the night mentioned at the end of my last chapter, so bone-weary that we fell asleep while we marched or slid over the snow, waking when we fell ; how two fellows threw up the sponge and lay down and froze to death ; how in a little hut on the way to Metz we all drank soup, one after the other, from the same Gold Flake tin.

I should like to tell how, when the thaw set in and trench foot became prevalent, men with bits of sacking on their feet limped through running water into Villers-pluich crying like babes, only to be sent back to the trenches because the line had to be held. I should like to tell of how I fell down a well in Bapaume—not right down, thank goodness, for my elbows caught on the sides —and how I spent a hectic day's leave in Amiens. But I must leave out a lot, because comparatively small as my war experience was, I did not know how much I had to tell when I first began to write of it.

My new company commander, platoon commander and C.S.M. were all Chelsea Rifles men. The C.S.M. was a good chap, and Lieutenant Blood was a fine-looking, gallant boy of twenty who had already been wounded twice. My skipper I didn't like, although, for a bully, he was not really ill-natured. He knew exactly how an officer ought to behave because he had once seen one impersonated in a musical comedy. He was foul-mouthed and used to encourage the men to sing smutty songs on the march because he thought it promoted high spirits. I was no prude and liked singing them myself when the spirit moved me, but I objected to organised obscenity. The best I can say of him is that he had once played first class rugger, and the worst is that he had about as much brains as a demented louse. Subsequently he was taken prisoner on the March retreat, and it served the Germans damned well right.

We had also acquired a new colonel, and I don't know where he came from. I don't think he had been in action before but had been kept fuming at the base. He was small and old and grey, brave as a lion, but quite incurably stupid. Later, when times were very bad indeed, he nearly got all of us killed, and used to specialise in dramatic orders which are so uplifting to the civilian who may read of them but so nerve-destroying at the time to troops already scared stiff.

Of course he was a martinet, and the first time I saw him was when he had us out on parade at an indecently early hour on the morning after we had just come out of the line. I wasn't going to sweat myself to make an elaborate toilet to please him or anybody else, and he paused and brooded over me on his way along the ranks. It happened that just at that moment the drums struck up " Colonel Bogey." Those acquainted with the Army *de nos jours* will not need to be reminded of the words the men sang to this tune ; and the others must remain in ignorance so far as I am concerned. As he stared at me he knew exactly what was in my mind, and I knew he knew. It put him right out of countenance, and he passed on without a word.

We were still in the same old sector at Cambrai when I went home on leave. By this time I had done well over a year out there and I was fed up to the wisdom-teeth. This may not seem very much but it was a fairly good innings for a front line soldier. *Experto crede.* I was now practically a stranger in the battalion, nearly all the old faces having vanished and many of them for ever. I know that Stanhope in *Journey's End* had done three years off the reel, but he was rather exceptional, as they all were in that monumental drama. Bursting into tears after dinner was as common in that mess as grace after meat in a pious household, but then the poor chaps were seeing earwigs in March, which must have been awfully unsettling. However, I must own that I have seen *Journey's End* nine times, and *Hamlet* only twice, and that I hope to see the former at least nine more times.

The average " innings " of an infantryman was not a long one before he " retired hurt " or worse befell him. You could tell by merely looking at the troops who had lasted out there long enough to get " Blighty " leave. There was a fair sprinkling of gunners, but the great majority were non-combatants. When you saw a foot-slogger complete with rifle and full kit you could lay a comfortable shade of odds that he was a storeman or that he had a soft job somewhere at Brigade or Division H.Q. or on the divisional train.

Speaking for the majority, the jolliest experience that a man could have was to go home on leave from the front. Speaking for myself, I had an even happier one later when I was invalided ; but that can hardly have been common to most, for the bulk of the fellows on the Red Cross train were suffering and had operations and painful dressings to look forward to, whereas at that time

I had little the matter with me. So for most of us it was going home on leave that was the experience of a lifetime.

I had hardly expected my turn to come when it did, although heaven knows it had been long enough in coming. We had come out of the trenches the night before to the huts in Havrincourt Wood—the huts from which, three weeks later, we turned out so hopelessly in morning twilight, with the broken line before us and nothing behind.

We had had what we called a good sleep and were cleaning up to go on some desolating parade when a sergeant poked his head into the hut and told me to report at B.H.Q. I wondered which of the few dozen misdeeds which I kept in that pigeon-hole of my conscience devoted to the Army had come to light, and what was going to happen. Outside the colonel's hut I found some ten or twelve other fellows all in the same disagreeable state of doubt.

It was soon dissipated. The " regimental " came out and, without so much as a smile, told us to parade in an hour's time for going home on leave. I hated the man, but just then I could have kissed him with only the least feeling of repulsion.

When I got back to my hut the other men seemed almost as pleased as I was, which begs the suggestion that they were glad to get rid of me ; but it was a kinder feeling than that. Had I any money ? I should need some on my way down the line. " Here, you'd better have my puttees ; they're better than the ones you've got on." " Let me give your boots another rub." " I say, you can't possibly go home in that old tunic—I'll swap with you." I felt like a village maiden on her bridal morning ; and if any village bride ever felt half so happy as I felt then she must have expected much too much of her husband.

But getting away was a slow and tedious business. We had to cool our heels while passes were made out and multitudinous ration cards dealt out to us. Also the M.O. had to look at us and give us each a certificate to the effect that we weren't lousy. This was the funniest farce ever devised by the Army mind. I for one carried on my person a large assortment of all the fauna on which Mr. Keating wages war—with the single exception, perhaps, of beetles. I believe we did get a bath of sorts on our way down the line, but at this distance of time I can't be sure. If we did it didn't do much good, and when I arrived in London I was still a walking pestilence.

At last we got the order, " Move to the right in fours," and the leave party marched away over the sleeper road to the railhead at Ytres. Never before had my pack felt so light, and my singing threw all the others out of tune.

Of course the disgusting train was late, but we boarded it at last and didn't in the least mind travelling in cattle trucks. The time of year was late February, but the sun was warm, for it was one of those spring days which come before spring is really due and before we return to snow-storms and east winds. We kept the doors of the cattle trucks wide open and sat sunning ourselves and swinging our legs over the footboards.

Having changed somewhere into another train, and into compartments intended to accommodate human beings, we arrived at a station beside a rest camp where we were to spend the night. I think the place was Bray, but I am not quite sure. I only remember that the civil inhabitants seemed to deal exclusively in rosaries and hard-boiled eggs, and that the huts with real stoves in them were much more comfortable than the average.

I was too excited to attempt to go to sleep, but sat up all night over a delightful stove with a man from another unit who was as absurdly hilarious as myself. We ate hard-boiled eggs, smoked and talked about home. Fourteen days in the England we had scarcely dared hope to see again seemed too good to be true.

Next morning we had to wait a long time for a train, and began to chafe miserably when we realised that we couldn't get home that day. I saw some of the men buying the commonest kind of rosaries at four or five francs each. They couldn't have known what they were or that they could have bought precisely the same article for twopence at any Catholic shop in England ; but the business-like inhabitants of Bray seemed to have realised that the average Tommy with ten or twenty francs in his pocket was the biggest mug in the world.

We got to Boulogne that night and went under canvas in St. Martin's camp on the top of the hill. After breakfast next morning we were paraded to march down and board the leave boat, but it would have been unlike the powers that were to let us go without a few irritating pin-pricks. We had to fall out again and clean up the camp, with dozens of the permanently base in fatigue dress watching us with their hands in their pockets. I don't know why the Commandant wanted to keep them there. Personally I would rather have kept pigeons or white mice.

It was again a beautiful day and the sea was like a mill-pond. Even then a good half of the men wasted their breakfasts on the way over. I stood on deck waiting to see the white cliffs, the memories of which had

so tormented Mr. Kipling's absconded company pro-
moters ; but in the sun and haze they came up pink.

On the station, after we had entrained, dormant
memories woke and held me entranced. It was like returning home after my first term at boarding school to
find all the dear familiar things not quite as I had
expected to find them—the rooms smaller, the furniture
commonplace—because idealism had cheated memory
while I was away. I was delighted to see on a sheet of
tin that jolly blue blot which advertised Stephens' Ink.
Until something over a year since I had seen that blue
blot nearly every day of my life, since then I had entirely
forgotten it, and here it was again waiting to greet me
with the familiar face of an old friend.

All the unlovely commonplace things visible from the
train became suddenly dear to me. I even laughed at
those two irritating figures who are caught in the act of
striding over so many railway-side fields carrying a
ladder between them. Not many months since I should
have said that a modern English villa of the approved
suburban type was the most hideous example of archi-
tecture to be found anywhere. Now, because there was
nothing quite like them in France, I loved to see them,
and blessed the sun for shining on their trim little back
gardens, for were they not as English as a cockney
accent ?

In the back garden of one such villa just outside Folkestone I saw a young woman cutting a ridiculous little
grass patch with a ridiculous little mower. I had scarcely
seen a woman for many months, for the line we had
been holding was at the further edge of the waste which
the Germans had made of the Somme country before
retiring ; and when we went out to rest it was only into

a blasted wilderness. But it was not because she was young and good to see, with hair and jumper as yellow as the sunlight, that I could have blown her a kiss ; it was because she was a symbol of the England I had loved and lost and found again.

We did not take very long in getting to Victoria, and I did not want to read or talk. I just wanted to look out of the window and whistle back to me a pack of memories. I knew that line well and tried to imagine myself a little boy again in a nice broad Eton collar coming home from my preparatory school. We passed through a grassy cutting where I had once sat beside a girl who fumbled with a bunch of primroses all through a long April afternoon, because I was trying to make love to her and she was almost as shy as I was. There were still primroses in that cutting and already some had begun to bloom on that first day of March. We shot through a station outside a dingy little town and another girl took the place of the first. I remembered changing from evening dress into old clothes in the station pub, because I had been dining with friends in Ramsgate, and was going to pretend as an excuse for inviting myself for the night, that I was passing on a walking tour. Strange, I thought then, what idiots boys can be when they are taken that way. Yet now at forty I can't look back with any pride to the nature wisdom of twenty-eight.

I was almost shy of getting out of the train at Victoria and mingling with civilians. I could imagine people nudging one another and pointing and saying : " Look. Soldiers back from the front." However, I need not have troubled, for nobody took the least notice of the horde of us that streamed through the barrier. They were as used to the sight of us as were the French. We were dingy reminders of a war three and a half years old, a war which wearied them to mention, which had deprived them of friends and relatives, exposed them to the risk of air-raids and, despite increased wages, was beginning to make them feel the pinch of privation.

Yet on the surface I found London much as it had always been. George Robey and Harry Lauder were still going strong. You could get a drink within the legal hours if you could find a pub with anything to sell ; and some of them still had plenty. There was a shortage of certain foodstuffs but no real hardship. Bread, fish and vegetables were not rationed, so that it was always possible to fill oneself. People grumbled at the quality of the bread, but I would sooner have an unlimited quantity of the war-time stuff than live on the mouse's portion of the white which was issued to us in France. At least, it was in England that I had my first satisfying meal for months, yet I met many civilians who had the neck to tell me that I had been living on the fat of the land.

My first act on arriving at Victoria was to jump into a telephone kiosk and ring up regimental headquarters to ask if they could let me have a complete change of clothes. Until I had this I wasn't fit to go home. The clerk at the other end said that he couldn't do anything that day as the Q.M.S. had gone. He said that they weren't supposed to do that sort of thing for overseas men, but he very decently added that if I cared to come round on the following morning he had no doubt that something could be wangled.

That kept me away from home on the first night. I made myself a little less offensive to mankind by having a hot bath, and then got on the District Railway and went round to my club. Just inside I met an elderly member whom I knew quite well.

" Hullo," he said, " they want you in the card-room. They're looking for a fourth at bridge."

" Right," I answered, " I'm on."

He looked at me curiously.

" You've been away for a bit, haven't you ? " he asked.

" Yes," I said, " I've been away for a bit."

" Ah," said he, " thought I hadn't seen you about lately."

So I hung up my equipment in the cloakroom and went in to play bridge with two staff captains who happened to be very decent chaps. The fourth was, oddly enough, the young subaltern who had befriended me in the refreshment room when we were on our way to Hesdin. I hadn't met an officer on terms of equality for more than a year, and for a few minutes I was ridiculously shy, but these good fellows soon put me at my ease.

As night came on and more and more members dropped in I met many old acquaintances, and the reception I got was beautifully mixed. To this day I hardly know which attitude of mind I found the more offensive ; to be regarded as a splendid fellow, or as a lucky lad who had had a nice picnic and was going to have some more of it. The old gentlemen who had given their sons were still extremely patronising. You see, *I* hadn't any to give.

The no-treating order was still in force, to the expense and disgruntlement of certain notorious characters, and this seemed to me to upset the social amenities without in any way curtailing the sale of drink. Only a nation which takes a morbid pleasure of submitting to petty

tyrannies would have put up with this sort of nonsense.
The Liberal politicians who dominated the Coalition
Government were in their turn dominated by the Nonconformist conscience, which in the happiest times has
never made for frivolity. Now that the country was at
war everybody was to be made as miserable as possible.
I wonder they did not make us all do penance by clos-
ing the public lavatories, but that pleasant thought
seems not to have occurred to the Minister of Public
Miseries.

The old men who came into the club were nearly all
in the Volunteers (or " Gorgeous Wrecks ") or else
serving as special constables. I must say that I admired
the latter. I shouldn't have enjoyed working hard at
my job all day and then tramping the cold wet streets
for half the night. The younger men who had not seen
active service or, for various reasons, any service at all,
were rather irritating. Most of them tried to imply that
they had been having just as rough a time as the men
in the trenches, and talked about air-raids and the bomb
which had fallen only three-quarters of a mile away.
One young man took twenty minutes to tell me how he
had been mentioned in despatches for something clever
he had done while with the A.S.C. at Grove Park.

Yet despite the normal appearance of the streets
I realised from the conversation of others that I had
come back to a rapidly changing England. Under the
surface there was a state of topsy-turvydom which even
Samuel Butler never imagined. With still more women
doing the work of men, with the working classes earning
more than they had ever dreamed and throwing away
their cash on pianos they couldn't play and clocks that
wouldn't go, with a wave of sex immorality sweeping

over the hitherto respectable classes and hordes of girls snaffling and marrying young officers for the sake of their blood money pensions, with the rich made poor and the poor made rich, I could foresee a pretty tangle to be unravelled after the war, especially after hordes of disgruntled and disillusioned men had been flung back on to society.

Still, for me there might not be any afterwards, and I had learned the art of living for the moment. I had fourteen days of freedom before me, and I meant to make the most of it. For the present I was sitting in my club in a comfortable chair, talking to more or less reasonable human beings and helping them curse the politicians.

Politicians seemed to be unpopular not only with civilians but with all ranks of the Army. They interfered with the schemes of the Higher Command who, to do them justice, would have shortened our miseries if they could by getting us killed off even more quickly than they had already contrived. We cannon-fodder disliked them for their bombastic speeches. Apparently *they* were never going to sheathe the sword until two provinces we had never seen had been ceded to a nation we didn't particularly like. It is very easy to be brave when somebody else is doing the fighting for you. My own courage as a civilian in 1914, when I seemed to have little prospect of being anything else, was little short of magnificent.

I found that people at home seemed to take a fiendish delight in asking me silly questions. The favourite one was, when did I think the war was going to end ? I always answered that we had a saying that the first seventeen years would be the worst. One old lady—I admit that she was very old—actually asked me if I had seen the

Kaiser out there. People seemed to forget the very short limits of a private soldier's range of vision, and to credit him with being in the confidence of his corps commander.

I already knew from the journals sent out to me that the politically-inspired newspapers had been feeding the public with bunk. It was not very amusing to run around half a dozen traverses of a trench, with a shaving brush in one hand and a razor in the other, to avoid the machine-gun of an airman who had come over almost low enough to knock off one's tin hat ; but it was not unfunny to read immediately afterwards that we had complete command of the air and that scarcely an enemy machine dared come over our lines.

I hate party politics and I hate all parties fairly indiscriminately, but I am bound to hand it out to the Conservatives. If their policy of compulsory Territorial service for all men of a suitable age had been adopted prior to 1914 there would have been no war. And what happened ? The Liberal adherents backed by the small but noisy band of red flag-waggers screamed with wrath at the idea of the country spending a few extra hundred thousands a year, and raged with fury at the thought of young Alf and young Bert wasting their time at drill when they might be at the cinema or the roller-skating rink.

Well, they had their way, and lived to see the spending of six or seven million pounds a day, while poor Alf and Bert died in the shambles which their fathers had prepared for them.

It seems that I am getting away from my "leave" although all these thoughts were in my head that first night in England. We had to thank the muddle-headed old men for all this colossal waste of lives and money—the old men who seemed even now so pleased with themselves. Yet we are all human and fallible. It may be that we of that generation shall some day, in the folly of our age, light the torch which shall illumine the steps of our own children to untimely death.

I slept in a hotel that first night, and I hope for the sake of the next occupant of my room that I left no living souvenirs behind me. Next morning began as another of those typical May days which somehow creep into March. I walked all the way up to the headquarters of my regiment because I enjoyed being in good old London streets, and bought things I didn't want for the sheer joy of going into the shops and asking for them. I saw that Swinburne's *Poems and Ballads* were now being published at three and sixpence, so I bought a copy for a girl whom I knew would cheerfully pay twenty times that amount rather than be compelled to read one of them.

At headquarters the good-natured Q.M.S. re-clothed me from my boots to my cap, and before putting on these delightfully clean clothes I had another bath for luck, that being my third in fifteen hours.

I had plenty to do while I was on leave. It was necessary for me to do a little work and earn a little money. There were innumerable people who expected me to visit them, and I had promised to call at or 'phone to the homes of half a dozen comrades with the usual news and messages. There were girls of whom I was fond, and I cursed having had to spend more than a year of my precious youth away from them. A couple of pub-crawls with the nucleus of some boon companions was long overdue. It seemed to me that the arrears of about sixteen months had to be crowded into fourteen days, and at the same time it was up to me to scatter a few rays of sunshine about the home.

Nothing worries me more than to have other people worrying about me. As I have already stated my battalion was not in the line when I first went out, and when we went up I tried to keep it from my mother and, in subsequent letters, to give her a hazy impression that I was helping to guard a pillar box on the Riviera. But busybodies had been at work, and anyhow mothers have a sixth sense about their sons. I hadn't been in the house five minutes when she smiled at me mysteriously and asked : " Where have you been ? " So then I had to own up, only to find that she knew it all already. I was an only child and her sole means of support. Had I gone west, God knows what would have become of her. But she had endured, and continued to endure, the anxiety with that Spartan fortitude which was the glory of so many women throughout the war.

Later in the day I went out to pay a visit, and once more I held an English girl in my arms. There's nothing to beat 'em !

CHAPTER XVI

All my life I have been at the mercy of well-meaning people, and the curse of well-meaning people is that however annoying they may be one cannot be rude to them with an easy conscience. Enemies can be slapped ; real friends understand plain speech ; but the merely well meaning must be treated with a starched politeness while one fumes under the starch.

While I was on leave all the people I knew slightly seemed to be throwing parties, to which I was committed by my poor mother who wanted me to enjoy myself while I was home. I would much sooner have found my own amusements, but one has often to sacrifice himself on the altars of others' good intentions. Parties were a hard frost because there were so few men about, and everywhere I went I felt like a Mormon elder.

In every house some young woman bleated a terrible ballad, which sounded like a Lenten hymn, entitled *God send You back to Me*. I was not frightfully popular with young women, so they couldn't have meant it for me personally, but this awful ditty always made me feel like a dipsomaniac at a Band of Hope meeting.

I noticed then and later that terrible, but quite natural, inclination to entertain soldiers instead of leaving them in peace. Previously I had seen wretched squads of convalescents taken from their nice comfortable hospitals and made to have tea and play games in environments which must have been foreign and awe-inspiring to nine-tenths of them. Soldiers did not know what to say to pompous old gentlemen and refined ladies, and the well-meaning ladies and gentlemen certainly did not know what to say to the men, nor how to amuse them.

Later, after I had become a casualty, I told the commandante of the English hospital—a white-haired old dame with a heart of gold securely concealed by a malignant aspect—that I wasn't going to any tea-parties. And she made me, just to show me that I jolly well had to obey orders. So I went like a sheep to the slaughter and was made to play fifteen games of draughts with well-disposed ladies who were probably at least as bored as I was. Imagine a man, highly-strung and sensitive as I was, being compelled to play fifteen games of draughts in the drawing-room, when he has a strong theory that his scandalous hospital mates are pinching the spoons out of the dining-room on the other side of the hall.

Still, if nobody had taken any notice of us I suppose we should have cursed an ungrateful country. We human beings are hard to please.

A number of " Cock and Hen " clubs seemed to have sprung up in London during the war. I was taken to two, the first of which was known to its enemies as the Gomorrah Club. It was very—oh very—literary, and although in those days a person whose work was so cheap as to be saleable was hardly eligible for membership, I was invited to join. It was run by a lady who was supposed some day to be going to write a novel. I believe she did, too. At least, I was afterwards invited by her to attend a lecture on " The Agricultural Novel, including

the works of Thomas Hardy and my own book which
—— is about to publish ! " Strangely enough, I missed
the chance of a lifetime and didn't go.

Another and a rather different club to which I was
taken was in a nice cosy cellar which looked as if it had
been furnished by Mr. Drage. Here people used to sit
on the floor and seemed not to mind listening to recitals
of one another's original poetry.

It was in this club that I rediscovered a friend, a man
slightly older than myself, who was slowly going blind.
He was very intense and precious, an artist to the finger-
tips, but a Jack of all trades and a master of none. Before
his sight failed he had been a mediocre painter ; he had
a fair bass voice, he could play the piano very well for
an amateur, write readable fiction, and had had one or
two plays put on on Sunday nights which West End
managers had slept on and turned down. Of course, he
was very precious and intense, and claimed to be
" psychic," whatever that may mean.

I said " good-bye " to him a few nights before going back
to France. For some occult reason he liked me, and real
tears came into his almost sightless eyes as he squeezed
my hand.

" I shall never see you again," he said, and added with
great intensity : " You will die a bloody death ! "

I am not particularly superstitious, but in the circumstances it was not a comfortable remark to hear, especially as I was of the same way of thinking. The nature of
my end still " remains to be seen," as the monkey said ;
but he was right in one respect, for although we met and
talked after the war he never saw me again.

One definite change I noticed, and that was in the
attitude of strangers towards me. When I joined the

Army people did not naturally assume that because one was a private soldier he was necessarily a guttersnipe. By this time most men of any education, and a good many of none, had got commissions, and the poor Tommy had returned to his pre-war status.

I had the tact not to butt into places mostly frequented by officers, but when I had a lady with me I did not see why I should feed at "a good pull-up for carmen." One evening I took a girl to a West End restaurant where I had been a fairly regular customer before the war. The staff had been entirely changed ; half of it, I suppose, had been interned and the other half was probably fighting against us. The place was full of officers and their lady-loves, and judging by the manners and accents of the former they were nearly all " Smiffs," late of Little Buggington Grammar School, who had been " clurks " in civil life, and were now throwing their weight about on seven and sixpence a day and half salary. Their obvious contempt for me was only exceeded by the still more obvious contempt of the lousy alien waiters who decided that the best way to treat me was to ignore me altogether.

In the circumstances I did not want a row, but I had to risk one, so I seized the arm of one of these dish-lickers as he was trying to pass me, and hung on to it while I spoke some brief, bright and brotherly words.

"When I came here before the war," I said, "I used to receive civility and attention. I propose to be treated with the same courtesy now. Whether it shall be done with or without the assistance of the manager is a matter for you to decide."

I was in terror lest he should bring the manager and lest the manager should ask me to withdraw—which would have made me look an awful fool. Fortunately, however, the waiter wilted.

" Oh, sair, sair," he cried, " I 'ave not neglec' you. You 'ave made a mistake."

" No," I said, "*you* have made the mistake. You may now bring two dry martinis and afterwards some hors d'œuvres."

So far as I can remember there was only one air-raid while I was home on leave, and I must own that I didn't much care for it. Danger of that sort seemed so out of place in dear safe old London. Nothing fell anywhere near me, but I found the general panic rather catching. Later when I got home I found my mother and aunt sitting huddled on the stairs, and pointed out to them that the house was only standing upright with the aid of the wall-paper and that if a bomb were going to hit it one might just as well be comfortable in bed.

For some time I had realised that my nerves were getting pretty bad and wondered how I was going to endure any more of the trenches. One night when I was seeing a girl home the wind caught some telegraph wires which crossed the road, and the sound was just like the whine of an approaching shell. I just stopped myself in the act of flopping down.

As my time in England shortens I become extremely miserable. There is nothing to look forward to when I get back. All the old faces are gone. Dave is home in England somewhere with trench fever. Young Lloyd was away on a course when I left France, and I was not to see him again until after the Armistice. We all know that there will be dirty work in the spring, for the Germans now have hordes of men released from the Russian front. I know that there is not the least chance of my getting a soft job. Bad soldier as I am, I am considered fairly reliable, so they are certain to keep me in the line until something happens to me. After all, others have seen three times as much service. I begin to get morbid fears of going off my head and being shot for cowardice.

Moreover I have developed a cynicism which sits uncomfortably on the shoulders of a born sentimentalist. I can't look anywhere without seeing injustice or reading or hearing hypocrisy and cant. We English suck up cant as a baby sucks up milk. I was brought up in the pious belief that we were a nation of sportsmen, and I am now undeceived—unless, after all, a sportsman is only a man who thinks it brave of his terrier to attack a rat. We have never engaged in any sort of war without squealing that the other side wasn't playing the game even before the first shot was fired. I am just old enough to remember the Boer War and all the silly tales of dum-dum bullets and firing on the Red Cross.

Sportsmen ! My God ! Go to a Soccer match and hear the rabble—our present governing class, God save the mark !—hurling filthy insults at the visiting team and mocking men who lie on the ground writhing in agony. The gentleman has been trained not to display his uglier emotions, but he is little different under his skin. This becomes apparent in the Army, where every man in authority is free to indulge his natural taste for bullying.

King's Regulations, when properly administered, were not unfair, although a man might easily go to prison for six months or more for an offence for which a magistrate would bind him over—or fine him five shillings if he were very severe. But how could a man collect his thoughts to say anything in his own defence when he was compelled to stand all the time at attention, as stiff as a ramrod, with some buttocks-kissing N.C.O. yelping at him every time he moved an eyelid ?

If a man went to prison it was to no ordinary prison. The detention prisons were staffed by the dregs of mankind on whose brutality complete reliance could be placed. Manhandling and torture were quite common. If the victim complained no notice was taken of him by the Commandant—who found it convenient to disbelieve him—and he was afterwards half-killed for his pains. The military police were a nice crowd, too. The only good word I have to say for the Australians is that they killed a lot of these swine ; but they didn't kill half enough.

Don't you know what went on in your detention prison, Mr. Commandant ? No ? But how strange ! Well, then, darling, I'll tell you a few things. You know, of course, that a N.C.O. has no right to strike a man ? But how many of the N.C.O.'s on your staff bashed the poor prisoners who couldn't hit back ?

Do you know what " Mr. Dunlop " was, sweet ? Well, I'll tell you, dear. " Mr. Dunlop " was the inner tube of a bicycle filled with sand, used for stunning prisoners who were goaded into answering back or were too ill to obey every command at the double. It was a good idea, angel, wasn't it ?—because it didn't leave any mark.

And of course, duck, when you saw a prisoner with black eyes and broken lips you couldn't believe that it had been done by any of the nice kind men whose business it was to look after the malefactors. You didn't know, of course, that you were presiding over a worse hell than any of the old convict hulks. If you say you don't know and did, then you are a liar and a scoundrel. If you really didn't know, then you were a fool and incompetent. But you didn't care a damn, any of you, so long as you could live in a place of safety, poison your carcases with drink, and keep your tawdry, dirty little mistresses—who, when you weren't about, received from common Tommies those favours which you were unable very frequently to bestow.

A friend of mine, a sergeant, spent forty-eight hours in a detention prison at one of the bases, while awaiting court-martial on a charge of which he was subsequently acquitted. Among the pleasant things he heard and saw was a young English soldier beaten almost to death and thrown into a dark cell alone with a Chinaman.

Three decent-spoken Tommies were brought into the cell next to my friend, who was able to hear every word uttered. Three inquisitors proceeded to torment them, hurling at them insults in the most filthy language in the hope of getting them to answer back. This for some time the men prudently and resolutely refrained from doing until flesh and blood could bear it no more and one of them was stung into making some retort which was quite mild in the circumstances. So then all three got a dose of " Mr. Dunlop " and after they had been stunned their inquisitors went away laughing at the fun they had had.

Yet we go on yapping about being a nation of sportsmen, the fairest people in the world, and purring pleasantly about the humblest private getting his full measure of justice.

At this time of writing we have not done booing the Germans for killing Nurse Cavell. Will nobody understand that if she did not knowingly and wilfully break the barbarous laws of war in the service of her country, well knowing the penalty, she would not have been the magnificent heroine that she undoubtedly was. If in similar circumstances the French had shot a German nurse I think we should have managed to repress our indignation.

But the crowning example of hypocrisy was to come after the war when the Unknown Soldier was buried in Westminster Abbey. I don't mean that the nation was insincere—indeed, I am sure the proceedings were a consolation to those near and dear to many of the missing—but the Generals who came to weep crocodile tears over the poor fellow's shrine were the very people who had made his life unendurable while he was alive, and probably one of them was responsible for his present condition. If he were not dead he would have been " crimed " for having lost his identity discs.

Everywhere I look I find cant, hypocrisy, lying, shirking ; my superiors abusing their positions and not doing their jobs ; young and fit men with commissions in non-combatant units, and damned pleased with themselves at that ; the willing horse being flogged and kicked to death. The arrogance of the men in the soft jobs—the military police for instance—towards the poor fools who were doing the real work was something that had to be experienced to be believed.

The joy of going home on leave was more than counter-balanced by the misery of going back. A voice kept on dinning in my brain : " You're one of the lucky ones. You've been out, and you've been allowed to have another look at England. But you won't be lucky any more."

Authority demanded that one should appear at Victoria at such a ghastly hour in the morning that it wasn't worth while going to bed. One very dear girl sat up with me all night and accompanied me, and I wished she hadn't, because I wasn't feeling at my best, and had to make some show of being cheerful.

It wasn't so bad when the train got under way en route for Folkestone. One of our fellows—or rather one of the Chelsea Rifles attached to us—got into the same compartment with me. He was a dark-haired fellow named Harrison, and he had come home on leave with me. It seemed that he had committed matrimony during the fourteen days, and he showed me photographs of the wedding, and seemed unduly proud of having had an officer for his best man.

His father-in-law's wedding present was a furnished house. It was one of those villas with which Jerry the Builder delights in beautifying the suburbs. They are all so alike that you don't need to be shown where the bathroom is. Looking at it from the outside I knew exactly how it was furnished ; the " Jacobean " dining-room, and the drawing-room chairs and chesterfield covered with chintz of a very " bold " design. I could almost smell that new chintz.

The bride was a nice-looking girl, and he was a nice-looking boy. Poor lad and lass ! They did not live together long enough to lose their illusions. He fell dead beside me only a few days later.

It had taken a long time to get to London from the line, but it didn't take long to get back. We were incarcerated for a few hours in Folkestone in a street of empty houses surrounded by barbed wire, crossed to Boulogne in the afternoon, and spent the night in St. Martin's Camp. The following night I arrived at our transport lines in Ytres.

I heard from the transport that the battalion was in the line in the same old place, and due to come out on the night of the 20th. There had been a pretty bad gas attack while I was away, which had thinned us out a bit, but some new drafts had arrived—some of ours and some of other regiments. More Chelsea Rifles, of course !

Two or three of our own officers had come out, and among them was a huge fellow and a fine athlete whom we called " the Babe."

Now the Babe, in spite of his physique and genial, breezy temperament, had obviously " worked it " to stay in England as long as possible, for he was a pre-war Territorial who had never yet seen a shot fired, except at a range. We thought that he, like so many of these big genial people, would be pretty hopeless in the line. We were wrong. In view of what I shall tell later, my considered opinion is that he stayed at home as long as possible *because he already knew the exact hour of his death.*

As the battalion was due to come out in forty-eight hours, I thought they would have the decency to keep me with the transport for the time being. But I was sent up the line with the rations on the following night. Going home on leave must be very bad for the *morale*, for although the night was quiet, I was as frightened as the rawest recruit when I set off on the familiar trek up the communication trench. The sweat ran out of my hair and literally blinded me. But that soon passed, thank God.

Not to improve matters, they sent me out to a bombing post, a section of unfinished trench which had been deepened to accommodate a few men, about two hundred yards in front of our line. This I found to be populated by part of the new drafts, all boys of nineteen, who were about as cheerful as orphans on Good Friday. The only man I knew was the corporal in charge, who was under open arrest for some very serious offence— such as not smiling when the colonel made a joke— and he was about as happy as a murderer who believed in hell on the eve of his execution. Altogether it was a nice cheerful sort of crowd to be flung into on coming back off leave, especially as we were beautifully isolated and a big German attack was expected at any moment.

The only cheerful and loquacious member of the party was a youngster named Clifford who had obviously been an office-boy on ten bob a week before being called up. His reminiscences of wine and women irritated me to the verge of insanity. Poor little devil! Probably the most dashing thing he had ever done was to take a junior typist to the pictures and treat her to some coffee.

We were relieved at about midnight on March the 20th by the Royal Fusiliers. I shan't easily forget those fellows who crept into our post, and gave us cigarettes and asked us what sort of a war it was. It must have been the last hours of their lives, for they couldn't have got away when hell broke loose a few hours later.

We marched to a light railway, clambered on to toy trucks, and went back to the old huts in Havrincourt Wood. In Havrincourt Wood one regarded oneself as being as safe as in England.

Fagged out, we made our beds and " got down to it," but nobody had time to close an eye before the show started. There came a sudden thunder of German guns, intensifying every moment, the authentic shriek of shells, and there were crashes and bangs all around the camp and on the road beyond.

We looked at each other and said " wind up," and

Pw   225

tried to settle down to sleep with the philosophy of soldiers who feel that any fighting that may be going on has nothing to do with them personally. But it wasn't a " wind up." It was the beginning of the greatest battle of the war.

CHAPTER XVII

It was strange to hear the din of battle in that hitherto peaceful wood, to march with trepidation up a road where we had once whistled and sung and accounted ourselves safe, and close by which, even last night, a light railway was running. We knew that this was no ordinary "wind up." We came upon guns already taken from their pits but still blazing furiously. By the roadside we passed a poor devil of an artillery driver who had been laid out, and I saw, not for the first time, that most tragic of all sights—a strong man dying hard.

He watched us as we tramped past, his face a mask of misery, and he cursed continually all countries and kings, all empires and emperors, and made me think of poor Mercutio: "A plague o' both your houses. They make worms' meat of me."

At cross-roads, close by one of our field batteries, a very brave traffic man stuck unflinchingly to his post. Fritz had got the cross-roads "taped," and our guns encouraged him to concentrate on the spot, but for some extraordinary reason we were halted there for about ten minutes. Shells rushed over and fell around us near enough for us to hear that venomous final hiss and to see the flashes of their explosions in the bright sunlight. Then something rather horrible happened. One smashed on to the hard road right into the middle of the first platoon of the company in my rear. God knows how many limbs and heads went up in the black geyser of flying earth and explosive, but even at a distance of a hundred yards the thinning of the cloud revealed a nasty sight. I have seen something reminiscent when, having seen a swarm of wasps all feeding from the same plum, I have put my foot on the lot. One's foot seems to miss some of the wasps, but others lie in a writhing, struggling mess.

I never learned the extent of the damage, but I heard that the platoon officer was killed outright. But evidently this company—I think it was C—was able to deal with its own casualties, for we A Company stretcher-bearers were not sent for.

Eventually we were marched on and into a prepared line of trenches near Trescourt ; when we rather surprisingly had a tolerably quiet day. I say " we," but the poor devils in front of us caught it badly. The Germans seemed to have advanced about a mile on that front, and we could tell where the line was because it was perpetually plastered by shells. Fortunately for us, Jerry seemed not to know where we were, although two or three of his 'planes came over spying. One of them got caught between two of ours and shammed being hit. He fluttered down like a bird with a broken wing, but quite close to the ground he recovered himself and flew off in triumph. We had only three more casualties in my company that day, and towards evening the strafe in front eased up, but there was hell to pay on our right towards Peronne.

An hour or two after dark the remains of the men who had been holding the new front line came shuffling past us along the road. They were by no means cheerful, poor devils. " You're the bleedin' front line now," one of them called out, " and I hope you bleedin' well enjoy yourselves."

The night too was quiet, just where we were, but the strain of waiting was pretty acute. Patrols went out and reported that the Germans had attempted to advance no further on our sector. The tide of battle had, for the time being, surged altogether to our right, and there, although we did not know it at the time, our men were falling back hopelessly outnumbered all the way between us and St. Quentin.

Another fine bright day dawned—the Germans had all the luck in the matter of weather—and passed uneventfully so far as we were concerned. We were very fortunate not to be attacked. But after nightfall there was a sudden panic. Apparently our right flank had gone and we were left in the air. We were marched away, any old how, leaving no line at all, but a sacrifice party consisting of an officer and six men. Their job was to wait until the Germans came and hold them off as long as possible by running about the trench and firing, in order to create the illusion that the position was still being strongly held. This was tantamount to a sentence of death, but I am glad to be able to say that four of these gallant fellows managed to get away.

That night we were marched back to the old huts in Havrincourt Wood, where we got a little sleep ; and in the morning we had actually paraded to do a working party, when there was another panic.

" Battle order immediately. Don't waste a second. They're right on top of us."

We didn't waste many seconds. In a few minutes we were marching down the road towards Ytres—the same road which I had taken to go home on leave only three weeks since. Eighteen-pounders, blazing away as quickly as they could be charged, were strung out in the open spaces of the field on our left. I don't know what became of the guns or the men who served them, for I saw none of them pass through our lines.

There was a prepared line of trenches in front of Ytres which we manned and we had not been in them many minutes when the first Germans showed themselves on the outskirts of the wood. Rifles spat and Lewis guns chattered, the battery out in front poured point-blank fire on to the edge of the wood, and then within a minute or two all was quiet again.

" I expect they'll wait until it's dark now," said a sergeant who was very generously giving me some of his cigarettes. " My God, we shall get it in the neck if we stay here to-night."

Jerry now knew where we were and his artillery acted accordingly. I soon had plenty to think about, because we began to get casualties. There was a Field Dressing Station in Ytres, but in the afternoon the doctors and staff began to pack up. We were told to leave any subsequent wounded by the roadside, and, if possible, ambulances would be sent for them.

This pretty ghastly time was not altogether unrelieved by humour. There seemed to be a lot of drink flying about in Ytres, although I was not fortunate enough to locate it, and some of the walking wounded were staggering along gloriously "blotto." One fellow with a punctured forearm, having first of all got hold of some rum, was tottering away with a bottle of whisky sticking out of each of the lower pockets of his tunic. But he was probably stopped and despoiled before he got very far.

Late in the afternoon some of the 47th Division

attached themselves to us, bringing the disquieting news that the Germans had come through on our right, and once more we were " in the air." They said that they had killed thousands of Jerries earlier in the day, but how true this was I never found out. Towards dusk we began to be shelled from our right flank, and slightly from the rear.

Blood, the lieutenant of twenty, was perfectly splendid. He seemed to be everywhere at once, and at the same time to do a sentry's work by keeping a sharp look-out in front. I shall not easily forget that boy's face, calm and immobile, silhouetted against the twilight sky as he looked out over No Man's Land. It is stamped on my memory as it were a head on a newly-minted coin. I did not see him again after that evening ; but months later somebody saw him, or his ghost, with two " birds " in Regent Street—and I don't suppose it was his ghost. I'm glad to think that he got through.

All the while I could hear what I took to be guns firing from the middle of Ytres behind us, and was comforted to think that we were not left without the cover of artillery. I should have been rather hot and bothered if I had known the truth. The R.E.'s had set fire to the station and sidings on which were many truckloads of shells, and what we actually heard was these shells exploding.

Still no direct attack came, but even the least intelligent of us knew that we were holding on much too long to an untenable position. Our gallant colonel, having already lost communication with Brigade, had received no orders to retire, and it was not until midnight that he did so on his own initiative—and probably only then under pressure of the company commanders. Then, of course, it was too late. We came to a sudden halt in the streets of Ytres. We were already surrounded.

C Company was on the north of the village, and they were bayoneted almost to a man without the rest of us knowing at the time what was going on. We heard the " *hoy ! hoy ! hoy !* " of Germans shouting quite close to us, but that was all.

The position actually was that Brigade had retired to Barrastre, and the Germans were already in Bus on our direct line of retreat. A very brave lance-corporal named Talland-Brown, who could speak German, volunteered to take another man with him and get through the enemy line to Barrastre to let Brigade know where we were and ask for instructions. Outside Bus he was challenged by a German sentry, and he replied in good colloquial German something to the effect of : " Shut your bloody mouth ! Do you want to get us all shot ? " So the sentry said, " Pass, friend."

While we waited I suddenly remembered how hungry I was—we had lost our transport and had little or nothing for three days—and I was also starving for a smoke. I knew Ytres through having been through it going on and returning from leave, and I remembered two large E.F. canteens in marquees close to the station. So I left the fragments of the platoon to which I was attached for purposes of rationing, and went off on the scrounge.

It was a good job for me I did so. It was pitch dark inside the marquees and I felt my way about, putting my hands into broken crates. I found bags of cigarettes but nothing to eat—except Epsom Salts, of which, at that time, I was not in particular need.

Suddenly the world seemed to come to an end with the first of the two worst explosions I have ever heard. I was flung down between two piles of crates, and after a moment or two a storm of missiles—mostly bricks, I should think—came crashing through the top of the marquee.

I picked myself up, badly shaken, and was hardly on my legs when the second explosion came, and down again I went.

Screams and yells were ringing out all around, and the inevitable cry for stretcher-bearers. My own company came first, so I hurried back to my platoon, or rather to the spot where I had left it.

I had seen a few ghastly sights but nothing to equal the one which awaited me. The road was strewn with fragments of men, torn-off limbs, and trunks of men which seemed only half to fill their tunics. It was the only time I ever saw a gutter literally running with blood. And the scene was lit up by the fitful red flames of the burning dump and station.

Only one man out of the platoon was left alive and he was the boy Clifford who posed as having been such a lad of the village. Now he was lying on his back, crying, and another fellow was hanging on to a severed artery in his thigh above a gaping wound from which the blood pumped at every heart-beat. I had nothing with me to make a tourniquet, and our clumsy attempts to hold the artery seemed useless. We could do nothing but watch him bleed to death. He died crying for his mother. " Mother " was the one and only word he uttered.

Whether this ghastly mess was caused by part of the shell-dump exploding, or whether the Germans had thrown some heavy stuff in among us, I do not know to this day. I suppose our officers knew, but we men were not concerned. Things happened, and afterwards we scarcely discussed them nor asked the how and the why.

An hour or two before dawn—when Talland-Brown

and his companion had got safely back with orders—we were led out of Ytres two or three hundred yards on our line of retreat, and told to dig ourselves in with our entrenching tools. This should have been done before. Indeed, I don't know why we weren't taken straight on to Barrastre. The German cordon around us could not have been a strong one, and we could have burst through it with fixed bayonets under cover of darkness and met practically no opposition.

One of my fellow stretcher-bearers, named Jones, was badly wounded and unable to move. A Company had no stretcher now—I can't pretend to remember what had become of it if I even knew—and I offered to try to take him out on my back. He replied that he'd damned sight sooner be taken prisoner, and in the light of subsequent events I am very glad that he declined the offer. I know I should have had to dump him, and the memory of that would have worried me to this day.

We dug in with showers of bullets whizzing harmlessly overhead. In good ground it is extraordinary how quickly one can dig with an entrenching tool a hole big enough to shelter oneself. In a very few minutes I was as snug as a bird in a nest and sound asleep.

When I woke up it was broad daylight. Above my head the air was still humming with bullets from either flank, but they must have been coming very high, for I saw a number of our fellows walking about quite unconcernedly. Well, let them walk about in it if they wanted to, I thought : *I* was quite comfortable where I was.

I lit a cigarette and reflected that exactly one week ago at that hour I had been eating a civilised breakfast in England and wondering how I should spend the rest of the day. I was quite happy and comfortable so long as I was permitted to squat at the bottom of my little pit and smoke, but I knew that something would happen soon, that I should have to get out into the storm, and that then I should be terrified.

Suddenly it seemed to me that the fellows walking about began to move hastily in one direction. I poked my head up to have a look, and an officer saw me and waved to me.

" Come on," he cried, " we're all going."

And go we did. It was the last time I did a non-stop run for two miles. What should have been done under cover of darkness was now done in full view of the enemy. He made no attempt to bar our progress, but he pumped bullets into us all the way.

There was no attempt at keeping any formation, and we ran helter-skelter, a herd of stragglers, the flotsam of half a dozen units. It was on this hurried retirement that we lost our nice American doctor, and Captain Kettle was wounded and subsequently captured.

Very soon men began to drop ; others, lightly wounded, fell behind and staggered on limping and moaning in the hope of saving themselves from capture. It seemed to me that cart-whips were being cracked about my ears, and I imagined that I could feel the wind of the bullets across my face.

One creature, however, was enjoying itself. This was a little brown dog who had attached himself to us, having probably been left behind in Ytres. He thought it fine fun to see men running, and frisked along, growling playfully at our heels, running from one man to another.

We had a huge burly R.S.M., late of the Scots Guards, whom I presently overtook. I thought he might protect me from one flank, so I kept pace with him. He had never liked me, and when he saw what I was up to he seemed distinctly peeved and tried in vain to shake me off. Now this was unkind of him, because it didn't increase his own danger : on the contrary, I was protecting him from the other flank.

By the time my lungs were bursting and my heart going like the piston-rod of an express engine we got out of the worst of the firing. Halfway up a gentle slope our Colonel halted and turned.

" The Blanks," he announced, " will fall out around me."

I thanked heaven for the respite and dropped panting at his feet. There was soon a crowd of us lying in all sorts of attitudes, gasping, wheezing and sweating. An officer came rushing up, and shouted : " They're coming on in thousands, sir. Are you going to make a stand."

Our little Colonel folded his arms and said :

" Certainly."

" Where ? "

" Here ! "

I nearly laughed in my despair. There was no cover of any sort, and anybody knows that you mustn't take up a defensive position halfway up a hill. I had come safely through a fair amount of danger, and now it seemed that this gallant old idiot was going to get me murdered.

However, other counsels prevailed. We sorted ourselves into companies again and were marched through Bus, already vacated by Fritz. Indeed, shells came screaming over into the village and threw up clouds of bricks and rubble. Just beyond, a battalion of marines fought the first rearguard action, lining a sunken road in front of two very active field guns.

We passed through the hut encampment at Le Transloy, where we had once spent a long rest. Here we were allowed to lie on the ground and stretch our limbs for half an hour while some morsels of food which arrived mysteriously from somewhere were issued to us.

While we were thus massed in the open a German aeroplane came over flying very low and chasing one of ours. I am not trying to cast aspersions on the courage of the British pilot, whoever he may have been, for I regard all airmen as heroes, and, more likely than not, his was not a fighting machine. He was a lucky man, for the German spotted better game in us, and, abandoning the chase, swooped upon us and let go with his machine-gun. We were lucky, too, because by a miracle he did no damage ; but the experience of being charged by an aeroplane in the open is not one to call for any encores.

Subsequently we continued the worst march I ever did. Heaven alone knows how many weary miles we covered, for the way by which we went, marching over broken country, would be impossible to find to-day. I heard later that we were supposed to be protecting the Bapaume-Albert road, for although Peronne had fallen two days since, Bapaume was still holding out, and all the trouble was coming from the south. We never saw a road except to cross it, and plodded on three-parts starved, thirsty and unspeakably weary over broken and wasted land, threading our way between the shell-craters of '16. On the way we drank shell-hole water, risking mustard gas, and although every drop of that green water must have contained billions of malignant germs none of us that I know of came to any harm.

Nobody fell out. Occasionally we heard the familiar, authentic whine of a shell, followed by a crash, and a shrapnel cloud bubbled out of the sky above us, as a reminder that others were keeping pace with us and not too far behind. We were still marching when night had fallen and at last struck a road near Courcelette where a kind of silent pandemonium was in progress. The road was chock-a-block with lorries and troops, going both ways and trying to pass each other. The congestion was denser than any traffic block I have seen in London, and the inky darkness made things worse. Imagination recoils from the thought of what must have happened if a shell or two had fallen among that mass of men and lorries.

So far we had been fed with absurd rumours. Our troops had advanced in the north and were halfway through Belgium. Down in the south the French had advanced about twenty miles. The Germans were being led into a very pretty little trap. But to-night most of us realised the appalling truth—that we were a defeated Army in headlong retreat.

CHAPTER XVIII

There had been much talk about reserves. What reserves had we ? A few drafts of untrained men coming out from home, a few composite battalions formed of the men coming back off leave, a few more composite battalions formed of men doing courses and the shattered remains of troops that had escaped the shambles between Peronne and St. Quentin.

The *morale* of most units was already gone. Men were deserting wholesale, pretending to be lost. They were swept into composite battalions where nothing was known of them, and from these in turn they deserted as soon as they found themselves about to go into action. There seemed not the least doubt that Germany would take the Channel ports. This did not mean that we had lost the war, but it meant that the war would drag on indefinitely.

I have never heard an American say that his country won the war, and I have never sneered at the comparatively small active part that America took. I, for one, am deeply grateful to our distant allies. In those dark days we had this for comfort : we knew that America was committed, and that, happen what might to us, her fresh millions must eventually wear down the war-worn Germans.

Subsequently when the Germans in their turn were on the run I could almost find it in my heart to be sorry for the poor devils. I know the taste of defeat, the weariness and the despair, but our misery could have been nothing to theirs. They had no new armies in training behind them. They indeed, as somebody said at the time, " had their backs to the wall—and no wall there."

Although my battalion had lost an entire company and the other companies were sadly depleted we hung together doggedly enough. There were no desertions even although, like cattle, we could smell panic in the air. But then it must be owned that, much as we had endured, other units had suffered far worse, even as we were soon to suffer. If we had been through purgatory we were to experience something more like hell.

That night we were halted in a sunken road and told to get some rest. Thank God for the sunken roads of France. Two field guns in the road blazed away over our heads intermittently throughout the night, but they didn't spoil my rest. We just fell down on the wet road-side grass in the lee of a bank and snored like hogs, lit by a red glare in the sky from hundreds of burning dumps which were now blazing all over the wilderness of the Somme.

Daylight revealed piles of debris along the roadside where other units had blazed the trail of defeat by dump-ing all that they no longer wanted to carry. I found and pocketed Rupert Brooke's *1914 and Other Poems* which I had not yet seen in volume form. Strangely enough that self-same book belonged to a friend of mine whom I did not even know to be in France. He was an officer in the Machine-Gun Corps attached to the same division as myself, and although we had been for days together at the same camp we had not seen each other.

We also found the fancy costumes of a concert party. and some of the fellows arrayed themselves eccentrically over their tunics, while others pirouetted with Japanese sunshades. One or two were actually in fancy dress when a sudden panic came and we had to fall in.

The two guns fired their last shots and began hastily to "pack up" and we were marched off into the wilderness once more. We had not gone far before we saw a solitary gun and two gunners. Seeing that we were retreating they fired a last shell, abandoned the gun, and ran for it.

We had not covered much more than a mile before we were halted, put into extended order, and told to lie down in the long grass. There was a road about two hundred yards away, and a ruined cottage on our right. The word came round that the Germans were coming, and it was to be our job to ambush them. There were still a few British stragglers trying to get away, and we took no notice of them. At last the word came round : "Two more, and the next will be Boche."

If we had only been well fed and not so desperately weary it wouldn't have been a bad war that afternoon. It was most exciting and exhilarating, and reminded me of games of hide and seek played as a child, when then, as now, I found it difficult to hold my water. For some while we had been conscious of the chattering of a machine-gun coming nearer and nearer. I suppose they had it on a lorry. It advertised Fritz's approach much in the same way as the crocodile in *Peter Pan*.

My sight is pretty bad for distances, and of course I had lost my glasses, so I did not see the arrival of the German advance guard. I think the firing order must have been given a little too quickly, and not much damage was done, for I was told that Brother Boche immediately took cover.

Apparently our job was not to try to hold him—we couldn't have hoped to do that—but merely to harass

him and retard his advance. A minute later we were
running like hares for the brow of a hill, with bullets—
which I don't think hit anybody—whizzing after us.

Down in the dip on the other side we again took cover
and waited, and this time I saw heads and shoulders
appear on the skyline. We were nearer to each other on
this occasion, and I think our fellows did some damage.
We hung on for about half an hour while a duel of rifle
fire took place. Two or three of our fellows got hit, but
it was remarkable how few, since we had no real cover.
Then, I suppose, some more Jerries must have come up,
for their fire became more intense, and we legged it
again for a further ridge.

Until nightfall we kept up this guerilla warfare,
making use of the undulations of the Somme country,
and making Fritz approach us over a skyline. I don't
suppose we hurt him very much but we must have
annoyed him a great deal.

We spent the night in what had once been a trench.
At some time in '16 it had evidently been flattened by
artillery, for it was not more than two feet deep, and
now overgrown with grass. We sent out a patrol, which
met and gave chase to a German patrol, but I was not
in that, and managed to get a little sleep.

Although I did not know it at the time we were then
very close to the banks of the Ancre. Just before dawn
we were marched away, crossed a very beautiful little
bridge over the river, and found ourselves in Aveluy
Wood.

When I was a very young man who loved the country
and was compelled to live in a ghastly Thames-side
suburb called Twickenham, I used to walk out towards
Staines, and at one point I always used to pause and

catch my breath. It was houses, houses all the way, until suddenly and without warning the miles and miles of them came to an end, and on either side there were open fields. It was like crossing a frontier. One had got out of London and into the country. The character of the inns that one met along the road was different after a mile or two of hedgerows. They were country pubs, and the men who came in and drank their ale talked country talk. Before me was the dear west which has always held my heart. I used to return home feeling that I had got half way towards the Land of Heart's Desire.

I recaptured something of this sensation of passing from one land into another when I crossed the Ancre. It was a boundary line between desolation and civilisation. We had travelled many weary miles over a war-wasted wilderness where every tree was blasted and every cottage was a ruin. Aveluy Wood seemed scarcely to have been touched by the war, and beyond, as we were soon to discover, were tilled fields and villages from which the inhabitants had only just departed.

We were halted in the wood which was literally carpeted with anemones, and as the light grew I read Rupert Brooke. I shall never forget *The Chilterns* for I read it there for the first time in brightening twilight.

The Germans seemed to have got their guns up, for a few shells went screaming harmlessly over our heads. Then with full dawn a miracle happened, for we were relieved. The —th Division had come up at last.

We were now happier than we had been for many days. Not only were we apparently going out to rest, but it seemed that the Hun had come to the end of his long tether. How could he possibly cross the Ancre, with a dense wood facing him on the other side? We even sang as we marched away between ploughlands and fields of pasture.

In a village—name now forgotten—we were taken into an orchard, and behold ! our cookers were there, and there was a hot meal which was as nearly satisfying as ever we got. What was more—*mirabile dictu*—there was a bottle of red wine for each of us. It was the only occasion in my experience when wine was issued to English troops in France.

After this delightful experience we were allowed to lie on the grass and snore like hogs for a little while ; and then we were marched off to a village only very lately abandoned, and billeted in real furnished cottages with real roofs and intact walls. I managed to bag one of the beds, and thought I was half way to heaven.

In a shed outside I found a barrel of cider, drank what I could, and filled my water bottle. I also found some leeks growing in the garden, which I ate raw and unwashed.

We were all about to go to bed, feeling extremely pleased with ourselves, when we were suddenly ordered to parade. The rumour leaked out that the worst, the impossible, had happened. The Germans were across the Ancre.

I know something of the tortures of Tantalus. I know what it is to think that one is going to get a little rest, a little relaxation from the continuous strain of nearly a week, to see a real bed in which to lie, and then to be marched off again into some other circle of the inferno.

We marched four or five miles into another intact but deserted village, incredibly eerie in the dark. We passed through it to the further outskirts, and there we received a dramatic and disconcerting order from our C.O., who

evidently had a taste for theatricals. We were to dig ourselves in with our entrenching tools and " No man is to retire or surrender. You are to hold on until you are killed."

I suppose we should have done it, too. I don't think
many of us were brave men, but we were at least well
disciplined. I had lost the helve of my entrenching tool
—I was always losing things—and digging with the odd-
shaped bit of metal itself was a good deal too much for
me. I was too utterly tired to care what happened, and
having scrabbled up a bit of earth, which wouldn't have
sheltered me from a pop-gun, I lay down behind it and
went to sleep. " If the bastards are going to kill me,"
I thought, " let them, and get it over."

That was the night of March the twenty-sixth. It may
be remembered that at this time the Germans hesitated
and grew infirm of purpose as they had done before.
Their infantry was too far in advance of their guns.
Success had been too easy. It was all too good to be true.
They were walking into some ghastly trap. Besides, they
were probably as weary as ourselves. I am no war his-
torian, but I am very sure they could have walked
straight through to the Channel ports.

I was grateful for my faculty for being able to sleep
in times of acute danger. This was not courage ; but
probably an inverted form of cowardice, and fear may
have acted as a narcotic. I snored while others looked
haggardly up the starlit road, down which the enemy
failed to come. When I woke, it was because somebody
prodded me with the butt-end of a rifle. We were to go.
We were to abandon the position which we had to-hold-
to-the-last-man-or-die. Well, I was quite pleased, but
I was sorry they had to wake me and tell me about it.

Still, there was more sleep coming, for we were halted

in the market-place and told to lie down. I found the paving-stones very cold after Mother Earth, but I managed to doze fitfully. Then came daylight, and we were marched away. Well, thank God we are going out to rest at last.

Thank God we are going out to rest.

But not a bit of it. We pass through another deserted village and are halted in another sunken road. The order comes to fix bayonets. Nobody knows what is going to happen. We thought we were going out to rest, and now —this ! We are all a little dazed and too tired really to care.

We climb the bank and get into extended order across the ploughed hillock which slopes down to the road. Bullets, not too near, begin to hiss past. We are going to counter-attack. Jerry won't come on, so we are going to have a slap at him. He is on a railway embankment close to Albert. I have no idea that we are anywhere near Albert. Nobody seems to know anything at all, and we are much too worn-out to care.

We start advancing " by sections," or to be more correct, by platoons, for we are sadly depleted. One section lies down and prepares to give covering fire, while another runs a few yards ahead. I am the left-hand man of the battalion, and am in luck's way through having to advance along the bottom of the slope.

However, if we are going to charge with the bayonet, I am entirely out of place. It is a stretcher-bearer's job to follow up behind. I am unarmed if it comes to any rough stuff at close quarters, having nothing but a satchel of shell-dressings. So I run over and ask the Babe what is going to happen and what I ought to do.

I have mentioned the Babe. By the process of elimination he was now my company commander. In fact,

I think he was the only A Company officer left. As I
have already written, we did not expect much of him,
but he had shown himself to be a fine officer. During
our series of rearguard actions he had stood up as large
as life, making a target of himself while he gave firing
orders, when we older hands were trying to get behind
blades of grass. This morning he was different, although
he did not seem afraid. He had the air of a fatalist going
to execution. He said : " I don't know where we're going or what's going to happen. And I shan't be with
you at the end of the day to know."

It may be a pure coincidence, but here seems to me a
case of a man who knew exactly when he was going to
be killed. The poor Babe was wounded a few minutes
later, and fatally hit while trying to drag himself away.
I did not see him go down, for I was attending to other
wounded at the time, but I heard about it afterwards.

Well, as that was all I could get out of the Babe, I had
to advance with the others, and I am afraid I selfishly
hoped for casualties which would legitimately keep me
in the background. I hadn't long to wait. We came on
to the brow of a hill, still on ploughed fields, and below
us was a road lined by poplars and stone telegraph posts.
There were men half-left of us on the road and, as senior
man, I shouted out to those nearest me to fire on them.

In the circumstances, I am glad that not one of them
was hit. After one ragged volley we heard : " Gaw, you
something bastards ! Wot the something hell do you
think you're doing ? " They were troops belonging to
another division on our left.

I hadn't to wait long for casualties, because on the
downward slope to the road the next five men to me all
dropped. Harrison, the youngster who had just been

married, caught it first. I heard a bullet hit his skull with the splitting crack of a chopper striking a block. He sprawled forward and must have been dead before he fell. I went to him and saw that it was hopeless and tried not to think of the wedding photographs he had shown me.

Close to the road was a haystack, and I saw one of our sergeants hiding behind it instead of going forward with the company. He was not actually one of our own fellows, but one of the Chelsea Rifles who were attached to us. I marked his name down for future reference in case I ever came into collision with him.

The Germans now started playing a dirty trick in deliberately aiming at a stretcher-bearer—and the stretcher-bearer was I. I could tell that I was receiving particular attention by the bits of earth which jumped up around my feet. I kept waving my hand and pointing to my brassard. But to do Fritz justice he was at some considerable distance and perhaps could not see what I was about.

The next man I went to was a youngster lying on his face on the road, and he was the first of two extraordinary cases which were to come my way on that same morning. I turned him over and found him to be breathing, although he could not speak, and I could not see anything the matter with him. When I had unbuttoned his tunic I saw that he had a bullet wound in the chest, right over the heart. I had always thought that men shot through the heart were killed outright, but he was certainly alive, so I applied iodine and a pad. I had no sooner done this, however, than his eyes rolled up and he was gone.

There was another fellow lying on his face about four yards away, and when I went to touch him he sprang up with a yell, and said : " It's all right, I'm not wounded, I've only fainted." My nerves were rather rattled by the fact of my knowing that German gentlemen were regarding me thoughtfully through their sights and getting unpleasantly near the target, so I skipped about half my own height and said about ten bad words. Of course, I ought to have kicked his backside, but I am glad to remember that I was tender to this poor frightened boy.

" Go on, old dear," I said. " I know how rotten it is, but you'll have to get on with it."

A few days later he came up to me and apologised. He needn't have worried for I told nobody, I never knew his name, and to-day I shouldn't recognise him if I saw him in the street.

The next man I found was groaning with a bullet wound in the thigh and a splintered bone. He had to be got away, and I had to find not only a stretcher but somebody to help me carry it.

By this time our men had gone forward and were trying to make headway up a grassy slope towards a railway embankment. They didn't get very far, poor chaps. Just on our left, while I was looking for a stretcher and help, I saw a crowd of men—I don't know of what unit— literally flung back by a storm of bullets. A machine-gun officer was trying in vain to hold them up with his revolver, exclaiming : " Now, you sods, I'm not going back to Boulogne for you ! "

There was a dugout on the far side of the road, and I saw an officer standing in the entrance. He belonged to the battalion on our left and had evidently established a company headquarters there. I asked him if he had a stretcher and if he could lend me any men, and to my

surprise he treated me with great courtesy, letting me
have not only a stretcher but three men, who weren't
at all pleased about it. He also told me that an Aid
Post had been established a few hundred yards down
the road.

We started carrying the wounded man out, stretcher on
shoulders, which is the most comfortable way of carrying
if there are four to do it. But we had a bit of bad luck, for
the first shells of the morning came over, and when we
reached the Aid Post we found it wrecked and deserted,
with a smashed-up motor ambulance just outside. I
don't suppose there were any casualties there at the time
but probably the driver of the ambulance had gone west.

This meant that we had to carry the unfortunate
casualty into the village about a mile further on, where
I spotted a red cross flag outside a farmhouse and, on
entering, found it was our own regimental Aid Post. We
had no M.O., having lost our decent American doctor
coming out of Ytres, and the place was staffed only by
one frantic lance-corporal who seemed at his wits' end.
The place was full of wounded belonging to other units,
he was nearly out of dressings, and not being an M.O.
he was unable to get in touch with an ambulance. He
pinched nearly all my dressings and begged me to tell
the first officer I saw of the plight he was in.

We started off back to the line, keeping to the sunken
road where one was safe from direct observation. On
our right, a composite crowd was coming up in support
of us, advancing by sections over the ground we had
already covered. I don't know why they—and ourselves
in the first instance—didn't stick to the road. However,
they didn't get very far, for two big shells—nine-point-
twos, I should think—fell slick among them, whereupon

they turned and fled, led by their officers, and tumbled into the road just by where we were passing.

One of the officers—and I regret to say that his badge showed him to belong to my division—relieved himself by the roadside of much water and wind, and then remarked : " Them bleedin' shells didn't 'arf put the wind up me. Git orf down that road by twos and threes." My God, what an officer and gentleman ! The order was obeyed with alacrity. I don't know what became of them, and I hope they were all court-martialled.

The worst of it was that I lost my stretcher-party, which scuttled off with the others. I had a mind to go too, but I knew that our line was still intact, otherwise I should have met the remnants of our fellows running for it, and if I had to be shot I preferred it happening in the ordinary way, instead of for cowardice and desertion. I am sure my people would have been sensitive about that.

I met only one man on my way, and I don't know who he was because his face seemed to have been ripped off. He ran blindly, reeling across the road from one side to the other. I called to him to stop, but he wouldn't, and since I was hampered with the stretcher he got past me and I did not drop it and pursue him. Since he could use his legs, and I did not begin to know how to dress his indescribable wound, it was better to let him go.

I had to find my way back to the company, and I found the remains of it in a roadside cutting, trying to find cover among the exposed roots of trees. They had been driven back there from the grassy slope above, where more dead and wounded had been left. Their cover was pretty poor, for they seemed to be in a horse-shoe, and bullets coming from the left flank were spitting and cracking in the earth and tree-trunks around them.

In getting to them I had to cross the road, and was once more made conscious of having attracted unwelcome attention. As I put on speed to get out of the worst of it I heard a dire, familiar voice shouting to me, " Run, X, run ! " It was, of course, the voice of the awful man Rumbold, who sat perched in the bank like a roosting fowl. Did the ass think I needed to be told to run ?

There I found M'Cracken setting off with another stretcher party. It was the first I had seen of him that morning but, white man that he was, I knew he had been doing his job. He too seemed to have " won " a stretcher from somewhere.

I learned that it was useless to attempt to bring in any wounded who might be left on the slope above the cutting, and as there were none of the makings of a V.C. in me I didn't try. There was plenty for me to get on with where I was, without the need to look for trouble. My next case was the second phenomenon I observed that day. This was a fellow with a hole in his forehead and some stuff like phlegm smeared across his temple. Because he was breathing and groaning it did not occur to me that this phlegm-stuff was part of the poor fellow's brains. I am afraid I knew next to nothing about anatomy or first aid, and I had always believed that a man with such a wound must have been killed on the instant, just as I had thought in the case of the man shot through the heart.

This poor chap lived for some considerable time, groaning at every breath. I like to think that he felt nothing, but he could not have been entirely unconscious all the while, for some of the grey stuff was on his sleeve which he must have raised to dab against the wound.

I could not raise another stretcher party until
M'Cracken returned with his, so I set off back for the Aid
Post with a couple of walking cases. I would have made
them go unescorted, but one of them had been shot
through the face, just under the bridge of the nose, and
in dressing him I was compelled entirely to blindfold
him. He was a very plucky fellow who obviously did not
realise the comparatively small extent of his hurt, for
presently he asked me quite calmly if his nose were still
on. I met him again in England about the time of the
Armistice and he carried two scars so small that one could
hardly see them. I should not have known him if he had
not started telling the story. It seemed he had taken me
for a Red Cross man, confound him !

The other was a youngster who had been shot through
both legs but was able to hobble. He was a nice boy
except that he persistently addressed me as Gus, which
was never any name of mine, and which I thought I
hardly deserved of him.

We started off arm in arm, and were fired on as soon
as we set foot on the road. I should not like to say that
Jerry knew he was potting at two wounded men and a
stretcher-bearer, but the unpleasantness of the fact
remained. I thought the three of us made too big a
target to risk going by the way I had returned, so I made
a detour, taking them up the road among the poplar
trees until I thought we should be out of sight and range
in the open country.

On the ploughland, which we presently crossed, I
saw for the first time the effect of shrapnel. One could
not see this very well in grassy places or ground pitted
with shell-holes, but on the comparatively smooth brown
soil one could see the stuff strike the surface, like handfuls

of pebbles tossed into a pond. But only one or two bursts came over, nowhere very near, and very high.

I next collected a German prisoner. I don't know where he came from ; he seemed to emerge from the ground like a novel kind of daylight spectre. He had been slightly wounded in the jaw and had already shed his rifle and equipment, and he seemed much more pleased to see me than I was to see him. Although he exhibited the utmost docility he was difficult to get on with, for he could understand neither French nor English, and my German consisted of once having been able to decline *Der, die, das*. I should think he must have been the biggest bonehead in the German Army, and the language of signs meant nothing to him. If I pointed to him to go in one direction he would look intensely stupid and turn the exactly opposite way.

But we got along somehow and on the way I saw a tragedy in the air, high up and about half a mile to my right. About half a dozen German'planes were around one of ours and machine-guns were hammering like Bedlam. Suddenly I saw a tremendous flame shoot out of our machine, which began to fall. Beneath it, and dropping like a stone, was the body of the unfortunate pilot who had been compelled to throw himself out. I suppose he was dead before he touched the ground.

In the Aid Post I found the lance-corporal in charge even more hot and bothered than before. He had run right out of dressings, and took what were left of mine.

" I can't cope with the work," he said, " and I'm going to detail you to stay here with me. We *must* get an ambulance. The Eastshires " (as I shall call them) " have got their Aid Post somewhere in the village. Some of their chaps are here, for they say they can't find it. Go and get hold of their M.O., ask him to get us an ambulance, and get as many dressings from him as he can spare."

Occasional shells were now falling on the village, which presented an extraordinary scene, owing to the French having just cleared out and left their live-stock behind. A flock of sheep and a mixed herd of cattle, mad with terror, galloped from end to end, bleating and bellowing. When a shell fell near them they turned about and rushed back in the direction from which they had come, until another shell caused them to " about turn " again. I don't know how long the poor devils kept it up.

No wonder the Eastshires couldn't find their Aid Post. The Red Cross flag, instead of being prominently displayed outside, was hidden almost out of sight, and I only found it by the merest chance. The M.O. evidently didn't want to be troubled, for there were no casualties about that I could see, and he was giving a tea-party to some infantry officers who ought to have been in the line. He had a staff of three men who were also blissfully idle. He was not in the least pleased to see me, and very reluctantly doled me out some dressings and promised to send for an ambulance.

The ambulance duly arrived, and the stretcher cases were taken away in relays. The driver told us the position of the Field Dressing Station, and the walking wounded, including the German, were sent off to find it.

However, four or five men had already died in the Aid Post, and I was sent off to find Captain Penny, the adjutant, and report to him. As I went, some Australians arrived in the village, and I learned that a division of them had been marching from the Ypres sector to relieve us. It looked as if we were going out to rest at last.

We were, but I was not at first affected. Captain Penny detailed me to remain behind in the Aid Post and look after the corpses until the chaplain and a burial party arrived next day. I had trained myself not to be surprised at anything, but the strangeness of the order fairly staggered me. Soldiers' dead bodies seemed quite well able to look after themselves, since nobody would want to steal them, and apart from a natural distaste for sitting up all night with corpses for company, I was not sure if the Germans or the burial party would arrive first.

However, it had to be done, and I was left alone, pretty well worn-out, and without any chance of the good feed which probably awaited the others in their rest billets. For the first time I had the opportunity to investigate my temporary home. There was a fire going in the little stove in the kitchen, and enough fuel to last for the night. I was grateful for this, because, as I may have forgotten to mention, the transport had our packs, including our overcoats, and had lost everything.

In the bedrooms all the household linen and spare clothes of the exiled family were beautifully folded and put away. For warmth's sake I looted a kind of woollen cowl with ear-flaps, which I afterwards wore under my tin hat, and I must have looked a damned funny sight in it. There were plenty of beds, but none for me, for I did not feel like turfing off a corpse and sleeping in its place, or lying down in a pool of blood left behind by a wounded man.

There was also a cellar containing many bottles of quite drinkable red wine, but, of course, no food.

I was not alone in the village, for it was now full of Australians, who were, I suppose, part of a battalion in reserve to the troops already in the line. They knew what to do with the livestock, for I saw some of them carrying sheep slung over their shoulders, evidently looking forward to a meal of fresh mutton.

Presently about half a dozen of them paid me a visit, and told me that their fellows had already advanced four miles. This was about the silliest lie I had ever heard, but as they were armed and I was not, and as they were six to one, and slightly drunk at that, I held my tongue. They spent a happy few minutes pointing their bayonets at me and making me say that they were the finest troops in the world. I don't mind owning that I said it, but it was a good job for me that they couldn't read my thoughts.

At the risk of giving offence to the undeserving, I can't help saying that I am sorry that the Australians were on our side. I don't mean that they were all rotters, for I met some very good ones, but their black sheep achieved an extraordinary prominence. On the whole they were brave men, but not nearly such fine fellows as they boasted of being. But they kidded simple people into believing their brag—including the gentlemen of the press, who buttered with praise all troops except the English county regiments and, later in the war, the Territorials.

The Australian private drew twelve times as much pay as most British Tommies, until ours was increased late in the war. On account of a separation allowance I did most of my soldiering for sixpence a day, while the Australian drew six shillings. Yet when I was home on leave the Strand was full at night of whining Australians, trying to cadge their fares back to camp from their poor English comrades, or trying to blackmail belated civilians. The way they repaid the hospitality extended to them when they arrived in England is still remembered by the parents of daughters and the owners of portable valuables. Their objection to saluting officers always struck me as funny, for the lower a man was in the social scale and the more ignorant he was, the more his pride rebelled at paying this simple and manly-looking tribute to authority. Still, I must say this for them : they did kill a few of our military police.

When my unwelcome guests had left the temporary mortuary I drank as much as I wanted of the red wine, and this, striking my very empty stomach, made me extremely drunk. So fuddled was I that when Jerry started shelling the village as if he meant it, I did not think of retiring down the cellar, even although one shell smashed into the left wing of the building and brought down all the glass in the windows of the kitchen where I sat carousing with the dead.

The burial party and chaplain arrived next morning on a lorry, and, hearing that I had had nothing to eat for nearly forty-eight hours, the Padre very kindly gave me a tin of sardines which I had to eat without the accompaniment of bread or biscuits.

Shortly afterwards there took place just outside the village the strangest interment I ever saw. Not more than a hundred yards from us some infantry were at work digging furiously, and shells intended for them were falling uncomfortably close to us. The Burial Service was never read quicker, and all of us were smoking. I am not sure that the Padre wasn't smoking, too.

Then we all legged it for the lorry.

CHAPTER XIX

Some kindly person in authority had decreed that I should have a few hours' real rest, and I was left with the transport at Mailly-Mailly. There I had quite an adequate meal—for the Army to have supplied—and slept for about fourteen hours in some delightful, thick, clean straw in a really luxurious loft. The remains of the battalion was in Forceville, and the transport moved thither next day, so I had to rejoin what was left of my company, then about five-and-twenty strong.

There I found that some new officers had joined us. They did not belong to the regiment, but they seemed to have seen a great deal of service with other units. They seemed very nice men, but I was destined to serve under them such a short while that I have forgotten their names.

We also received a new draft of men, which must have made the battalion nearly four hundred strong, for the strength of my own company was increased to ninety. They were not our own men, but about as mixed a bag as one could hope to find anywhere.

Life in Forceville looked like being tolerable at first. A canteen where one could buy cigarettes, chocolate and biscuits was opened. A few French peasants still remained in their dingy tumbledown cottages, but I think they were soon made to go. We saw refugees from other villages miserably pushing prams and wheeled boxes which contained the best of their portable possessions.

These scowled at us and made rude remarks such as, " Inglis no bloody bon. Inglis parti tout-de-suite. Inglis run away." Poor devils, no wonder they were fed up ! We couldn't bear them malice.

The civil inhabitants of Forceville, such as they were, had very little to sell. At one cottage where one or two of us called in the hope of buying eggs we were greeted by a scowling old dame who remarked in the fashionable Franco-English : " Australian coupy poule's throat. Œufs na poo."

However, we managed to find an inhabited cottage which through some oversight seemed to have escaped the notice of the Dominion troops, for chickens were running about in the garden. So Talland-Brown, his companion in adventure that night at Ytres, another man and myself, went in and asked if we could have a chicken killed and roasted.

The old lady, who seemed singularly tender-hearted for a Latin peasant, replied that it was her husband who caught and killed the birds and that he was out, but that if one of us cared to catch a bird and wring its neck she would pluck and roast it for us. We all looked at each other and each remarked rather sheepishly that he wasn't very good at that sort of thing. Then the extraordinary fact emerged that although the four of us (two of whom— Talland-Brown and his friend—were expecting decorations for bravery) had had a pretty rough time, none of us had the guts to wring a chicken's neck. Eventually we managed to prevail on the old lady to perform the brutal but necessary act.

In Forceville we got our first letters for more than a week. The people at home seemed to have the " wind up " pretty badly, and I don't wonder, for the newspapers

couldn't have looked very well in those days, and Haig's
" back-to-the-wall " message had already been published. But the worst, as regards the chances of a complete
break-through by the Germans, was already over.

As for myself, I felt that I was coming to the end of my
tether, and I felt in my bones that something would
happen to me in the next few days. For some time I had
felt my nerves, such as they were, beginning to go, and I
felt that unless I " stopped one " soon I should go off my
head and do something which might necessitate a court-
martial and a firing party. Other men in other units had
been through three times what I had been through, but
please remember that I was naturally timid and highly-
strung and never had in me the makings of a soldier.

I was now, so far as I could discover, the only front-
line soldier left in the battalion who had been with it in
every stunt. Only one other original member of A Company remained, and he had been left on the nucleus for
the Passchendaele show. We still had Rumbold (no
longer will I call him " the awful man," poor chap) ; but
he had not joined us until just before Passchendaele and
he was away sick when we were at Cambrai. The only
man who really beat my record for longevity with the
Blanks was young Lloyd the signaller, for although he
was not with us through the retreat, he having been
absent on a course, he fought in a composite battalion,
and having afterwards rejoined our crowd, he went
through with it triumphantly until Armistice Day.

But looking around me at the new faces, and feeling
friendless and lonely, it seemed to me that my number
was rather over-due to go up. Well, mercifully, I hadn't
long to wait.

Forceville was not at that time one of those peaceful

villages beyond the sound of gunfire where one could sometimes forget the war for a few minutes on end. The German artillery made it as uncomfortable for us as they could by strafing it heartily at unexpected times. I was billeted in some foul byre on the usual louse-ridden, stinking straw. Behind us was a barn containing some of our transport. One night a shell came over and killed two horses and two men. I saw the two horses being dragged out next day, and they were a nasty sight.

Our sanitary man was wounded while digging a latrine and blown into the empty pit. On another occasion, while we were on parade, a shell knocked down part of a wall only two or three yards away. By a miracle not one of us was touched, but a gunner standing on the road about thirty yards away was badly hurt.

We spent about five days in Forceville, and then paraded once more to go up the line. While we were marching some Australian transport shouted after us : " That's right. We've done our bit, so now go and do yours. But you're ——ing slow about it."

Now we'd been bearing the brunt of the retreat while these loud-voiced fellows were on the march, so having comrades with me, and armed ones at that, I turned round and cursed them for a pack of Botany Bay bastards. The effect of this remark was almost awe-inspiring in the language it evoked. An Australian dislikes being called a " Botany Bay bastard." I wonder why.

However, it was not the Australians we relieved, for we were marched to a bit of front that was new to us, near a village called Mesnil, between Aveluy Wood and Ingelbelmer. We found we were to hold a line of posts in fallen-in trenches—relics of '16 or earlier—overlooking the River Ancre and the weald beyond.

Here the conditions were frightful. We had no protection at all from the weather, little cover from shell-fire, and we were so extremely close to the Germans that it was dangerous to show our heads during the day, and those who wanted to move had to crawl about with bent backs through the eighteen inches or so of water which perpetually laved our feet. And of course it rained. My hat, how it rained ! So naturally the water around us deepened perceptibly.

Our brave, well-meaning but not very intelligent colonel came round at stand to on the first morning in a drenching rain-storm. He found us soaked to the skin, with our feet in miniature ponds, and asked coldly and not very intelligently : " Can't you men keep dry ?" He might just as pertinently have asked the same question of a fish in the Zoo aquarium.

Half A Company was in the front line, and the other half was in the supports on top of a chalky hill behind us. M'Cracken was in the supports, so that we met only at night. We soon found that it was impossible to evacuate casualties from the front line during the day, because the communication trench climbing the slope had been battered to pieces and one was in full view of the Germans.

Nor were we long in getting casualties. Jerry strafed us mercilessly with trench-mortars, whizz-bangs and five-nines for several hours each day and night. This increased our miseries, apart from the mere danger, because after a man had bled the water in the trench took on the colour of blood. By day we could do nothing at all except crouch down and wait. And at night when I tried to shift the wounded I found that nobody loved me.

I had the utmost difficulty in getting officers to lend me men for stretcher-parties. There was a raid going out or else the men were wanted for working parties, and the line had somehow to be held. Many times I could have cried like a fractious child. One of the new officers said he would recommend me for something if I would only stop grumbling—which I didn't. Most stretcher-bearers got the M.M. if they lasted long enough, but I didn't, and didn't deserve it, so I am not barking at sour grapes.

The worst time we had in that enchanting spot was my penultimate day in the line, to wit April the 6th, and, unless I am in error it was the Saturday between Good Friday and Easter. The post to which I was attached was seven strong, including myself, who didn't count as a combatant. We occupied two bays of the trench, with a low traverse between us. I was in the left-hand bay with three newcomers who were strangers to me. In the farther bay were Sergeant Fullerton, Rumbold and another of our own fellows named Crossby.

Soon after breakfast Jerry started an intensive bombardment which lasted for about three hours. It was about as bad as anything of the sort that I had hitherto endured. We crouched in the mud and water, our tongues and palates coated with the fumes of explosive, waiting for the inevitable shell to fall into our midst. The German gunners seemed to know exactly where we were, and how they missed us for two and a half hours, lobbing shells just a yard or so in front and behind, is one of those mysteries which I should ascribe to Divine Providence had not the seemingly inevitable happened at last.

I heard a yell from the farther bay, crawled round to

see what had happened, and found myself wading in blood and water. A shell had burst right on the parapet. Fullerton and Rumbold had been untidily killed. They were half kneeling, half resting against the parapet, and as the skulls of both of them were smashed they could have known nothing about it. Crossby, who had called out, was in a pretty bad state, wounded in about four places, and I did my best for him. His most serious wound was a hole in his wrist, for I could not stop the bleeding, but at last I managed it by plugging it with a piece of Army biscuit, a bit of work which might not commend itself to the College of Surgeons, but it was none the less effectual.

He was still able to use his legs, and like most wounded men he was naturally in a hurry to get away. I had great trouble in dissuading him. It was possible for any-body who was fairly nippy to use the communication trench by daylight, but for a man who could only hobble, and with that strafe going on, it was sheer madness.

He then begged me to take him somewhere else, and again I tried to dissuade him. " There's been one in here," I urged, " and it's long odds against another." But the poor chap was so urgent that at last I helped him round into the bay which I had lately vacated.

Here there was another nasty scene. During my absence a shell had pitched right inside and my late three companions were all mangled and dead. I hap-pened to have been in the right bay at the right time on each occasion.

While Crossby and I were looking at each other—and I wonder how we did look—the shelling suddenly ceased. Crossby was again urgent to get away, but I was still more urgent that he should wait. After a minute I heard the chattering of Lewis guns from our supports, and from the front line away on my left, and the staccato cracking of rifles. Mingled with this came the sound of Germans cheering, as I had heard them that night in Ytres. Just for a quarter of a second I poked up my head and saw a long line of Germans with fixed bayonets running up the slope towards the trench. Their left flank man would have been about fifty yards distant on my left.

I own that I was panic-stricken. I realised that if they turned to their left I was the only sound man for perhaps a hundred yards. I had a stark terror of the bayonet, and I knew that their leading man was as likely as not to poke me in the guts before discovering that I was unarmed and innocuous. I suppose I ought to have hared off to the right, dragging Crossby with me if I still had the nerve to encumber myself with a wounded man, but I was so petrified that I simply didn't think of it.

Crossby kept on asking me what had happened, but I was physically unable to answer, and just crouched and waited in an agony of apprehension.

A measure of comfort came after a minute or two. A bombing party from our right came splashing past, led by " Jock," who carried himself as if he were leading a raid on the football field. After another minute I heard the smash of bombs bursting, and the piercing whistle of their fragments. Then came another of those strange hushes.

I took another peep. A battalion of New Zealanders were on our left flank about a hundred and fifty yards away and the only man in sight was one of them, at about that distance. He stood up, his head and shoulders visible above the low parapet, and for a moment he was still as a statue. Then one of his hands shot high above his head. I suppose there must have been a bomb in it and that he shouted something for the effect was almost uncanny. From all around him in the tortuous maze of shallow trenches the heads and raised hands of Germans sprang into view.

The raid had failed. I daresay the Germans thought that they were getting into deep trenches where they could move about unseen. Our rifle and Lewis gun fire had made a mess of them, and I afterwards heard that we and the New Zealanders had taken over fifty prisoners.

But we had suffered too, apart from during the preliminary bombardment. I was soon in request. One very gallant boy of nineteen had stood all the while exposed, working his Lewis gun while the rest of his crew, all children of the same age, had dropped around him. Two of them were dead, and the third was shot through the right lung.

That poor lad is on my conscience to this day. I had been told that if a man were shot through the lungs his only chance was to be left quite still where he had fallen in the hope that a clot of blood would form. I could not bandage him without turning him over and pulling him about, so I left him exactly as he was. He died a short while afterwards, and I don't know if I could have done anything to save him ; and if I could it was not my fault that I was ignorant of the means. But his ghost still worries me when I wake in the small hours of the morning with an active conscience and a touch of liver.

All that day my feet had been aching pretty badly, but I took little notice at first. Aching feet are, after all, only a minor inconvenience. But I noticed them still more during the night, which I spent yanking stretchers to the Aid Post which was in a sort of cave on the other side of the hill.

We had a new American M.O., and I didn't like him. He was very young, and he had a little round face with about as much expression and intelligence as an uncut cheese. Moreover, I came to the conclusion that he was " windy."

During the night we had a bit of good news, hall-marked " official." We were being relieved for another short rest on the following night. This was the barest humanity. Living flesh could not have endured much more than four consecutive days and nights in that place. I think the Royal Welch Fusiliers took over from us, for I saw what looked to be an advance party, and I hope they had a better time than we did.

Then dawned April the 7th, a red letter day in my memory.

CHAPTER XX

It was a fine morning. The Ancre flowed blue and peaceful below us at the bottom of the slope. I remember that we had rissoles for breakfast, and that the fellows in the new post assigned to me drank my rum ration, alleging that I had not been provided for. I think I used more bad language over that rum than ever I used before or since. After breakfast we received another strafe.

It was not so bad as the one of the previous morning, but pretty bad. In the midst of it a sergeant came creeping down the trench and said to me : " Come on, you're wanted."

I followed him, bent and hobbling, conscious that my feet were hurting more than ever, and asked him what was the matter.

" Oh," he answered wearily, " there's a nice bloody mess along here." And there was ; the first adjective in this case being entirely literal.

Another shell had fallen on the parapet of one of our posts. Two men had been killed outright, a third badly wounded in two or three places, and the fourth sat on the fire-step, his face the colour of mud, with both his legs blown off, one just above the knee and the other below.

He was quite conscious and seemed not to be in pain, and strangely enough there was no arterial bleeding. But he presented a problem which was beyond me to solve. I simply did not know what to do with those exposed splinters of bone and the flesh that hung in rags like the ends of tattered garments. How could I dress wounds like that ? What could one begin to do ?

The poor chap begged me piteously to do something for him, and I had to tell him I couldn't. But the shelling had now ceased, so I told him I would go and get the M.O. to come up and see him. I gave the sergeant some dressings, and asked him if he would look after the other wounded man while I was away.

As I have remarked, it was not dangerous to go up and down the communication trench by daylight so long as one was fairly nippy in crossing the exposed places. The thing to do was to run from boulder to boulder and take cover until the aim of any German gentleman who might have seen one would be sure to waver. In spite of my burning feet I can promise that I was as slick as a young gazelle.

The M.O., when he had heard what had happened, shook his head.

" He can't live," he said, " so I won't come up the line."

" No, you blighter," I thought, " you don't like that communication trench."

" He'll be dead by the time you get back," the M.O. continued, " but I'll give you some morphia tablets in case he isn't. Don't give him more than two."

The M.O. was certainly right. The poor chap had passed out. So I gave the tablets to the other man and marked his forehead with a large M in indelible pencil to show the people at the Dressing Station that morphia had already been administered. Then I sat in the mud and thought about my feet, which were now hurting almost unbearably.

Our bit of front was quite quiet, but there was a lot of firing going on in Aveluy Wood on our right, and it must have been from there that I picked up a stray bullet. It must have been nearly spent and had a very steep downward trajectory to have got me in the way it did. It got me over the right kidney.

Strange what one's nerves will do. I felt it go right through me like red hot wire and come out through my belly, and actually opened the front of my trousers and pulled up my shirt to see the hole from which it had emerged. But there was no hole there. I had imagined it all—or nearly all.

Meanwhile I had called out that I was hit, and I wonder how much quaver there was in my voice. A man squatting close inspected me from the rear.

" Yes, you have been," he said, " but I don't think it's anything much. It's only a graze. Looks to me as if you've stopped a spent one. You'll probably find it in your bags. *That* won't get you home. I'll put some iodine and a dressing on for you."

This was comforting in one sense but not in another. I told him he could put a dressing on for me with pleasure, but that as regards the iodine he could go to hell. I'd seen other chaps wilt when I'd used iodine on *them*.

While this inconsiderable scratch was being dressed the sergeant who had first called me that morning came up.

" Here," he said, " you'll have to go down to the Aid Post and get an anti-tetanus inoculation."

Now I loathed the idea of that anti-tetanus stuff, much good as it undoubtedly did. But this was an order and I didn't want to find myself in trouble when I came out of the line. So I proceeded to obey, but when I got up my feet seemed to be bursting through my boots, and I found that I could hardly crawl. I knew then that I could not possibly march out with the battalion that night.

On my way down I went into company headquarters and saw the skipper, telling him of my plight. " I believe," I added, " that I've got trench feet."

He looked rather worried, supposing, I think, that he would be held responsible.

" I don't say it's your fault," he said quite kindly, " but I suppose you know it's a crime to have trench feet."

I could, if I'd dared, have said something quite amusing, although just then I didn't feel particularly funny. All I said was : " Look at the conditions, sir."

" I know," he said, " I know. I'll try to keep you out of trouble if I can. Well, you'll be seeing the M.O."

I got up the communication trench somehow, but much too slowly for my mental comfort. Thank goodness Jerry was kind, or else he wasn't looking, for nobody tried a pot at me. On the other side of the hill I ran into—or hobbled into—our colonel, who pointed an accusing finger at me and asked me what was the matter. When I told him he raved like a defrauded money-lender.

" How dare you have trench feet ! What's your name and number ? Why haven't you looked after yourself ? You know very well it's the duty of every man to take off his boots and socks every day and rub his feet ! "

I told the old fool that it was impossible during the day when we could not show ourselves. I could have added that the only possible way would have been to lie on our backs in the water and hold our feet in the air, an attitude not convenient for massage.

" Why haven't you done it at night ? " he demanded.

I told him that I had had to spend my nights organising stretcher parties and trying to get the wounded away. He passed on, muttering that I should hear more about it, but to do him justice I never did. Nor have I seen him since.

The M.O. had a look at my scratch and applied some iodine and another dressing, and I asked him to look at my feet, saying that I had already reported at company headquarters that it would be impossible for me to march out with the battalion that night. He was new to the job, and I don't suppose he knew what a trench foot was.

" No," he said, " I don't think you've got trench feet, but if you can't march, you'd better start off now and take two days' light duty with the transport at Mailly-Mailly. If your feet aren't better then you can report sick again. I'll give you a chit."

He did ; and so it happened that, thanks to him indirectly, I left the line for ever. Had he attended to my feet and sent me away on the first ambulance I am sure I should have been all right in a few days, and either court-martialled and shot for cowardice—I was feeling very much that way—or killed in the ordinary manner within the next few weeks. I don't know how far Mailly-Mailly was, but it was some distance beyond Ingel-belmer, and I started off with the feeling that I had been set an impossible task. I was in pretty bad pain.

The road to Ingelbelmer was running like a shallow trout-stream after the recent rains, and this considerably increased my unhappiness. I got along somehow, moving like a duck with bunions ; but I hadn't gone far when I heard the booming of guns, the screaming of shells, and

Sw

half a dozen fell one after another plumb on the road two or three hundred yards ahead.

This gave me cause for reflection. If they were going to bump the road I felt morally and physically incapable of getting any further. Anyhow, I decided that I must get off that road and make my way to Ingelbelmer across the fields, even at the expense of covering more distance. So I climbed a bank on to a ploughed field, and I could see Ingelbelmer quite distinctly from the top, because of the trees around it. So I started off on a semi-circular route.

The ploughed field, however, was worse for making progress on than the road. At every painful step my boots picked up a few pounds of clay and I could not endure any attempt to kick it off. But I floundered on for some distance, when, to my astonishment and dread, a string of shells burst right across the field in front of me. It seemed to me that this must be my unlucky day.

Ignorant as I was of what had attracted the shell-fire, I wondered why the fools of Germans wanted to shell that field. They couldn't be wasting pounds and pounds and pounds' worth of good stuff on one poor devil like me. I discovered the cause a few minutes later when I slid down a bank on to a field on a lower level, and found some New Zealanders crouching underneath it. They were evidently in reserve to us. I was about to go on, when one of their sergeants called out to me roughly and asked me where I was going. Too weary to answer him I held out the chit from my M.O. Then his demeanour changed. What gentlemen, what fine fellows, those New Zealanders were !

" Could you do with a drop of rum ? " he asked.

" My God ! " I answered.

He brought me a tooth-glass full and watched me drink it. Rum out there was grudgingly issued, and, under the conditions in which these fellows lived, it was more precious than rubies. No saint who gave half his cloak to a beggar did a finer thing. Think of that, you Nonconformists, when you howl " temperance " hymns in your tin tabernacles. If that sergeant is still alive and these lines should happen to meet his eye, he may remember, and now know that I am eternally grateful.

The rum put new life into me (sorry, Mr. Stiggins !), and I managed to drag myself into Ingelbelmer, but I knew that I couldn't get much farther. My intention was to get beyond the village, where I should be in compara- tive safety, and wait by the roadside until I could get a lift on a passing ambulance. But I was hardly in the village before three or four shells came over slick into the heart of the place.

It was very unpleasant to be in the streets of a town or village which was being shelled, because the danger was multiplied by showers of bricks. So I tried to put on a spurt, and that finished me. Black cotton-wool came floating up before my eyes, and I had just the time and presence of mind to lean against a wall. I seem to remember sluttering down it before everything went black.

When I came to I was on my feet with my arms around two necks. A voice, soft as a woman's, was saying in one of my ears : " What's the matter, old man ? Feeling bad ? What's the matter ? "

I told him, and he asked me if I could walk a little.

" Lean on us as hard as you like," he said. " Our Aid Post is only just round the corner."

They were New Zealanders, of course.

275

I wish I could remember the name of the man who spoke to me. It began with Mac, and I promised to write to him after the war, but to my shame I let it slip my memory in a few hours. Still, I haven't forgotten the man himself.

They half carried me into a farm-house kitchen, where two men were lying on stretchers and a man with a bandaged and slinged arm sat in a chair drinking tea. There was a doctor and a staff of two or three.

" What's the matter ? " the doctor asked me.

I showed him the chit from my M.O., at which he glanced once and snorted.

" Had your feet dressed yet ? "

" No, sir."

" Get his boots and puttees off, one of you. Got any tea and biscuits ? "

So while my puttees and boots were coming off I had hot tea and a packet of sweet biscuits. Afterwards a packet of cigarettes was given to me. These were the New Zealanders, please—not our own people. My feet came out of my socks so swollen that I could not think why my boots had not burst, the soles very puffy and soft and in colour the dirty whitish grey of a conger eel. Soft pads were applied to them and afterwards bandages. Then some queer-looking footgear was immediately improvised with cardboard soles and loose canvas tops.

The doctor glanced at the chit I had had from my M.O., muttered something under his breath, and tore it up much in the manner that a decent-minded man would tear up an anonymous letter.

" Stretcher case," he said ; and turning to me he added : " There'll be an ambulance here in a few minutes. Have some more tea ? "

I tried to thank him, but he wasn't the kind of man to be thanked. My feet were easier now, so long as I kept them just touching the ground, and I felt weak and drowsy and happy, and I was already beginning to dream of getting back to England.

Presently the ambulance arrived and I lay down on a stretcher and was hoisted into an upper berth. The two other stretcher cases followed, and the man with the damaged arm sat on the side of another. Off we went, and we had just reached the further outskirts of the village when a shell came over and burst very uncomfortably near the rear of the ambulance. It was the last I ever heard burst.

I don't know where we went to that night, but I have a vague memory of alternately dozing and waking somewhere under cover where I lay on a stretcher with a blanket over me. My feet were burning and worrying me quite a lot. Next morning I have a dim recollection of sitting on a little station with scores of other bandaged men, waiting for a train which never seemed to be coming, and being fed with bread and butter and tea out of a plated pail.

Of the train journey to the big Casualty Clearing Station at Doullens I have no recollection at all, but I remember getting there and being carried on a stretcher into a reception tent, where an orderly, who hailed from Lancashire, gave me about a quart of anti-tetanus in the arm, despite my vigorous protests. " Eh, an' you'll 'aave three more doases," he explained with great satisfaction.

I was lying on the ground, waiting to be taken into a ward—if a large tent can be called a ward—when a nurse came up and spoke a cheery word to me. She was tall, pale, thirsty-ish and hopelessly unattractive ; but what a good sort to be in that stinking hole ! I remember thinking what a pity it was that no man would be likely to fall in love with her.

She smiled archly, touched my ribs with her toe, and said very wistfully : " Well, I suppose you'll be going back to England now, to see your best girl again."

I told her I hoped so, but very strongly doubted it.

Next morning I was carried into a Red Cross train bound for Étaples. I must say that the appointments of the train were excellent. My stretcher was fitted into a berth beside a wide window, so that I could lie and watch the countryside. When I got tired of that, there was a paper-back novel in a rack beside me. I preferred looking out of the window, for the novel was a very dire one by a popular authoress. Still, I appreciated the kindly thought which had placed it there. There was plenty of tea and a little bread and butter, and I was supplied with cigarettes, so I was perfectly happy.

At Étaples we were lifted out of the train and I was dumped down outside a hospital for a few minutes before being carried in, and I saw a very pretty girl in a neat blue uniform standing by. Now I had never seen a member of the W.A.A.C., for although they were by that time no novelties, I had not been near a camp while I was home on leave, and had never seen one to my knowledge. So I thought she might be one, and I sat up on the stretcher and said: " Excuse me ; are you a ' Whack ' ? "

The answer came in an unmistakable accent, accompanied by a laugh : " No, you impertinent fellow, I'm a V.A.D."

It was a Canadian hospital to which I was brought. I was laid out on a slab at the entrance, like a cod at a fishmonger's, while a doctor examined a ticket on my chest, and then I was carried off and put to bed in a ward, where presently I was given a welcome sponge-down by a morose orderly. He treated my request for something to eat and drink with all the contempt which he evidently felt it deserved. I had had scarcely anything all day, and it seemed I was to have nothing now.

I might have slept a bit if they had not put into the bed on my left a youngster who was either as mad as Bedlam or swinging the lead with extraordinary velocity. I am inclined to think that he was one of those who would go to any lengths rather than face fire again, for he had lost his identity discs and his numerals, and nobody seemed to know anything about him. He howled like a dog all night, and had I been quite sure that he was shamming I would have got up and bashed his face in. Relays of doctors came and questioned him throughout the night, but he remained impervious to the Third Degree. Like Tennyson's infant, crying in the night, his " only answer was a cry "—damn him !

At 2 a.m., just as this ululating funk-hound—who hadn't a scratch on him—had almost howled out his strength and had allowed me to doze, I was wakened to be washed all over again. Why *do* they do this sort of thing at such an hour in all hospitals—even civilian ones ? The life of the patient may depend on his getting a little natural sleep, but nevertheless he is wakened and washed. The routine must be carried out, you see, and damn everything else !

After breakfast—or after most of the other men had had breakfast, for I had none—a sullen orderly came and dressed my feet and put a new pad on my back, where a dry crust had already formed. I may as well state here and now that no doctor or nurse ever looked at my feet during the five days I was in this hospital. This, however, was all to the good, for they improved with a distressing rapidity, having regard for the fact that I wanted them to take me back to England.

Nine a.m. in that place was hell upon earth. Screens were around half the beds where men were performing an operation, offensive to most of the senses, which is normally done in private. The other half seemed to be having their wounds dressed and were screaming the place down. Why couldn't they dope the poor devils, instead of sneering at them for cowards? Men like these didn't cry out for nothing.

When the last of the screams, sobs and moans had subsided a sister came round to my bed, and looked at my ticket hanging over the top, which stated the nature of my complaint, and a sort of condensed Army biography.

" Oh," she drawled through her nose, " you're not one of aour boys."

" I'm not a Canadian," I said, and wanted to add : " Thank God ! "

She regarded me with intense disfavour—as if I could help being chucked into her beastly hospital.

" They never seem to send us aour boys," she bewailed through her left nostril. " Now aour boys are so different from yours."

" But how true ! " I murmured.

" Aour boys won't put up with what yore boys will. They're manly. If they've got a complaint to make they stand up at attention before the C.O. and tell him about it."

" It's a pity you haven't some of them here," I told her. " Then they could stand to attention before him and tell him about the food."

She fixed me with a glassy stare.

" *You* haven't any complaint to make about the food, sure-lye ? " she said.

" Not yet," I said, " because I haven't seen any. But still," I added soothingly, " I only arrived yesterday afternoon."

To do her justice she then got busy. By an oversight no rations had been drawn for the influx of casualties of the previous day. But within half an hour I had some breakfast. However, it is not wise to score off a sister, and had she borne malice there might have been a different and unpleasant sequel to my story.

Perhaps the women who had come out to nurse their own countrymen had some cause for complaint. I was in a big ward, and there were only two Canadians in it. The orderlies were not Red Cross men, but privates in British fighting units.

One of the orderlies, a young London Scot, explained this to me.

" They won't send us home," he said, " and they've given us this job until we're fit to go up the line again. All the Canadians who come here go to ' Blighty,' but they don't send Englishmen home if they can possibly help it."

This was bad news.

" And where do you suppose I shall go ? " I asked.

" Oh, I expect you'll go to convalescent camp in Trouville for three weeks, and then up the line again."

" That doesn't suit me," I said. " I've had enough of this vulgar brawl for a month or two. I'm what they call ' war-worn.' I'm going to get back to ' Blighty.' "

" I bet you don't," he laughed.

" I can't bet much," I said, " because I have only fourpence, but if that's any good to you, you're on."

The following morning he came and asked me to pay up.

" You're marked for Trouville," he said.

" I'm not there yet," I answered. " Anyhow, they can't shift me just at present. My feet are improving at a most disgusting rate, seeing that nothing is being done for them, but I can only just hobble about. When I leave here for Trouville you can have your four-pence."

I could always hobble just outside the hut for func-tional purposes, and on my way back that morning I met a W.O. attached to the hospital. So I asked him frankly, " Can you get me marked for England ? "

He came to business at once.

" I can," he said, " and that will cost you two pounds."

Cheap at the price, of course, but I'd only fourpence in cash, and told him so.

" But," I said, " I could send it to you from England."

He shook his head at that.

" Some of you boys haven't played the game," he said, with the sorrowful air of a philanthropist, who was begin-ning to lose his faith in human nature.

He was quite adamant, and I went back to bed to think things out. I didn't see why I shouldn't have another look at England. It wasn't dodging the war, because they'd send me out again soon enough directly they were short of men. Meanwhile there were quite a few hale and hearty young fellows to take my place for the time being. I felt that, for a month or two at least, I'd done my shift.

That afternoon a chaplain walked into the ward, and I saw that he was popular. All the nurses were around him like flies around a honey-pot. I beckoned the London Scottish orderly over to my cot.

" Tell the padre I want to speak to him," I said.

" He's the R.C. padre."

" Never mind. I'm an R.C."

Presently the chaplain came over smiling.

" What can I do for you ? " he asked. " I'm the Catholic padre, you know."

" Splendid ! " I said. " I'm a Catholic."

He looked at the ticket over my cot, and said : " So you are." And then, as Rider Haggard would have said, a strange thing happened. My name caught his eye and he exclaimed : " You don't write stories, do you ? "

Now this was quite extraordinary. In those days my obscurity was so complete that I don't think I had hitherto met more than three strangers who knew my name in connection with my work. That he, of all people, should be the fourth, savoured of the miraculous.

I told him that it was the only means by which society permitted me to make a living, and he mentioned a short story of mine which he had just read, and which had been published so recently that, having come straight down from the line, I could not possibly have seen it in print. So I began to tell him the plot.

" Well," he said hastily, " what do you want ? "

" I want two months' rest," I said. " I want to see England and my people again. I want you to get me marked for ' Blighty.' "

" My dear fellow," he answered, " that's got nothing to do with me. I can't do anything."

" Yes, you can, Father," I said. " You're popular."

" But——"

" Yes, you can, if you want to," I insisted. " You're popular."

He argued, but it was useless. Presently he wavered.

" If you get home," he said, in the tone of one trying to refuse alms to a beggar likely to spend the money on drink, " I suppose you'll only write some more stories."

" Never mind," I replied, " you needn't read them."

This point of view seemed not to have occurred to him before, for he brightened considerably.

" Well," he said finally, " I'll do my best."

Next morning when the doctor came round accompanied by a nurse, the nurse remarked :

" Oh, doctor, this is the man who writes stories."

I pricked up my ears at this. It sounded to me like a code. The doctor began to regard me as if I were a five-legged sheep.

" How are you feeling ? " he asked.

" Oh, not so bad, sir," I replied.

" Can you walk ? "

Now this was rather a trappy question. If I said I could, he mightn't think it worth while to send me home. If I said I couldn't, there mightn't be room on the boats for stretcher cases until too late.

" I can just walk, sir," I said.

" Oh, you can *just* walk ? Very well."

He passed on, and I spent two hours of intense anxiety until the London Scot, half angry and half amused, came up and threw fourpence on to my counterpane.

" You wicked old (pervert) ! " he exclaimed. " You've been marked for ' Blighty.' How did you work it ? "

" Work it ! " I exclaimed, trying to appear indignant. " What do you mean—work it ? "

" Well, there are only four men in the ward marked for England—the two Canadians, another Englishman and you."

I picked up the fourpence, lay back, smiled serenely and tapped my forehead.

" It's there where you want it," I said.

But I lived on thorns for the next day or two, and didn't even venture to score off the W.O., who was two pounds out, for I should undoubtedly have sent it to him. Plans were always being changed, and at any moment I might have found myself booked for Trouville once more.

However, at two o'clock on the Sunday morning, exactly one week after I had left the line, the two Canadians, another man and myself, were routed out of bed and given ill-fitting clothes to put on. I was slightly above average height and build, and I was given the cut-away tunic of a badly nourished Highlander of about five feet two.

We were all walking cases, and wearing large smiles; we shuffled down to a waiting train and clambered on board. As it happened, we got out of that hospital in the nick of time, for it was bombed a few nights later and many patients and nurses were killed.

The swine who were responsible for this were not the German airmen, but the magnificent gentlemen with red tabs who, in spite of repeated warnings, allowed hospitals and ammunition dumps to be very near neighbours. I suppose there was an inquiry, but in our country we can be sure that those who were responsible were exonerated, and probably decorated, while the wicked German was reviled by the Press and everybody else who knew nothing about it. People who lost relatives, men and women, in that raid, have to thank some purple, belching old General who ought to have been publicly castrated and hanged.

The train crawled with us to Calais, and there each of us received two bars of chocolate and a packet of Gold Flake. I don't know who was responsible for these gifts, but if they were the result of private philanthropy they must have cost the donor a pretty penny. Let me record my gratitude.

I had one nasty shock as we were climbing up the iron steps on to the upper deck of the pier. Two doctors stood at the top, questioning the men as they came through, and I saw one or two being sent off in a direction opposite to that of the waiting boat. Were they stopping men from going home even at the last moment ?

But no. They only wanted to know if one had wounds which might require dressing on the way over. Those who had were sent on to another boat which was taking the stretcher cases.

It was the happiest voyage I am ever likely to have. It was misty, it rained, and the sea was choppy, but I stood on the wet deck and presently saw the cliffs coming up through the grey weather, like the ghosts of something loved and lost. I loved every plunge of the bows and beat of the engine which brought me nearer. The harbour seemed to swim out to meet us with a wide-mouthed smile of welcome.

It was customary for Authority to find out where you lived, and then send you to a hospital as far as possible from your home, in order that the hospital people need not be troubled by visitors. Thus, if you lived in Cornwall, and said so, you could rely on being sent to the north of Scotland. But I had heard that the first train always went to London, so I was one of the first half dozen up the gangway.

The information was only partly correct. The train certainly went to London, but it didn't stop, and threaded its way round through the maze of suburban stations, until it struck the Great Western main line. Then the truth was revealed to us by a train attendant. Some of us were booked for Gloucester, others for Cheltenham.

The other fellows in my compartment were all from the North Country, and when we passed through Slough, I told them that we were within two miles of Windsor Castle and might be able to see it. These fellows all thronged to the window in the hope of seeing " where the King lived," but they were disappointed, for one cannot see the Castle from the line.

Even the men in pain were in high spirits and they sang the old choruses, coarse or sentimental, according to the whim of the moment, until twilight fell and drowsiness came upon us all.

We passed through Reading ; and the upper reaches of the Thames, so well-known and so dear to me, played hide-and-seek with us.

I kept my face pressed close to the window, not wanting to talk, only to think, and be drowsy, and revel in a new-found, delicious happiness. Dim squares of fields swung into diamond shapes as we passed ; the lights of an inn gleamed dully behind red blinds ; scattered cottages leaped to meet us and ran past ; unexpected vistas of the river showed grey in the gathering gloom.

I had been a bad soldier, and a bad soldier is necessarily a bad patriot, but I realised then, as never before nor since, that I loved England almost better than I loved myself—that England was worth fighting for, worth suffering for, worth dying for. Oh, I'd got my grievances against individuals and institutions, but they weren't *England*. It was the land that called to me, welcoming me like a mother. I could have buried my face in the grass of an English field and kissed the soil from which I sprang.

Twilight deepened to dark and I grew too tired even to think, but I clung to consciousness as long as possible to enjoy while I might the perfect hour which I knew would never come to me again. Then nature very gently and kindly withdrew it from me.

And so I fell asleep and woke up in Cheltenham.

THE END